HOME

OF THE

HAPPY

HOME
OF THE
HAPPY

A MURDER ON THE CAJUN PRAIRIE

JORDAN LAHAYE
FONTENOT

MARINER BOOKS
New York   Boston

HarperCollins books may be purchased for educational, business, or sales promotional use. For information, please email the Special Markets Department at SPsales@harpercollins.com.

The Mariner flag design is a registered trademark of HarperCollins Publishers LLC.

FIRST EDITION

Designed by Jackie Alvarado

All insert photographs courtesy of the author unless otherwise noted.

Library of Congress Cataloging-in-Publication Data has been applied for.

ISBN 978-0-06-325796-2

25 26 27 28 29 LBC 5 4 3 2 1

For all of Aubrey LaHaye's descendants,
but especially for my dad.

List to the mournful tradition still sung by the pines of the forest;
List to a Tale of Love in Acadie, home of the happy.

—Henry Wadsworth Longfellow, *Evangeline*

Contents

Author's Note

The story in your hands is built from what remains of a devastating event that occurred thirteen years before I was born. These remnants include old newspaper articles, boxes of documents from the Evangeline Parish District Attorney's Office, redacted fragments of correspondence records from the FBI's investigation, the court transcript of *The State of Louisiana vs. John Brady Balfa* (1985), and the memories of law enforcement, the community, and my family almost forty years later. Though this account is delivered with a deep dedication to accuracy and faithfulness, the book, at its heart, is my interpretation of the information as I uncovered it, and not intended to be a perfect representation of events as they occurred.

The narrative follows my investigation of the 1983 murder of my great-grandfather, Aubrey LaHaye—a first-person narrative occasionally interspersed with scenes drawn from a past I was not present for. These scenes I assembled meticulously using interviews and records of everything from words said to clothes worn to a particular day's weather. Still, there are inevitably details and exchanges lost to time, and I have sparingly used my imagination—informed by knowledge of the world of Evangeline Parish and its people, largely my own family—to fill in gaps and portray situations with the nuance and complexity of life. In addition, while all conversations depicted in the book are drawn directly from records or from sources' memories, in some places I edited dialogue for purposes of clarity and pacing. Where there are conversations drawn from my own memory, such as those with my father, I have on occasion created composite scenes to illustrate the crux of many conversations that took place over the course of years.

A note on names: As you will soon discover, the social world in which this story takes place is a remarkably small one. A rural parish largely populated by a collective of multigenerational families, Evangeline is a place where someone you meet on the street is more likely a cousin than not. It is equally common to encounter others with whom you share a last name, but no (known) shared lineage, or a lineage that goes so far back as to have been forgotten. No names have been changed in this book, and thus you will notice that many characters share last names, or even full names, and may bear no significant relation. I have provided footnotes to indicate instances where this occurs.

In addition, when referring to members of my own family in the text, I do so as I would in life. This means that I grant Great Uncle Glenn, Great Aunt Janie, Great Aunt Tot, and Great Uncle Sonny the simpler, more familiar honorifics of "uncle" and "aunt." My dad's four siblings (Danny, Suzette, Jay, and Nick) and their spouses are named as such the first time they are referenced as aunts and uncles; but I also refer to my father's living first cousins (Jody, Richard, Sandy, Billy, Dusty, and Anne) and their spouses as "uncle" and "aunt" instead of "cousin once removed."

As much as this story is about a murder, and about a place, and about a family—it is also a struggle for knowledge, for answers, for truth; a struggle that continues far beyond these pages. It is a grappling with things unknown, and things that might never be known. And how we carry on despite it. I have laid these gaps, these questions, bare. They are in many ways at the very center of this story, my family's story—which has become, these past eight years, my story, too.

PART I

The Murder

"It's Him"

THE DAY THEY FOUND MY GREAT-GRANDFATHER'S BODY, THE Bayou Nezpique was draining. It was a cold, wet winter in Evangeline Parish—the gray weight of it seeping into each and every sodden air particle.

On the Nezpique Bridge, a ten-year-old boy stood with his father and mother, taking his turn testing the family's new hunting rifle.

It had rung true thus far, ripping through the beer cans, the dangling branches, a lone rubber boot buried on the bank. The boy pointed to a strange, dark mass at the bayou's center.

"What's that, Dad?"

"Hmm . . . dunno, son. Maybe someone killed a deer, dumped the carcass here. Why don't you see if you can shoot a hole in it?"

The new gun stood upright almost as tall as the boy. The father got down on one knee and helped him poke the barrel between the bridge's wooden rails. The boy closed one eye, leveled his aim.

"Now careful . . . careful. Take your aim, and one . . . two . . . three . . . now, shoot."

The forest reverberated from the sound. The target careened, dipped, then bobbed in protest.

"Good job, boy."

Leaning over the railing, the father asked the mother, "What do you think it is?"

"Looks like trash to me," she said, prying the gun from her son's hands. A minute later, she split a hole beside his.

Squinting, the father noticed a rope, stretched taut around one end of the shadowy shape. Taking his turn, he found it in the scope. And he fired. The twine popped, and the black mass rolled.

He froze, "Is that . . ."

The woman's hand raised to her mouth. "That's . . . that's an ear."

It kept turning: an elbow; a hand; dark, wet hair.

She grabbed her son, whose face had faded dull as the sky. She spun him around, burying his head in her belly.

The man stared, stunned, at the crumpled body, and he recognized it. "That's Mr. Aubrey. It's him."

Tell Me Again

I DON'T KNOW HOW OLD I WAS THE FIRST TIME I LEARNED OF MY great-grandfather's murder, only that I was enough of a child that the telling was draped in the distance of "the olden days." The mythology, first delivered most likely by my father though I cannot remember for sure, was made louder in the way it was whispered—the way I understood that this is something we do not speak of.

And we didn't, for almost a decade afterward.

Even today—consumed as I am by the event's minutest details—a ghost version of my childhood imagination, illustrating the unsaid, lingers over the facts as I know them now:

Aubrey, "PawPaw" they called him, floating belly-up, arms outstretched, framed by lily pads and cattails. My father on a tall horse, discovering him.

Emily, my mawmaw, spread-eagle, tied by her wrists and ankles to her bedposts, wailing.

Now I know PawPaw Aubrey's resting place in the Bayou Nezpique[1] was narrow, claustrophobic, more river than lake and more ditch than river. It was winter and everything was brown—the water, the leaves, the mud. My father never saw his grandfather's body. And MawMaw Emily—well, I know now that she asked the abductor if she could sit upright, ever dignified, on the bed's edge while he tied her wrists to the frame. I know that she insisted the man handled her "gently," and that she likely never even screamed.

Still, I can conjure these false scenes as readily as the new ones, as memories. The myth feels as real to me as the truth.

After all, even now, there is still so much we do not know.

I am twenty years old before my father tells me the story again. I'm home from college for a weekend, the two of us in the kitchen.

---

1 Pronounced "Nip-ee-kay."

I tell him I've been writing, and that I've been writing about home.

Everyone else in the usually bustling house has gone to bed. It is just us, on each side of the island in my mother's farmhouse-style kitchen, nibbling on brownies my little brother has underbaked. Dad is still in his scrubs, leaning one arm's weight against the counter, glasses hanging loose around his neck.

We're talking about chasing chickens at the *courir*, about Cajun music and the old record shop in town. About all the things I've only just realized the rest of the world does not know about Evangeline Parish, Louisiana. He's laughing. And then he's pondering, green eyes suddenly serious.

"You know"—he looks down at his hands—"if you're looking for a story about this place. A story that needs to be told . . ." He pauses. "Have I ever told you about how my grandfather died?"

A vision arises: *MawMaw Emily splayed upon her bed.*

"Some of it . . ." I say. "But tell me again."

Day 1

I N THOSE PREDAWN HOURS, A SOUPY FOG SPREAD ITSELF across the Mamou prairie—soaking up the first struggling strands of sunlight, then dissolving them into extended gray. In houses up and down LaHaye Road, men rubbed their eyes and peered out their windows toward the flooded rice fields, listening for migrating ducks. Unable to see even into their backyards, they dialed each other, one by one, to call off the morning's hunt.

Presiding over all of it were the three LaHaye castles: Aubrey and Emily's Acadian-style cottage at the center, flanked on each side by their sons' manors. My uncle Glenn's to the right, my grandfather Wayne's on the left, grandiose behind their collections of sprawling oaks. The farmer and the doctor and their wives—the Dupré sisters, Aunt Janie and my grandmother Susan. In between each house extended open expanses of pastureland, populated by LaHaye Brothers' Angus cattle—some of the finest in Acadiana. The driveways were full, the college crowd in for the holidays.

At 5 a.m., at the heart of it all, Emily's alarm went off. A reminder to reset her chime clock, which had been stopped for weeks. Plugging it back into the wall, her eyes caught a glimpse of her reflection in its glass face—a flickering outline of her sleeping-capped, denture-less state. She squinted, turned away.

The old house creaked as she shuffled into the kitchen, awakening to its familiar morning whispers: water rushing, splashing into the coffeepot, a measuring spoon clanking against the edge of the canister, the old man sighing from the bedroom.

The cold air gripped my great-grandmother by the waist and led her back to bed. Since Aubrey's retirement, there was no longer any hurry, no suit to lay out. They were still learning this new, slower routine. Breakfast could wait a bit longer.

She curled up beside him like when they were young, living in that cold little house on the *Platin*, dirty chickens clucking through gaps in the floorboards. Aubrey grunted, rolled over, gave a lazy smile, and squeezed her, eyes still shut. Emily breathed in the coffee's first curling fumes.

Rap. Tap. Tap. Three knocks ripped through the warmth of her half sleep. She opened her eyes. Aubrey didn't budge. Reluctant to leave the heat of his body, Emily convinced herself she'd imagined it.

Rap. Tap. Tap. More urgent this time. Unmistakable.

She rose. "Aubrey, someone's at the door." She waited for him to roll into a sitting position, rubbing his eyes. The knocking came again.

Emily walked through the kitchen, into the living room. Didn't turn on any lights in the still lightless morning. Before she reached the front door, she could already see through the panes that there was no one there. She paused.

The hammering returned—this time from the den. Whoever it was had moved to the side door. *What could anyone want so early?*

From the bedroom, Aubrey cautioned her: "Be careful, Emily."

She passed back through the kitchen, stealing a look through the window over the sink, flipping on the porch light. A subject materialized: a man, dressed in dark clothes and a funny hat, his pale skin bathed yellow.

She opened the door a crack. "Can I help you?"

It was a quiet voice that responded, one accented with a Cajun dialect not unlike her own, "I'm so sorry to bother you, ma'am. I . . . I had myself a little accident down the road. I was hoping I could use your phone to call a wrecker."

Emily released some of the tension in her shoulders, opened the crack an inch wider, turned back toward the bedroom. "Aubrey! Please come see." She looked the stranger over, a young man, around her grandsons' ages—familiar looking.

Aubrey's hulking presence entered the doorframe. He extended a hand: "Good morning, sir, and what is your name?"

"Hey, Mr. Aubrey, I . . . I had me a little accident."

Nodding, Aubrey leaned back and put his hands into the pockets of his pajama pants, the way he did when he assessed a potential borrower at the bank. "And now who did you say your people were?"

"I'm a Vidrine . . . you know," gesturing behind him. "I live right down the road."

"Where do you work?"

"I work in Mamou."

"Well . . . Surely, I must know you then? Come in, come in."

Emily opened the door and stepped backward, inviting him across the threshold. Turning to her desk, she gathered up some phone books, handed one to "Vidrine." Flipping through another, she asked him, "Which wrecker do you want?"

"Pierottis'll do just fine."

Finger on the number, she was reaching for the phone on the wall when Aubrey choked out the words: "Oh, no no no . . . no."

Emily turned around, and the phone book hit the ground.

The man was holding a knife to Aubrey's chest, pressing a crease into his shirt.

Practically whispering, the stranger spoke, "I don't need the phone. I'm here for money."

Aubrey's eyes, wide, locked on Emily's, which were still glued to the knife. *It's small*, she couldn't help but notice—nothing more than a pocketknife.

"Look . . ." she said, emerging from the initial shock. "Sir, we don't have any money here. You know nobody keeps money in their houses any—"

"—I've got a little bit," Aubrey interrupted her, turning toward his captor. "Em, go get my wallet in the bathroom."

Before she could move, the stranger's free hand grasped her arm. "*Ohhh nononono.* How do I know you won't go and get a gun?" Shaking her head, Emily told him there was no gun in the house. He was vibrating with a manic energy, but his eyes were soft—gentle even. "No," he said. "We'll all go."

Her body acted dutifully, leaving her stunned spirit behind, moving into the hall, through the bedroom, one step after the other. The men followed awkwardly, the knife never budging. From the blue tile countertop, beside their toothbrushes, Emily grasped the worn leather wallet. The stranger snatched it from her, looked inside, shook his head. Two hundred dollars.

He pocketed it, then turned back to Emily. "Okay, now this is how this is gonna go." He pointed to her. "I'm gonna tie *you* to the bed right here."

Something about the way he said it—with reluctance and a certain sense of duty—it alleviated her fear, just a little. *He only wants the money,* she thought. *He'll tie us up, and he'll leave. This will all be over soon.*

"Well, come on then," he said.

She took a breath and stepped forward to the corner of the bed. The stranger kept Aubrey close, moving the knife away from him and pointing it toward her. "I don't want to hurt her," he said, "but if either of you move an inch . . ." He produced a coil of rope from under his jacket, grabbed her arms, and drew her clenched fists together.

"Would . . . would you let me sit down, please?" she asked, gesturing toward her arthritic legs. He paused, looking at the old woman in front of him, grimacing without her teeth in, barefoot in her nightgown. He nodded, stepping aside so she could arrange herself on the bed before starting to wind the rope around her wrists, pressed together, prayer-like, blood pulsing on each side of shaking soft skin. As he tied the knot around the bedpost, she noted to herself that it was a poor one.

The knife returned to Aubrey's chest.

"You aren't going to tie me up too?" he asked.

"Not here," the stranger said. "You and me, we'll go to the front."

As the stranger pushed him toward the door, Aubrey looked over his shoulder to catch Emily's eyes one last time. There, she managed to find a familiar reassurance, a promise, as though he were saying: *It will be okay, Emily. Of course, we will be okay. We always are, in the end.* Then, he turned away.

She listened as they walked through the den to the front door, the stranger's steps heavy, Aubrey's padded, still barefoot. There was a creak, and then a slam as the screen door shut. The rumble of a vehicle starting up, then fading away.

The house was, so suddenly, silent. The brightening sky had begun to seep through the windows. At the bedpost, Emily took a deep shudder-ing breath.

Quickly and quietly, afraid he'd come back, she worked the rope, rubbing her wrists back and forth against it, loosening the knot. She managed to catch a corner with her thumbnail and pulled, breaking loose.

Free, she lurched to the phone on the bedside table, dialing 911. "Hello? Hello. Please help me. I'm in great trouble. I've been robbed, and . . . I think he took my husband with him."

"Ma'am—"

"No, I've—" Her voice cracked and then shattered as she started to hyperventilate: "I've been . . . I've been robbed. They took . . . my husband. I need, I need you to help me, I need you to call the sheriff."

"Ma'am, can you tell me where you live?"

"Everyone in the parish knows where Aubrey LaHaye lives!" she screeched. "Please, please just call the sheriff."

She called her eldest son next. Within minutes, Glenn and Janie were racing across the pasture—leaving their twelve-year-old daughter alone at home, assigned the task of rallying the rest of the family.

The deputy sheriff Thomas Lupkey met Uncle Glenn at the side door around 6 a.m., about thirty minutes after the stranger had first knocked.

Emily hadn't yet left the bedroom. She sat, perched on the edge of the bed. Her hands wouldn't stop shaking. Lupkey sat beside her, pulled out his notepad, and asked her to recount—for the first time of what would be dozens—what had happened. She told him of the knock on the door, how the stranger called himself "Vidrine," and that the knife was a folding blade. He jotted down:

Subject described w/m round face, dark complected wearing a beret type cap, black in color. About 5'10" 175 lbs in weight. Was wearing a flannel shirt. No description of vehicle.

He gathered Aubrey's description, too:

w/m, five feet eight inches tall, 230 pounds, blue eyes, gray hair (receding hairline), glasses, potbelly, last seen wearing blue pajamas, no shoes.

He turned to Glenn, "Have you called Rudy yet?"

"Oh yeah," he said with a nod. "He's on his way."

As if on cue, two vehicles pulled into the driveway. The first belonged to my grandparents—Aubrey and Emily's second son, Wayne, and his wife, Susan. While Glenn looked the most like their father—with his round apple cheeks, heavy brow, and broad shoulders accented handsomely by Emily's dark features and curly hair—Wayne's composure, every move so very thought out, so quietly orchestrated, so gentlemanly, was all Aubrey. His thin frame was tense, jerky even, as he rushed inside to his mother. Susan followed shortly behind, nervous hands pulling at her blond bob, repeating over and over again, "I can't believe this, oh Lord, oh Lord." Janie, all seriousness and strained temples, her dark lips a thin line, caught her sister in the kitchen. "Let the men speak to her first," she said.

The other car belonged to Detective Rudy Guillory. Guillory was a Korean War vet who'd gotten his start in law enforcement at the FBI Fingerprint Identification Section in DC and at Quantico. He spent twenty years working with the Louisiana State Police before coming on, in 1974, as the official investigator for the Evangeline Parish District Attorney's Office in his hometown of Ville Platte. Besides his extensive training, he excelled at the job in part because he was so damn likable. He was only fifty, but already balding with a soft, grandfatherly belly that contributed a certain jolliness to his demeanor. He was easy to trust—well known by most everyone in town. He was also one of Glenn's best friends.

The deputy filled Detective Guillory in on Emily's account, then asked him if he thought this had anything to do with Guaranty Bank in Mamou. Aubrey had retired only weeks before, after serving over thirty years as the bank president.

Detective Guillory shook his head, "I don't know what this is. But yeah, that's what I'm thinking too. Would you secure the scene here? Have Wayne and Glenn take Mrs. Emily to the outdoor kitchen and ask them to stay there for the time being. I'm gonna run down to the station and make some calls."

"Yes, sir."

Within the next hour, my aunt Tot arrived with her husband, Sonny DeVillier, coming from their home in Eunice, a small town about fifteen miles south. Aubrey and Emily's only daughter, the middle child, Tot was a classic midcentury beauty in her youth, a princess of Evangeline. Middle age had treated that inherent elegance well, as had the wealth her husband, Sonny, had accumulated as a lawyer, banker, and investor in St. Landry Parish. Even on this day, in the rush and panic of that morning, Tot wore jewels on her wrists, sparkling through the cigarette smoke swirling from her bright red mouth.

The DeVilliers were followed in quick succession by a stream of grandchildren, nieces, and nephews. The college students who had already headed back to Baton Rouge and Lake Charles and Lafayette were called homeward—a chorus echoing across Louisiana: "Someone took PawPaw."

Just before 7 a.m., Susan used Emily's telephone to call her house— where four of her five children were still sleeping, including my father, Marcel, age eighteen. She told the school-age children they'd be skipping and instructed them to instead get over to morning Mass at St. Ann's in

Mamou. "Then y'all come over to PawPaw's after. Pray hard. Something bad has happened."

They arrived late, but the service was mostly unattended anyway. The LaHaye children kneeled in the back row, hands folded, heads bowed— every shift and shudder echoing throughout the empty congregation. Their mother's call had been brief, and they still weren't all that sure what was going on when Father Nunez announced the Mass would be offered up for the intention of Aubrey LaHaye and his family.

Back at the house, everyone huddled around the pool table in the outdoor kitchen. The air was stretched taut. Some congregated in the center of the living space, crowding into the couches and onto each corner of the coffee table. Others paced and gripped the countertops. Janie started to brew another pot of coffee. Emily had around six hands on her at any given time.

When the phone rang, it sounded like it was coming from another dimension. For the first two waves of sound, everyone could only look at one another. It was Janie who made her way to the wall. She answered, and her eyes widened.

She turned to Wayne, standing beside her. "It's . . . them, I think. It's them." No one moved. She held out the phone. "They say they want to talk to one of the men." He took it from her, looked to Glenn across the room, and gestured toward the main house. Glenn nodded and headed out the door. Wayne gave him a moment to pick up the main extension, then answered, "Hello?"

The voice on the other end was soft-spoken, "Are you one of the sons?"

"I am."

"Okay. Look here, now listen, I'm the one that's got your daddy."

"Okay," Wayne's hand went up to the back of his head. "Just . . . just tell me what you want."

"A half a mil." Wayne was silent. "And Dr. LaHaye, you should know, I'm not alone in this. Do *not* call the cops. I'm telling you, don't do it. There are four of us, and we mean business here."

Wayne's shoulders sagged inward, his thumb and forefinger reaching behind his glasses to rub his eyes, "Surely you must know that's the first thing we did. We called the cops immediately."

There was a beat of silence, then, "We'll tell you what you need to do."

"Yes, just tell us what you want us to do."

"We'll call back at nine. We'll have instructions."

At this point, Glenn's voice poured out, ragged, "Before you get any-thing, we want to speak with our father. We want to know he's okay."

"Sorry, sir, but that won't be possible." There was an edge now, a breathier tone to the voice, a gravelly touch of urgency, increasing by the second. "You can't be making demands here, you see? We are the ones in charge. It's us running this show, Mr. La—"

Cutting him off, Glenn's voice raised to match, managing to get the last word before the dial tone, "We want our daddy back alive! We ain't gonna pay a dime for a dead man, you hear me?"

When Detective Guillory returned to LaHaye Road around 7:20, cars were lined all the way up Emily's driveway, spilling into the yard and the road. If you didn't know better, you might think it was a holiday, or Sun-day dinner. Except that it was a Thursday, and the sun had only just come up from behind its film of weepy gray clouds. He'd made calls to the Louisiana State Police and the FBI, who were each on their way.

When he opened the door to the outdoor kitchen, as he had for hun-dreds of card games and suppers before, the detective was greeted by a frigid, dull silence, a collection of familiar faces stricken by fear like he had never seen working in this quiet parish. Glenn made his way over to him, breaking through the tense portrait to tell, in a frantic flurry of words, of the kidnapper's call.

Detective Guillory directed him back out to the patio, Wayne follow-ing behind. As he pulled out his notepad to take down their statement, the air around them seemed to roar, the trees bending. All three men looked to the sky, where a helicopter was breaking through the lingering fog, descending upon LaHaye Road, shoving a shuddering breath across the petrified prairie.

By 8 a.m., the LaHaye homestead was packed with more than a hundred people, most of them members of the Evangeline Parish Sheriff's De-partment and Louisiana State Police force. An FBI task force of thirty-five agents was called to action by way of the Hobbs Act, a federal law prohibiting the extortion of United States bankers. The agents were headed by Baton Rouge Supervisory Special Agent Ed Grimsley—a forty-three-year-old veteran from North Carolina, whose Hollywood good looks lent a dizzying layer of unreality to the already-outlandish situation unfolding. Grimsley had never worked a major case in a town quite so remote—hadn't seen a single motel on the way in. And he was wondering where he was going to put up all these agents if they had to stay overnight. Someone from the community donated their portable trailer home, which was rapidly set up in Aubrey and Emily's driveway as a micro-investigatory headquarters.

Leading the parish's efforts was Sheriff Ramson Vidrine.[1] The fifty-two-year-old sheriff was well known in the community as a physician-slash-politician-slash-professor and ambled about in thick glasses and a cowboy hat—bearing the familiar potbelly of the area's rice-and-gravy-fed patriarchs. One of Evangeline Parish's prized sons, he had spent years representing his hometown as a state senator and as the state health officer. He'd returned to Evangeline for good about a decade before, working briefly as the parish coroner before deciding to run for sheriff. He was well acquainted with the LaHaye family and knew as soon as he stepped into the yard that this case would come to define his career.

Upon arrival, Sheriff Vidrine and his deputy Floyd Soileau[2] got to work helping Detective Guillory recover evidence from the scene. Soileau collected the rope in the bedroom, still twisted around the bedpost. They scanned the house and, unable to find any other evidence of the intruder's presence, they brought Emily back in, hoping she might direct them to any disturbances they'd missed. As Detective Guillory started to process the kitchen for fingerprints, Emily turned to him. "Rudy . . ." she said, "I'm pretty sure he was wearing gloves."

With nothing else to go on, the detective deemed the crime scene clean and invited the family back into the house, allowing the FBI to take over the outdoor kitchen as they prepped Glenn, Wayne, and Emily on what to say when the kidnappers called back at nine.

Half the agents were then dispatched to Guaranty Bank. After the ransom call, Glenn, who worked as a loan officer at Guaranty, had called up his dad's contemporaries—convincing members of the board to write checks. After all, Aubrey was still a board member himself. The $500,000 was pooled in no time, but the cash was more money than was stored in the bank's vault. Employees were sent driving across the parish to cash the checks at other local banks. Guaranty's vice president,

---

1   Pronounced "Vee-dreen," the name's commonality with the one Aubrey's kidnapper claimed was not a matter of concern to anyone—it being one of the old French family names of the area and extremely common.

2   Pronounced "Swallow."

Harold Monier,[1] and his nineteen-year-old son Greg locked themselves in a small, un-air-conditioned closet in the back of the bank to count it all out by hand—copying each and every bill on microfilm so the FBI could track the serial numbers later.

"Dad, where are we going to store this?" Greg asked.

"Well, in the vault, son. Where else?"

"No, Dad, that ain't gonna work. The time lock . . ."

Harold looked at him, realizing what he was saying. The vault's lock only opened every twelve hours, at 5 a.m. in the morning and 5 p.m. in the evening. The ransom call was supposed to come at 9 a.m.

"Shit," he said. "Shit, shit, shit."

"We're going to have to sit with it," said Greg.

"Yeah, we are. Until they call back."

Back at Emily's, all was silent and still. In the outdoor kitchen, Emily, Glenn, Wayne, and Tot all huddled around the phone, the FBI's recording equipment set up and ready to roll. The minute hand shifted past twelve, 9:01. The silence screamed.

The rest of the day was spent in an agonizing vigil, each room hot with the short, awful breaths of unspeakable anxieties. No one wanted to speak too loud or too long, in fear they might not hear the ringing. And the phone did ring, incessantly—each time effecting a visceral reaction throughout the house: hearts stopping, voices sucked right out of the air, the agents jumping out of their skins to answer. Each time, though, the agent would listen, then make eye contact with Wayne or with Glenn and shake his head. The media, most often; nosy neighbors; Aunt Margot, who lived in California; numbers that called and hung up without a word. One call, immediately dropped, was traced back to the Louisiana State Penitentiary at Angola. Another caller, rendered untraceable, said Aubrey was being kept in a trailer in Mamou. And around ten p.m., a woman called, claiming to be clairvoyant. "I've had a vision of this crime," she said, offering a description of the spot in St. Landry Parish where "they" were keeping him. Despite themselves, with nothing else to go on, the investigators added the information to their short list of leads.

On that list was the vague account of La Nysse—a farmhand employed by Aubrey and other landowners in the community, who claimed

---

1 Pronounced "Moon-ee-yay."

to have seen a pickup leaving the LaHaye house around 5:30 a.m. as he was driving by. He'd noticed lights pulling out of the driveway but hadn't thought anything of it. It was duck season, anyway—there was nothing unusual about trucks pulling out of driveways, headed to the blind, before dawn. When interviewed by the FBI, he couldn't remember a single identifiable detail of the vehicle, only that he had seen it.

Harold and Greg Monier decided to stay overnight at the bank, guarding the cash, ready should the ransom call ever come. They slept on the floor of the bookkeeping room, right under the teller's window. All night long, Greg imagined the kidnapper peering through it, watching them.

In the Home
of the Happy

N THE TEN YEARS I SHARED THIS EARTH WITH MY GREAT-grandmother, MawMaw Emily, I never once wondered where her husband was. It never occurred to me that she might have ever been anything other than a single, strict old woman sitting straight as a board in a floral cushioned rocking chair.

If I could only see her again, I would begin by asking her to recall her father's folktales—told in the evenings after long days spent working in the fields. Considered a tradition bearer of his time, a holder of the "old ways," Marcellus Deshotels played a fiddle upside down, like a cello, because he was left-handed. He and his wife, Atile, raised Emily and her siblings in a small laborers' community down the road from Mamou called L'Anse Grise, where they lived as sharecroppers according to the rhythms of harvest and planting, the simultaneous poverty and abundance of subsistence. A hard life, and simple, but happy—it was a distinctly "Cajun" lifestyle, in which the homestead was the center of the world.

In a book on Cajun folklore, I find one of Pépère Marcellus's old stories—a tale about an alligator disguised as a bridge, secretly eating the town's livestock for generations. When a young boy discovers the truth while fishing, the townspeople decide to kill the monster, bludgeoning it with cannonballs. When they do, the water goes down three feet, and everyone in town receives new shoes. The bayou where it all happened, they say, was the Bayou Nezpique.

Born upon the Nezpique, MawMaw Emily would spend the rest of her life trying to escape it, to forget it. The bayou fed her family, in grain and in story, throughout her childhood; but it never gave them quite enough. And when it flooded, it took everything with it.

Decades later, after she had married into the owning class, she would wring her hands over the fact that her grandson, my father, the namesake of her father, Marcellus, planned to make a home beside the bayou, instead of on LaHaye Road. She couldn't believe that instead of settling

on the promised land she and PawPaw Aubrey had built for their descendants, he'd chosen to live upon the Nezpique.

"That was where the poor people lived," my dad remembers hearing
her say of L'Anse Grise. No matter that my dad was coming home to
start a medical practice, with a wife who had plans to do the same. Nor
that the distance between the Nezpique and LaHaye Road was barely
five miles.

Of course, though she'd never speak of it, for MawMaw Emily the
Nezpique would forever represent monsters far more sinister than poverty. Beneath its frigid January waters, for ten days, the Nezpique had
hidden the love of her life—bludgeoned to death like that gator, tied up
like a pig, sunk to the bottom.

Born on the cusp of the twentieth century, Emily Deshotels and Aubrey
LaHaye were among the last generation of Louisianans to speak French
before English, to claim their identity as "Cajun" or "French" *before* American. The age of assimilation began with them, the draw toward the
country western music on the radio, the television—bringing the rest of
the world, bright and shiny as it was, into their homes. The world wars
ushered in a new patriotism, forcing the men out of their homes on this
isolated, French-speaking prairie and into American military uniforms.
And when they became parents, Aubrey and Emily remembered how
they had been beaten in the schoolyards when they forgot the English
word for "play" or "home" or "bathroom." Their children would grow up
speaking English, as would every generation after them.

By the time I was growing up at the beginning of the next century,
the term "Cajun" and the culture it represented had been almost lost,
then revitalized through various preservation efforts, then commodified
across Louisiana and beyond. A form of it lived on in our isolated little
towns in Evangeline Parish, though, struggling away thirty miles from
any interstate and much farther, it sometimes seemed, from the rest of
the world and its influence. I heard Cajun French all around me as a
child, the secret language of the "old people," spoken in fragments in the
gas stations and on the radio. It was the language of the music—songs
we all knew, even if we didn't know what the lyrics meant. And I understood that long ago, in the before times when no one had cars or running
water, MawMaw Emily had known French. I wish I could remember
hearing her speak it.

Still, I understood that I, too, was "Cajun." In a certain sense, "Cajun" was all my generation knew of ourselves. In those later aughts, the mostly white upper-middle-class students attending Ville Platte's private Catholic school possessed bloodlines thickly blended—each of us emerging from tangled branches of the Acadian, French, Spanish, and German ancestries that came together on this prairie two hundred years ago. Rarely did the traces of our Atakapa-Ishak and Black Creole forebears reveal themselves on our fair-complected faces. But they live on in us too. All these classifications have largely been lost to the ages—buried within the mixing of peoples. In Evangeline Parish, if you were white, you called yourself Cajun.

This designation was what connected us to one another—most of us fifth, sixth, seventh cousins, our parents and grandparents able to trace the lineage all the way back to some single shared ancestor. Cajun defined our funny, flat accents, our crawfish pond horizons. It was why we poured Slap Ya Mama seasoning into a pile on our lunch plates and dipped everything in it. Why all the local restaurants played fiddle music on the radio. Being Cajun had something to do with how we smoked our meat better than anyone else in the world, and the way the entire city smelled like roux in the mornings. It was why we all had big families and mawmaws who cooked the best rice and gravy, why our neighbors knew when we missed Mass on Sunday. Why on the first weekend of October, the high school football game was pushed to Thursday to accommodate the first day of squirrel season. We didn't even really know, yet, that the rest of the world was any different.

The first time most of us gained an inkling of where it all came from, what had been lost, was in sixth-grade English class—each of us taking our turn reading aloud stanzas from a packet of stapled sheets: Henry Wadsworth Longfellow's *Evangeline: A Tale of Acadie*. We'd begin all together, a chorus of young Cajuns remembering:

> *Ye who believe in affection that hopes, and endures, and is patient,*
> *Ye who believe in the beauty and strength of woman's devotion,*
> *List to the mournful tradition still sung by the pines of the forest;*
> *List to a Tale of Love in Acadie, home of the happy.*

Through the recitation of this myth, this love story crafted by a New Englander who had never been to Acadie nor Louisiana, we discovered for the first time where we came from, the New France—Nova Scotia, Prince Edward Island, New Brunswick. "The Home of the Happy." Acadie. Our French ancestors had come to the New World as early as the 1600s, promised bountiful fishing and a thriving fur trade in this land of fertile pasture and abundant orchard, guarded by the brilliant blue Atlantic and all her riches. Longfellow paints a portrait of paradise: a village of oak and hemlock cottages with roofs of thatch, lovely girls wandering the streets in handspun skirts, singing as they went. *L'Angelus* rang through the valley twice a day, re-creating the Immaculate Conception and reminding the world of miracles. There, in Acadie, *"the richest was poor, and the poorest lived in abundance."*

My father planted us beside the Bayou Nezpique, despite MawMaw Emily's protestations. The short distance between our home and LaHaye Road granted my Texan mother, swollen with my early beginnings, space to form roots apart from the claustrophobia of our family, time for her to seep into the land. The history of this place, of our ancestors' lives here, rarely crossed their minds. But I like to believe the ancient oaks and pecans scented our blood in the air. That, despite our English, they recognized the old French songs of Marcellus Deshotels in my and my brothers' childish shouts and screams, in my father's thick, thick Cajun accent.

The Nezpique ran along the border of our pasture, which rose like a tiny forest out of the infinite, treeless farmland. The bayou held its own magic, trickling away on the far side of the field, cradling our little world. In the springtime, we'd walk there without shoes, baking beneath the vast Louisiana sky. The stand of woods upon her banks welcomed us over the threshold: a dark, wet world canopied by myriad trees all wrapped up together—a private room carpeted in luxurious emerald moss. My brothers would leave their hoop nets overnight, and the entire family would feast on catfish fried crisp and flaky the next day. My friends and I imagined fairies hiding between the waves and knots of a cypress's foot, dancing on the canopy above our heads.

Later, when the magic of childhood wonder faded into something else, I'd run to the Nezpique and back, twice. Two miles. My mom, terrified someone would try to pick me up from the lonely road, would park her Suburban at the end of our driveway until I was done.

Longfellow's *Evangeline* begins where the Eden ends, on the heroine's wedding day in 1755, when the British ships arrived.

Through the fictional characters of Evangeline and her lover, Longfellow imagines a microcosm for the real-life deportation campaigns against the Acadians, an event now known as *Le Grand Derangement*, or the Great Upheaval. After a century of being passed back and forth between France and England, the settlers of Acadie felt less French than they once had. But they certainly didn't feel British. When the British lieutenant governor Charles Lawrence demanded the Acadians sign an oath of unconditional allegiance to Britain, they flatly refused. Such allegiance would require them to bear arms against the French if called upon, as well as their allies and helpers in Acadie, the First Nations tribe, the Mi'kmaq. It would require them to abandon their Catholic faith in favor of the Protestant Church of England.

As punishment for this disloyalty, the British destroyed the Acadian villages and forced them by the thousands onto their ships, which "[bore] *a nation, with all its household gods, into exile. Exile without an end, and without an example in story.*" In Longfellow's telling, the soldiers burn Evangeline's village to the ground, slaughtering its cattle and leaving the corpses to rot. Her father, an elder, dies upon the beach as he watches it all go up in smoke. In the chaos, she is separated from her beloved Gabriel, who she'll spend the rest of her life searching for.

Years later, I'll find the real Acadians' names on lists, on blogs, in books—exhaustive efforts of the dispersed, generations past, trying to recall that lost Acadie. We're spread across the globe now, our ancestors dropped without resources and as outsiders into the new British colonies. Many were shipped back across the ocean to a home that no longer recognized them, nor wanted them. They died by the thousands on the journey, of cold, disease, and hunger, *"friendless, homeless, hopeless."*

At least twelve of my ancestors were among the few who escaped the initial deportations—only to be captured and held in prison camps in Halifax. After the British achieved their goal, transforming Acadie into an extension of New England, they finally allowed the refugees to leave on their own accord. This group of two hundred Acadians set their eyes on the bottom of the continent, on Louisiana.

The Spanish colony, which had a few years before been ruled by the French, promised a Francophone culture rumored to welcome Catholics and new settlers. In the summer of 1765, the refugees arrived on the Southwest Louisiana prairie, the home of the Atakapa-Ishak people, where the grasses were as tall as their horses. Here, the Acadians built temporary huts and fought rampant disease. They learned to hunt and to farm this strange new soil, to fish the intricate lacework of rivers and bayous surrounding them. Many died, many left. But the ones who stayed dug in their heels, and they sent word to their fellow refugees around the world.

Welcome once more, my friends, who long have been
friendless and homeless,
Welcome once more to a home, that is better perchance
than the old one!

Over the course of the next century, the Acadians, who came to be called "the Cadiens" and then "the Cajuns," became known for using every piece of the pig, for catching bugs out of the bayous and making them delicious, for singing the saddest songs and telling the tallest tales and throwing the most raucous of parties. The European settlers and the Creoles of the area couldn't resist falling in love with them. The region they occupied—spanning South Louisiana from the Gulf through the bayous to these prairies—became defined by their distinct presence and given a name: Acadiana. And in 1910, two years before Aubrey LaHaye was born, they named the piece of it my ancestors called home "Evangeline."

In that classroom, we did not learn of the Acadians' Mi'kmaq allies, or of Halifax, or the names of our ancestors. We learned only of an idyllic, ever-faithful woman, banished from her home into a wanderer's existence, spending the rest of her life searching, without rest, for her lost love.

In the bored way of preteens, without clearly registering it, we absorbed from *Evangeline* an understanding that we had lost something, long ago. With this loss came an inheritance—a new comprehension of our Cajun identities, shaped by survival and reclamation. That day, the word *resilience* quietly seeded itself into each of our emerging selves, fated to grow and trail behind us so long as we claimed this story, this people, this place.

Day 2

WHEN I IMAGINE HOW MY GREAT-GRANDMOTHER MUST have spent that first night without her husband, I see her stubbornly refusing to retire anywhere but her own bed—despite the constant, screaming reminder of its emptiness. She wouldn't have slept a second. Hours before daybreak, she'd have abandoned it, recalling how long it had been since she showered and how so many strangers had seen her in pajamas the day before. She'd turn the water on hot, almost scalding, and stand beneath it for what must have felt like hours. She'd have taken her time, wrapping up her hair in curlers, selecting a dress for the day. What shade of lipstick do you wear to send off a search party?

Just when the pleasure of such privacy might have started to impress itself upon her, she would have felt the weight sinking back in, starting upon her shoulders, and spreading out across her chest. I see her leaning against the wall, sinking to the tile floor, wheezing.

As early as 5:30 a.m., twenty-four hours since the stranger entered her home, Emily was sitting at her kitchen table, holding a cold cup of coffee in both hands. The room was buzzing: Susan stirring up a bowl of cornbread batter, bacon frying on the stove, Detective Guillory shouting out orders, various officers passing in and out. Someone had brought in early editions of the local papers, the front pages reading "Mamou Banker Grabbed at Home," "Son Wants Proof Father Is Alive Before Paying, Officer Says," "Ex-Mamou Banker Kidnapped." They were calling it Evangeline Parish's first-ever kidnapping case. In the newspaper for the nearby town of Opelousas, the *Daily World*, reporter Monte Williams quoted a sheriff's deputy, who said: "We don't know a damned thing more than we knew yesterday, but we're still looking."

No one had slept. Glenn, Janie, Wayne, Susan, and Tot had stayed overnight, sitting in the outdoor kitchen with the officers and agents, sustained on coffee. All of Aubrey's grandchildren had stayed in their parents' houses, even the adults who had homes in the area. No one wanted to be alone. Each house had an agent on guard, as well as an FBI-issued gun.

The agents and officers who remained worked through the night, canvassing the immediate area, pulling at strings, rotating through naps on Emily's couches. As the hours stretched onward, no one spoke of the possibility that the abductor might have already killed Aubrey. They focused, instead, on the fact that he did not have access to his blood pressure medication. If the kidnapper didn't kill him, a heart attack soon would.

"Can I get you anything, ma'am?"

Emily startled, a trance broken.

She looked up at the handsome young man in front of her, one of the agents. *His name is Ellis*, she remembered. Her voice came out hoarse. "No, dear. Thank you. Thank you for all you are doing." He offered her a half smile, tapping the table in front of her. "We'll find him, Mrs. Emily. We'll find him." She turned back to her cup, the exhaustion on her face shifting subtly into a manic determination. "Of course, we will."

At 6 a.m., hundreds of local volunteers—friends, neighbors, the grandsons and their friends, the local farmers—gathered in the outdoor kitchen, where the FBI laid out a strategic plan of search parties led by deputies, agents, and officers. Because some of the older volunteers still spoke only French, Sheriff Vidrine translated Grimsley's instructions to them: "*Si tu trouve un corps mort*"—If you find a body—"*touch li pas.*" Do not touch it. "*Va chercher un maison à coté, demander pour fair un appel sur le téléphone et puis pélé nous-autres à l'office du Sheriff.*" Find the nearest home, ask to use their phone, and call us at the Sheriff's Office.

They spread out on horseback and in squad cars, ATVs, and boats—through the rice paddies and out to the duck camps, through the forests and into the trailer parks, knocking down doors and wading through swamps. Above them, helicopters churned the sky, searching for a suspicious-looking pickup truck.

Throughout the day, a steady stream of vehicles passed down the remote LaHaye Road, slowing to ogle at the activity, the FBI, the helicopter. *Things like this don't happen here.* Officers stopped each sightseer, asking for license and registration and to disclose if they traveled this way frequently—particularly during the hours of 5 a.m. to 7 a.m. "Do you pass here every day? Every week? Did you pass here yesterday, at this time? Did you see anything out of the ordinary? Anything at all?"

Guaranty Bank stayed open, and the lobby stayed full. People stood idly in groups of twos and threes, whispering, coming in to make small withdrawals just for the chance to ask the tellers, "Have y'all heard anything?"

Whenever they went on break, the tellers and the clerks started combing through Aubrey's records. Were there any big transactions? Any unusual deposits? Was Aubrey, or the bank, suing anybody? *Who did he piss off?*

That afternoon, at the FBI's recommendation, Aubrey's children invited local media to the courtyard at the front of the house. The goal, the FBI had explained to the family, was to appeal to the kidnapper's conscience. Wayne, milder mannered than his hot-tempered older brother and better known across the community as the town doctor, was selected as the more sympathetic spokesperson. After introducing himself as Aubrey's son and physician and thanking the dozen or so newspaper and television reporters for coming all the way out to the country, Wayne pulled out the statement they had spent the last several hours perfecting. His siblings and their spouses stood behind him—Glenn glowering at the crowd, hands in his pockets, Susan actively weeping. Addressing the kidnapper, Wayne intoned, just a little too quietly: "I feel you cannot know the grave medical danger our father is in right now, because he has been unable to take medications for his illness." He struggled not to look down, to train his eyes on the cameras. "Our only concern now is for his safe return. Please reestablish contact with us by calling the number you called earlier, or by getting in touch with someone who can."

Things Unspoken

BY THE TIME MY DAD DELIVERS THE BOX OF OLD NEWS-papers, I've already read most everything available online about the Aubrey LaHaye murder case.

A wave of insomniac obsession had me, night after night for weeks, cracking the pitch dark of my bedroom open in a blue glow as I waded through thousands of results for "Aubrey LaHaye Murder Mamou" in digital newspaper archives. A small-town kidnapping and murder of a seventy-year-old, rich, white man—the trove of news coverage was deep, stretching from the tiny *Mamou Acadian Press* all the way to a brief article in the *New York Times*. My computer became clogged with those digital scraps, and I pored over them meticulously—filling a notebook with de-tails and phrases that jumped from the screen. The "agitated" unnamed neighbor interviewed on the first day, who worried over why the kidnap-per had not worn any disguise. The way the journalists described Maw-Maw Emily and PawPaw Aubrey's home as "fashionable" and "spacious." I draw three question marks beside the note "two white men believed to be robbers forced their way into LaHaye's home"—a supposed misprint that ran in several outlets those first few days. In large script taking up a whole page, I copy out a reporter's description of the scene that first morning, with everyone: "huddled prayer-like around the phone."

A dissonance clangs within my chest each time I read the names I recognize so well, MawMaw's, my grandfather's, my grandmother's. Each time I recognize the courtyard in the photographs beneath the headlines—the same house my dad's older brother Danny, my *parrain* (godfather), inherited, where we to this day gather for Easter, Christmas, baptisms, birthdays, bridal showers. The bathroom, my dad swears, still smells like it did when PawPaw Aubrey was alive. A must of old per-fume floating in roux. In the newspapers, I see the branch behind Agent Grimsley's head, and I know the tree it belongs to. I wonder if I'll ever be able to stand in that kitchen again without reaching my mind out into the walls, asking what they remember. I wonder how Parrain Danny was able to sleep in that bedroom for all these years, to forget what happened there. His grandchildren now race through the hallways, play pretend in PawPaw's old office. Four generations past, the shadows have diminished to nothing.

I read the reports again and again, trying to reconcile the layers of my reality with this one. The revelation feels ridiculous, and almost embarrassing—that this story had felt so distant, so mythic, when I heard it as a child. Somehow, I had failed to realize *it happened to the people I love*. My dad was only a few years younger than I am when he saddled a horse to go looking for his grandfather's body.

This is not the story I know of my family, this is not the legacy they delivered to us. Bad things don't happen to the LaHayes—with our giant beautiful families living in the giant beautiful houses out on beautiful LaHaye Road. Aubrey and Emily's progeny are Evangeline Parish's doctors. They are the region's nurses, its teachers, its farmers. They are active members and generous donors of the local Catholic churches. The name LaHaye can get you out of a speeding ticket all over the state or trap you in an hour-long round of stories with an old man who used to be *padnahs* with your uncle. For a period, most of the babies in the parish were delivered by my grandfather, Papa Wayne. As they grew up, they'd visit my uncle Nick when they got the flu, a whole generation developing schoolgirl crushes on the handsomest of the LaHaye men, their family doctor. Many of them would be taught kindergarten by Aunt Sandy, whose doting lilt in her voice would forever be associated with the alphabet, and they'd fix their lisps during speech therapy with Aunt Dusty. Later, when their parents divorced or became addicted to drugs or enmeshed in some other crisis, they would go to counseling with my grandmother, Mommee Susan. And to this day, almost every Viagra prescription in town goes through my dad, the town urologist.

For more than twenty years—from the 1990s through the 2010s, there was a LaHaye in almost every class from kindergarten through twelfth grade at Sacred Heart Catholic School in Ville Platte. As a lot, we were well-behaved. We were creative. At the top of our classes. We were the baseball stars, the homecoming queens, the valedictorians. Some of the deepest fears of my generation are to be the first of the LaHayes to get divorced, or the first to bear an ugly baby. LaHaye babies are notoriously beautiful, and they grow into beautiful children, who are expected to become beautiful teenagers, beautiful adults. That one of us might bear an unhealthy child, or be unable to bear one at all, is unthinkable.

How did I miss this? I ask myself. This devastating moment, so deep and so ugly, transmitted as lore so as to disintegrate to nothing. I realize I've almost never heard anyone speak of Aubrey at all. To me and my brothers and my cousins, it was almost as though he had never existed, much less been killed so spectacularly.

Except he had, and he was: the evidence was laid out before me, in this cardboard box, wide and wilted, the bottom taped up to keep it from breaking open.

Mommee Susan tells me Aunt Tot spent years collecting these clips. Papa Wayne inherited the archive after her death in 2002, stored it in the attic, and tried to forget about it. He failed, though, because when my dad came asking, almost twenty years later, he knew exactly where it was. Later, as I carry my questions across Louisiana, I'll discover dozens of these archives still exist, scrapbooks of Mamou's most sensational crime, kept for decades by family members, friends, acquaintances, and fascinated strangers alike.

I imagine Aunt Tot cutting out the portrait of her father with a pair of kitchen scissors, carving a perfect line atop the headline "LaHaye Body Found in Bayou Nezpique." Thirtysomething years later, I'm there with her, my fingernail dragging across the type, line by line, trying to understand what happened to us.

Day 3

O N THE THIRD DAY, A WAVE OF TENTATIVE HOPE WORMED its way through Emily's house. A tip came in. The caller, reporting from the Breaux Bridge area about sixty miles southeast of Mamou, told of a suspicious vehicle on LA 314. Inside the silver Mazda RX-7, the young driver had appeared exhausted, and his passenger—a white, slightly overweight, elderly man—looked as though he was gagged.

The bureau put out a call to agents based in towns along the routes leading east and west from Mamou to Mississippi and Texas, asking them to check the parking lots of every motel along I-10 and US 90—searching for a silver Mazda RX-7. *Maybe this is it*, everyone dared to think. *Maybe he's still alive.*

The FBI hoped, today, to get something more out of Emily too. After three stressful attempts at crafting a composite portrait of the abductor based on her traumatized, piecemeal descriptions, they still didn't have one she was satisfied with. One of these interviews was recorded as follows:

> Mrs. LaHaye describes the subject as a white male in his early thirties, with dark skin, round face, clean-shaven, 5'11" 165–170 pounds, slim build, wearing glasses ... wearing gloves. ... a dark, light weight type jacket, a dark colored tan-type cap, fitting tightly over his head. She advised that she observed no jewelry and no glasses and did not recall him having any facial hair. Mrs. LaHaye describes the subject's features of his face as being clean, unscarred. And describes his eyes as 'sweet eyes.' She advised that he spoke in English with an accent that is very common to the area in which she lives. Mrs. LaHaye advised that the subject was very polite, used no foul language, and did not treat them roughly.

Even in this description, one of the most detailed of the many, Emily contradicts herself. First she tells the officer that the subject was wearing glasses, then later she says clearly, "no glasses." This second assertion would stick; glasses would never be spoken of again.

Each time they attempted to create a composite, the officer would sit down with her, pulling out clear plastic sheets depicting detached lips, eyes of every color and shape, left ears, right ears, and piles of dumpy little chins. He'd lay out fragments to form what is meant to be a sort of bare-bones everyman reflecting her description, which Emily offered like a recitation. The result was a cartoonish rendering that looked both unhuman and something like every white man you've ever seen. He'd ask her about the nose: Was it protruding? Pointy? Did the nostrils flare? Each step of the way, Emily would hesitate, rubbing her hands together, shaking her head. "It's not right. This doesn't look like him. I'm sorry, I'm sorry. I'm sorry I can't do better than this."

By Saturday, she was thoroughly frustrated by the whole thing. When the FBI agents asked her if she would sit for one more session, she protested. "I don't know what else to say," she told them, her eyes red from lack of sleep and tears shed. "I would recognize the man if I saw him, but I'm telling you I can't describe the way he looked." This time will be different, they explained. "Mrs. Emily, have you ever heard of hypnosis?"

The agents prepared a clean, empty room at Guaranty Bank for the process, which they hoped would break through Emily's anxiety to reveal something new. But so frayed were her nerves by this point that the specialist, try as she might, couldn't get Emily into a trance state at all. Following the pendulum, she would close her eyes, appease the specialist, answer the questions, but her consciousness was firmly set in that little room, where she felt plainly ridiculous. They tried three times, and she told the same story—almost word for word—she had told since day one. *He knocked on the door. He had car trouble. It seemed like Aubrey knew his family. I grabbed the phone. I turned around, and there was a knife to Aubrey's chest.* "Tell me again what he was wearing, Mrs. Emily," they'd say. Much was made of her mention of a hat. "What kind of hat? A baseball cap? A top hat?" "It was round, like the Girl Scouts wear," she told them. The agents in the room looked at each other, perplexed.

Later, in the kitchen at the bank, one of the agents looked up. "A beret!" The other men in the room turned to him and frowned. "Like the Girl Scouts wear! A beret."

About an hour later, the agents brought Emily in one last time. "Mrs. Emily, did the hat look like this?" Someone had gone to a store in town, and now entered the room with a black beret on his head. Her eyes lit up, and she nodded in recognition. "Yes," she said. "Just like that."

In the far corner of the room, one of the deputies said aloud what many of the Mamou residents were already thinking: "Feryl Granger always wears a beret."

Though never stated in an official capacity, the name had already been hovering around most conversations of the investigation. The notorious Granger had grown up starting shoot-outs at the Mamou bars and was rumored to be a contract killer for the Dixie Mafia out of Biloxi, Mississippi. At the time of Aubrey's kidnapping, though, he was imprisoned in the Huntsville Texas State Penitentiary. He could not have been the man who took Aubrey, and there was no definitive reason for connecting him to the crime—but it was undeniable that there was something distinctly "Feryl" about the whole ordeal.

Despite Emily's insistence that the composites weren't quite right, the investigators took what they had and deemed them official. They took copies back to her house to share with the search parties and the family.

As the agents distributed the portraits throughout the packed den and kitchen, Aubrey's granddaughter-in-law Cindy and nephew Bob, both employees at Guaranty Bank, stood elbow to elbow by the back door. When Cindy got her copy of the drawing, she gasped. With her hand to her mouth, she turned to Bob and whispered, "Doesn't that look like that kid who came in last month? That PawPaw turned down for the car loan?"

Bob looked at her, then back down at the flyer. "You're talking about John Brady Balfa."

Balfa was a skinny, floppy-haired twentysomething from Mamou whose dad was a farmer and a carpenter, his mom a hairstylist, and his uncles famous Cajun musicians. Most of Mamou had watched him grow up, the way they watched most of the kids from the bigger families in town grow up Sunday after Sunday in church, playing in the city sports, and through the local high schools. He was the same age as the older LaHaye grandkids, and the town had collectively celebrated when he'd been elected student body president at LSU-E, the two-year Louisiana State University campus in nearby Eunice, a couple years before. He'd later transferred to the university's flagship campus in Baton Rouge, and most people had lost track of him since, though he still showed up around town on occasion. Over the past year, he'd been visiting Guaranty Bank, applying for different loans—coming in each time a little more frazzled, a little more desperate. Aubrey, who almost never turned anyone down, had to tell him no. And Balfa had been pissed.

"John!" Cindy nodded. "Yes, John was his name. Oh . . . Bob, you don't think it could be him?"

"I see what you mean, Cindy; it does look familiar. But . . . surely not?"

Later that same day, Ramona Johnson in Guaranty Bank's note department was making copies of the composite to pass around town. As she stood over the machine, Johnson watched the face shoot out on top of itself, again and again. A familiarity registered. Coming out of the printing room with the stack, she set it on her desk and grasped the sheet off the top. "Hey, Joyce, come over here for a sec," she shout-whispered across the room to her coworker. "This . . . This is John Brady Balfa's face, right? Isn't it?"

Joyce Reed held the paper up close to her eyes, "Oh yeah! I do—I see that!" Handing it back to Johnson, she asked, "You don't think it could be him, though? I mean he's just a kid."

Johnson stared at the picture, "I . . . I really see him in there. You know I went to high school with him? That would make him about the right age, actually. A little younger."

"Yeah . . . Gosh, Mona, if you're serious—you might go ahead and tell one of those FBI guys about it. You never know what could help?"

"Oh, I don't know . . . You know what, I'll bring the yearbook in tomorrow, and we'll all take another look, just to be sure."

At Emily's house later that evening, the calls ramped up, responding to the composite that had now been plastered on every storefront, meat market, gas station, bank, and feed store in Evangeline Parish; and shared with every media station in the surrounding area, through which it entered the television screens of every home within a hundred-mile radius.

By this point, Wayne's statement from the previous day's press conference had already made its way across the country—printed in newspapers large and small, from the *San Francisco Examiner* to the *Evening Sun* in Baltimore, from the *Billings Gazette* in Montana to the *Fort Lauderdale News*, from the *Los Angeles Times* to the *New York Times*. The composite would follow suit, staring back at an enraptured audience with cold, empty eyes.

The Nose Isn't Right

N ONE OF AUNT TOT'S CLIPPINGS, THE COMPOSITES TAKE UP half of the front page. I place these side by side with an image of John Brady Balfa I track down in the LSU yearbooks, taken a few years before PawPaw's kidnapping. He's got a shock of black hair, setting him apart from the beret-capped man in the drawing. His face is too skinny, I think, too angular. The nose isn't right. The eyebrows, though, and the ears—they're similar. I guess. It's amazing to me that anyone *saw* in the composite this man whose face gazed out at me from the yearbook. That they recognized him. I stare at the two images until my eyes hurt, trying to decipher what I'm missing, because I *must* be missing something, something strained from MawMaw Emily's devastated memory and replicated effectively enough for Aunt Cindy and Uncle Bob and Ramona Johnson to see it.

I think back to something my dad told me that night in the kitchen. "We don't have the full story," he said. "There are things about this that we might never know. But what's crazy is some people really, truly believe the guy they put away didn't do it. That he's innocent."

There's a paper that stays toward the top of my pile, the disheveled mountain of newsprint on the side of my bed. I keep coming back to it. In September 1985, a journalist interviewed John Brady Balfa's parents before a pretrial hearing. "There's no motive, never was," insists his father, explaining that his son could not have possibly killed Aubrey LaHaye. His mother tells the interviewer she does not believe the case will even make it to trial. "Something, someone will come up and prove him innocent."

"He didn't do it," his father says. "He couldn't have."

Day 4

ON SUNDAY FOLLOWING THE ABDUCTION, ST. ANN CATHO-
lic Church was filled to bursting—families from across the parish
squeezed into every pew, resisting the urge to ogle at the poor
LaHaye family up at the front; to point at Mrs. Emily; to whisper about
the handsome men in uniform who sat behind them—taking up three
pews of their own.

My father sat in between his brother Danny and his uncle Glenn.
That morning he, Danny, and their sister, Suzette, had made the decision to stay in town until they found PawPaw, even though LSU's spring
semester started the next day. Dad was considering not going back at
all, perhaps enrolling at LSU-E so that he could keep living at home.
The boys had each been going out every morning with the search parties,
spending those endless days on horseback and in cop cars.

On the other side of Danny was their mother, Susan, eyes squeezed
tight. No one believed in prayer's power more than she, and most of the
family believed she had God's ear. That she had hardly ceased praying
for the past three days seemed to carry its own weight in hope for everyone else. Looking to her, my dad was reminded to bow his own head,
lowering it to rest on the pew in front of him, his hands clasped above
as though he were begging. And he was. *God, let us find him today. Let us
bring him home to MawMaw.*

All around him, the congregation recited, "Lord, I am not worthy to
receive you, but only say the word and I shall be healed."

Marcel lifted his head, having heard something strange to his right, a
choke on the word "healed." He discovered his uncle Glenn, the toughest,
hardest man he knew, weeping. His right hand splayed over his face, his
shoulders jumping, and a terrible childlike sound coming from his throat.
And the horror of it all hit my dad like a train, as he realized: *Uncle Glenn
doesn't think we are going to find him.*

\\\\\\

AFTER THE COMPOSITE HAD CIRCULATED, REPORTS OF LOOK-
alikes arrived in a torrent. The FBI set out to locate, interview, and clear
each one. In addition to the composite-driven potential suspects, officials drew up a slate of area characters with criminal records and bad
reputations.

It didn't take long for John Brady Balfa's recent run-ins with the law
to earn him a star by his name, falling into both categories. One of the
agents went to his father's house, a few miles down the road from Emily's.
They found his teenage brother Tim on the property and asked where
John Brady was.

"Oh, Brady's in jail," Tim told them. He'd been arrested in Longview,
Texas, on January 7, the day after the abduction, facing charges of rape.
The agents asked Tim if there were any photographs of his brother in the
house. Five minutes later, he emerged with John Brady's LSU-E student
body president portrait.

"Handsome boy," the agent said. "Is this how he looks now?"

"Well, he's got a mustache," answered Tim.

"Hmm. Okay if I take this? We'll get it back to y'all."

"Sure."

Sheriff Vidrine had his own top suspect. Calvin Ware, a known burglar,
had recently escaped the Evangeline Parish Jail. The Oakdale native, a
legend for having escaped Angola in 1979 by swimming across the Mississippi River, had weaseled his way out of the jail twice the previous
fall while in custody for stealing four hundred pounds of sausage and
tasso from a local slaughterhouse. The second time, for which he and two
other inmates had scaled the wall around the exercise yard using their
bedsheets, had stuck—so far, at least. By the time of Aubrey's kidnapping, the other two escapees had been apprehended, but Ware had been
on the run for three months. His talent for evading capture, people said,
stemmed from a childhood spent helping his father train bloodhounds;
Calvin was the bait.

Still on the loose, desperate, matching Emily's descriptions, and possessing history with the LaHaye family (he'd once rented a home on the
LaHaye estate), Ware enjoyed a place at the top of the potential suspect
list. The FBI sent out a teletype informing agencies in all surrounding
states to be on the lookout for him. They showed Emily a photograph

of Ware, asking her if it resembled the man who had entered her home. With more certainty than she had shown during the composite phase, she shook her head. "That is not him," she said. "I can see the resemblances, but that's not him."

Still, Sheriff Vidrine wouldn't let it go. He kept naming Ware in the press as a "prime suspect." Each time, Agent Grimsley would clarify: "We have not referred to [Ware] as a suspect, we have no suspects."

That night, the sheriff gave another interview to the press. "No clues, no news," he told them. "I really don't know where to go from here. If it was a spiderweb, we'd hang on. And we won't stop."

American Dream

ODAY, EVANGELINE PARISH IS A QUIET, STAGNANT PLACE. Beyond the farmland where my brothers and cousins and I spent our childhoods, the towns and villages that make up the parish are littered with abandoned warehouses, boarded-up windows, ghosts of bustling downtowns past. There is no movie theater, no bowling alley, no shopping mall. Any restaurant that opens offering anything finer than a burger struggles to survive more than a year or two. In the few nightlife dives deemed "safe," you're as likely to meet an eighty-year-old man as a high school cheerleader. Walmart is the only full-fledged grocery store for miles. Most educated people who live within the parish work in one of four fields: education, health care, agriculture, or manufacturing. Some folks try to make their way selling insurance. The business owners who do the best own the meat markets. In 2018, *USA Today* reported Evangeline's parish seat, Ville Platte, as the poorest town in Louisiana.

When PawPaw Aubrey was growing up in Evangeline Parish, though, at the height of the area's tilt toward Americanization and all the aspiration it carried, everything felt brand spanking new.

Aubrey was born only two years after Evangeline became Evangeline, a new parish sectioned off from the existing St. Landry Parish, named for Longfellow's heroine. The town of Mamou was officially incorporated the year before he was born.

He grew up a witness to the way good ideas make money in a new world. In the single comprehensive history of Evangeline Parish, a 1972 tome titled *The Opelousas Country* by Robert Gahn Sr., Aubrey's father, John LaHaye, is cited as one of the parish's pioneers, and in his obituary is "regarded by many as one of the most influential and important men in the early history of Evangeline Parish."

Old man John, whom my family calls "Pépère" John, had his hands in enterprises ranging from cotton farming and carpentry to raising livestock and training wild horses. My papa Wayne tells me Pépère John can be credited with building almost every single road in Evangeline Parish. More famously, he and his business partner, Gus Miller, dammed the Bayou Nezpique to irrigate over three thousand acres of rice fields—in the process creating one of Louisiana's best hunting and fishing sites still in operation today, Miller's Lake.

As John LaHaye acquired his wealth, he invested in the enterprises of others—doling out private loans to friends and neighbors at a going rate of 8 percent interest. The man was illiterate and didn't speak one word of English. "He never wrote a sentence," Papa Wayne tells me. "I don't think he ever wrote his name, just 'JL.' To think about what he accomplished without that ability, it's shocking."

When PawPaw Aubrey is spoken of today, it is often as John's reincarnation—"Except a little bit warmer," stipulates my father, "just a little bit." Of John's four sons, Aubrey looked the most like his father—small framed, but with broad shoulders, carrying their weight in their bellies. Chiseled, hard faces weighed down in perpetual seriousness by thick, heavy brows.

Thrust into the momentum of a developing parish and the vacuum of opportunity it presented, Aubrey knew a good blueprint when he saw one. Upon his father's, he laid his own vision. He possessed John's knack for numbers and his business acumen, but he also had the advantages of an education, amplified by the ability to speak English. As soon as he came of age, he launched himself into the industries his father had prepared him for: cotton farming, rice farming, cattle raising, road building, and lending.

"They could see the whole picture," says my aunt Cindy of PawPaw Aubrey and Pépère John. "All at once." They could watch the weather and predict a good crop year, knew which sort of soil was best for planting cotton and which for rice. They were able to judge whether a man would pay back a loan, just by looking at him.

In June 1931, one week after her high school graduation, Aubrey married his high school sweetheart, Emily. And their American dream began.

Aubrey's father recruited him and his friend Leslie Ardoin[1] to settle with their new wives on a plot of land he owned near L'Anse Grise, where

---

1   Pronounced "Ard-wehn."

Emily had grown up, to sharecrop some of the first commercial rice farms in this cotton farming community.

People grew rice in Evangeline, sure. They grew it for their table—tossing seeds into the bayous near their homes, into the ditches, and waiting to see what emerged. They called this "providence rice," or "rice by the chance." Food made from little work and earnest prayers; food provided by God.

Pépère John, a man of great providence, saw opportunity for something bigger.

So Aubrey brought Emily to their first home, a cottage on a swath of pastureland they called the *Platin*. "We had nothing during those years," MawMaw Emily told my aunt Cindy once. For extra money, Aubrey and Leslie would go out into the ditches and catch the bullfrogs that lurked there, hoping to sell their tender, meaty legs at market. In 1934, when Aubrey's younger brother Elvin graduated from high school, he and Aubrey entered a business partnership with Leslie.

They started buying up as much land as they could afford. In addition to the cotton farms they acquired, they bought less-desirable, lower-lying lands for cheap—seeing their potential, under John's guidance, as rice plots. Much of this land could serve doubly as pasture, and the brothers began to populate it with herds of cattle.

After seven years and two babies, my papa Wayne on the way and, finally, plenty of money in their pockets, Aubrey and Emily made the move to a permanent homestead, on the road that would someday be called LaHaye. With the new home, they purchased acres and acres of land surrounding it—extending south to Mamou and north to Vidrine—encompassing a nine-hundred-acre lake that would later bear the name LaHaye, too. This would be their home. This would be their farm. Living five miles from the land her father had sharecropped, Emily was no longer digging up potatoes in someone else's dirt. This place, it was all hers.

Day 5

S O MANY PEOPLE WERE COMING IN AND OUT OF EMILY'S house that on the fifth day the plumbing broke down.

Because there were so few hotels in the area, the FBI agents were now living in the family's houses down LaHaye Road and in the trailer parked in the driveway. And they were eating better than they had in all their lives.

An assembly line of volunteers had been established in the outdoor kitchen making ham sandwiches, but in Emily's ever-crowded kitchen, magic emanated. A rotation of dutiful granddaughters and great-nieces and in-laws manned the massive pot, dishing out gravies, gumbos, biscuits, and roasts at all hours of the day. The smells—the spicy richness of burning roux and frying meats—allowed the chaotic space the grace of a haven, for the strangers and the family alike.

On occasion, Emily would become restless and make her way into her kitchen. Ignoring the "just sit down Mrs. Emily"s and "You don't worry about that"s of her daughters-in-law and her granddaughters, she made space on the countertop and immersed herself in the daily practice of bread making. Hours later, when the familiar smell of her French pan loaf began to waft from the oven, everyone stopped whatever they were doing to breathe it in.

Agent Grimsley decided he had to ask for the recipe. As she measured out flour, he said, "Mrs. Emily, my wife is a wonderful cook—I'd love to have her try to make this incredible bread of yours. Is the recipe a secret?" Emily laughed, the first time anyone had heard such a sound since the nightmare began. "No, *cher*. There's no secret. But there's no recipe either. I just do it like I always have. You're welcome to stand right there and watch if you like." Grimsley pulled up a chair, drawing from his front pocket the same notepad he'd been using to mark down clues and interviews, phone calls and leads. "I think I'll do just that."

In between the meals, the relentless vigil carried on. Besides the kitchen, the house was unrecognizable, stretching at its seams. The phone never stopped ringing, never the kidnappers. What had been MawMaw and PawPaw's house now felt like it would always be a crime scene, an FBI headquarters, a paparazzi horde. A site of mourning.

The one reprieve, one source of comfort, and at times even a shimmer of joy, were the babies: Emily's great-grandchildren, oblivious to the tragedy. The oldest was four—dashing in between the dozens of legs in the living room, then collapsing into deep, unadulterated naps upon various shoulders. The two one-year-old girls teetered about, blond and cherubic, blabbering on. And then there were the new babies, each less than six months old—being passed around to their great-grandmother like life rafts.

My father and the other young men, unable to match their sisters' and mothers' sense of duty in the house, sought their purpose outside of it—going out with the search parties every chance they got. Guided by members of the Sheriff's Department, they had already followed countless leads, checking out the suspicious movements in the rice field, the noise at the old camp, the light left on in the abandoned house, some footprints in the woods. Now, their objective was more aimless, more general. Covering ground. At this point, the authorities seemed to be trying to keep them busy.

They searched in silence, against the gentle background noise of hooves splashing through puddles, four-wheelers humming ahead. An armada of young, angry men balancing on a thin thread of hope and despair. Glenn's son Richard would bring his homemade machine gun with him every day, and the FBI never said a word about it. On one of the ATVs rested a suitcase, packed with clean underwear, socks, shoes, a suit, and a tie for PawPaw when they found him.

The LaHaye Farm

O N A SUNDAY AFTERNOON, MY UNCLE RICHARD AGREES TO take me on a drive. I want to know what the farm encompassed when he and my father were growing up. In his sixties now, Uncle Richard is the last of the LaHaye farmers, though it's been almost twenty years since he's farmed anything. Once known parish-wide as a hurricane of a man, not to be messed with, he now wears a jolly belly, glasses, and a gray beard, and his grandchildren call him "Peg." But he still knows the land like the back of his hand.

The first place he takes me is the old LaHaye Lake, which you can still find on Google Maps, though it is no longer a lake and no longer entirely the LaHayes'. For the first time, I realize how big it was, how *different* everything would have looked back then. Where those endless, rippling fields of green now extend there would have been only water, as far as the eye could see.

Most of the farmers in Evangeline Parish today are rice farmers— John and his sons' success revealing the opportunity of this water-logged savannah. Rice farming requires flooding, so to live here is to follow the rhythm of the water coming in, the water coming out. Planting season, harvest season, flooding season, crawfish season, duck hunting season. Ebb and flow, work and play. Skies in the water and sun-colored crops.

Before the days of mechanized irrigation systems, LaHaye Lake was the farm's water source, controlled through an intricate system of canals and earthen levees that followed the contours of the land. A pump at one end pushed the water, after a heavy rain, from the surrounding community into the lake. With farmland encompassing the lake on all sides, whenever the family needed to flood one field or another for the rice crop, they'd dig into the levees until there was an opening big enough to let the water through.

We move on, and Uncle Richard shows me where the cattle pen used to be, right off LaHaye Road, the slaughtering station. He takes me to each of the old barns, tells me about how the hay bales used to be square, not round, and how the barn at PawPaw Aubrey's house alone could hold two thousand bales. He remembers every levee, every canal. He names the plants growing in the ditches beside the new rice crop and recalls how when he was a boy, they'd send him and his older brother, Jody, out to pull all the weeds across the entire crop. Today, chemicals keep the unwanted flowers in the ditch.

"So much in agriculture has changed," he says. "The landscape looked so different; you have no idea." During Uncle Richard's time as a farmer, from 1980 until the early 2000s, the industry evolved in monumental ways. Laser leveling, pesticides, irrigation systems. Four-wheel drive tractors. Four-wheelers! "I got my first four-wheeler in 1987," he says. "Up until then, I would saddle up five horses every morning to go out into the fields."

The farms are more productive now, he admits, by far. But the land has suffered because of it. The culture too. "When I was farming, we ran water all over the place, and there was fish and frogs and turtles and everything else, and now that's all gone." He remembers that the fields held low, wet spots—tiny swamps they'd call *marais*. "There was some all over the farm. When it rained a lot, we'd go catch frogs and we'd catch turtles, all that. But now it's all laser leveled. All that's gone."

Uncle Richard tells me about how, mere months before PawPaw Aubrey died, he and Uncle Elvin agreed to separate the estate so that it could be better divided among their heirs. To do so fairly, exactly 50/50 as they had always done, they had to drain the lake. "Nothing was ever quite the same after that," he tells me.

Driving the backroads of the old LaHaye estate, Uncle Richard slows down past a set of century-old oaks. "This was once a homesite," he says, one of the many scattered throughout the old rice fields. This is where PawPaw Aubrey and Uncle Elvin's laborers lived. "Some of the little houses," he tells me, "were made of cinder blocks."

To say that Aubrey grew up on the post–Civil War version of a plantation wouldn't be an exaggeration. John LaHaye's farms were almost entirely labored over by Black workers, many of them descendants of enslaved people who, unable or unwilling to travel north after emancipation, were forced to abide by St. Landry Parish's Black Code. These laws required all Black people who lived in the parish to find a white employer.

This employer was legally given absolute control of their Black workers' movements, their living arrangements, business ventures, and access to firearms. Though the laws were quickly repealed, the social structures they established—which essentially preserved the racial hierarchies and cheap labor white landowners enjoyed before the Civil War—lasted much longer. Pépère John's laborers did receive compensation for their work, but never enough for them to leave and make it on their own. He provided them with housing and with food, establishing a community entirely dependent on him. The men helped to plant and harvest the rice crops and to herd cattle, and the women worked as nannies and house-keepers in John and his family's homes.

When Aubrey and Elvin began to develop their own properties, the descendants of John LaHaye's workers came to work for them and their families under much the same arrangement, with slightly higher pay. "They 'lived for' MawMaw and PawPaw," remembers Uncle Richard. "If you asked them what they did for a living, they said they 'lived for Mr. Aubrey.'"

Uncle Richard pulls out a list he's written of their names: Alton and his wife, Ocelia. Bébé and Violette Chapman. Pell Chapman. Stanley Jack. Junior Mitchell. Calvin Chapman. Fedah and Tonya. Herman Le-Day. Ronnie Simon. Alton Simon. Litton Green.

This isn't all of them. I only have pieces of their stories, told from the perspectives of my father and my uncles. But I do know that PawPaw Aubrey and Uncle Elvin and their descendants' prosperity and comfort is largely owed to their exploited labor. And that though Aubrey's legacy shines for his contributions to his community, the people and projects he invested in, that legacy and those investments never did extend to the Black population of Evangeline Parish.

Knowing all this, perhaps it shouldn't have jolted me as much as it did, finding the July 1969 news article with Aubrey on the front page, stand-ing with his hands in his suit pockets at the podium at the Evangeline Parish School Board's anti-integration rally.

For all his vision, PawPaw Aubrey could not see beyond a world made for him, a world structured around white people owning, and Black people working. He could not see it. Or he didn't want to.

Day 6

JANUARY 11, 1983

ARLY TUESDAY MORNING, THE MEDIA FRENZY HAD RE-
turned to Emily's courtyard. Dozens of newspaper, television, and
radio reporters clustered around the three LaHaye siblings, who
this time all stood behind Tot's husband, Sonny DeVillier. He introduced himself as Aubrey's son-in-law and attorney.

"I have been asked to serve as family spokesman in announcing a
$25,000 reward to be paid for such information received from this date
onward that results in the return of Mr. LaHaye."

The siblings had reluctantly agreed with the investigators to ensure
the callers' anonymity and protection, in the interest of finding their father, or at least his body. After thanking the media and the investigators,
Sonny referred any additional questions concerning the investigation to
Agent Grimsley. He closed with: "Members of the LaHaye family are
continuing their tense vigil, sustained by their faith, their family, and
their friends. Their anxiety is great, but their hopes undimmed. We wish
there were more to report."

Following the lead on John Brady Balfa, Agent Grimsley had arranged
with FBI agents in the Tyler, Texas, office to send interrogator Lloyd
Harrel to question him at the Gregg County Jail in Longview. Harrel
met Balfa in the interrogation room, where he sat in a folding chair
in his county jail-issued gray jumpsuit. He was well groomed, thin
as a rail, with thick dark hair and an impressive mustache. His Adam's apple bobbed when he spoke, and his movements were agitated,
annoyed even. But his eyes widened when Harrel explained he was
with the FBI, that he had not come concerning the pending rape
charges.

"Have you heard anything about the kidnapping of that old man in
Mamou? Mr. Aubrey LaHaye?"

Balfa sat back in his chair. "Oh yeah . . . I did hear something happened a couple days ago. They were talking about it on the radio."

Harrel pulled out a form, then passed it across the table. "I'm hoping you might be able to help me out, share anything you might know about the crime."

"Well, sir, I can tell you I don't know anything about it besides what I just said. I heard it happened, and that they hadn't found him yet."

"Then this should go quickly." Harrel smiled. After asking Balfa to read aloud from the document, which explained his Miranda rights, he said, "Now, we've got that settled. Okay if I ask you some questions?"

Balfa agreed, still insisting he didn't have anything to offer.

"Well, let's start with your whereabouts on the morning of January 6. Where were you when you woke up?"

"I was at my daddy's house, in Duralde, on the outskirts of Mamou."

"Who else was there?"

He answered that his father, his little sister, and his little brother were all at the house, but they hadn't seen him. "I left at about 5 a.m. to drive to Texas."

"Walk me through the morning, will you?" What time did he wake up, did he eat breakfast, did he go tank up his truck?

"My alarm went off, I put my jeans on, and went to my truck. I had packed and tanked up the night before. Got breakfast on the way out."

"And what was your business in Texas? Where were you going?"

"I was going to see my girlfriend. She lives in Atlanta"—a small town in northeast Texas.

Harrel asked Balfa for the name of the place he got breakfast—"Food, Etc."—and whether he'd made any other stops on his way out of town.

"Yeah, I stopped to pick up some laundry in Eunice."

"What was the name of the establishment?"

"Uh, Manuel's, I think."

"Did anyone see you there?"

"Damn . . . I mean, I don't know."

"Mr. Balfa, if someone can confirm your whereabouts at that time, it'll be easier for us to eliminate you, and I'll get out of your hair that much faster."

Balfa shook his head. "Okay, okay. I mean the guy I paid, I guess he was the owner. He was an old guy, probably about fifty or so."

"All right. What about a receipt? Any proof of the transaction?"

"Uh, yeah, I think I got a ticket."

"And what will the ticket say? How many pieces of laundry, how much did it cost?"

"Shit, man. I think it was six shirts. I had them washed and starched. I remember getting a dollar back in change—I had handed him a twenty."

Harrel made the notes. "Great. Any idea where we can find the ticket?"

"I'm sure it's still in my truck."

"And what kind of truck was that, that you drive?"

"It's a green Ford."

Balfa went on to say that after getting his laundry, he went straight to the Best Western in Atlanta, arriving just before noon. He purchased a one-night stay and took a shower before meeting his girlfriend, Debbie Kinney, at around 1 p.m. in the parking lot. The two drove around town until about 3 p.m., in her sister's car, before he went back to his truck and drove to a worksite in Lodi to speak with his boss at Sunland Construction—a pipeline company. Balfa said he stayed there until about 6 p.m. before heading back to the hotel to change for a double date with Debbie and her sister that evening.

"Where did y'all go?"

"To see a movie in Texarkana."

"What time?"

"I think we left her parents' house at about 7:15."

"What did y'all see?"

"*Tootsie.*"

"And afterward?"

"We went to eat pizza—I don't remember the name of the place."

"Then?"

"We went back to her parents' house and dropped her sister off."

"Debbie came back with you?"

Balfa sucked his teeth. Harrel was expressionless. "She did."

"And spent the night?"

"No. She followed me in her car, then left about three or four in the morning."

Only then did Harrel crack the smallest of smiles.

"Tell me about the next morning."

Balfa said he woke up at about eight thirty or nine to learn his bondsman was trying to reach him. His bond check had bounced, and there was a warrant out for his arrest. He called the guy and agreed to surrender himself at Debbie's parents' house. He left the hotel and spent the day there, until law enforcement came for him in the evening.

"And you've been here in jail ever since?"

Balfa raised his cuffed hands, "Right here, ever since."

Harrel leaned forward in his chair. "Well, thank you, Mr. Balfa, for your cooperation. I have a few more questions before I can let you go. Now, do you *know* Mr. Aubrey LaHaye?"

"I know who he is, but I don't know him well. I know he's a big deal in Mamou, is always in the papers doing a bunch of 4-H farm stuff."

"Do you know where he lives?"

"Somewhere outside of Mamou. I don't know the exact house or anything."

"Do you think he'd know who you are?"

"Yeah, probably." About a year before, he'd run into some problems in Baton Rouge with bookies and was struggling to pay his tuition and other bills. Had written some bad checks. He'd asked Mr. Aubrey for a loan, "and he had basically granted it to me," he said. But then someone from the booking department interrupted their meeting to let Aubrey know about the checks. "Then he turned me down."

"Got it."

Harrel pulled out another document and passed it to Balfa. "This is to give us permission to search your vehicle, as well as Miss Kinney's. We'll try to locate that laundry ticket."

Looking over the document, Balfa frowned.

"You know, I don't know about all this . . ."

"Like I said, Mr. Balfa, if everything you said is true, it'll only help us eliminate you."

Balfa's leg had started to jiggle. "I'd like to talk to my lawyer first," he said. "Sorry, sir, you don't understand. The cops here . . . they're treating me like shit. I didn't do anything. I just don't trust all this."

"Okay, Mr. Balfa. That's fine. Speak with your lawyer. We'll send someone to come talk with you tomorrow. We'll have them bring a polygraph test to confirm your statement—if you'd be willing to comply."

Balfa started shaking his head. "No."

"No, you won't do the test?"

"I don't trust those things at all. I've taken them for jobs and gotten screwed. I'm not taking that."

"Mr. Balfa, this is the FBI, we have some of the best equipment available—I'm sure much better than whatever was used—"

"No, Mr. Harrel." Balfa's voice was getting higher pitched. "I'm sorry. I'm not saying anything else. I need to speak to my lawyer."

The Greatest Man
That Ever Was

P AWPAW'S MURDER . . ." MY DAD TELLS ME, "IT'S CHANGED everything about who we are. All our lives were changed, forever." Attending the annual LaHaye-Dupré Christmas at Mommee Susan and Papa Wayne's house, these words echo in my mind. The "Nativity" play is about to begin. Children are wailing over "We Three Kings," and Papa Wayne stands beside me and laughs, his hands in his pockets. "Maybe this will go smoother than last year's," he suggests. I smile. "I doubt it." And all I can think about is the photo of him standing in Parrain Danny's yard, begging the abductor to bring his daddy home. I understand, suddenly, that I will have to ask him, all of them, about it. About this thing that we don't talk about. This thing that has changed them, forever.

When I ask Papa Wayne to tell me about his father, he comes alive— listing out PawPaw Aubrey's many achievements, his accolades. He regales me with the origins of our people, naming all the ancestors displayed in the black-and-white portraits in the hallway. We talk for hours and hours before I realize we haven't even gotten to the murder yet. I don't want to ruin it, don't want to bring in the darkness just yet, to dampen the excitement in his eyes. I tell him we'll continue another time.

And so, on I go, carrying my list of questions onto my family's porches, into their kitchens, asking them what they remember, reminding them of what they've forgotten.

PawPaw, I loved PawPaw, my uncle Jody tells me, smiling. *He was the greatest man that ever was.*

In most of the memories my family members hold, PawPaw Aubrey remains firmly immortalized in his most recent self, his grandfatherhood. A fat old man in a suit and cowboy hat, driving to the bank every day and sitting in his recliner in the evenings, smoking a cigar.

He could stand on his hands! Mommee Susan recalls, laughing. *Oh yes, big ole guy. He would stand on his hands and walk on them, and the kids would laugh.*

He always had the same kinda car, says my dad's youngest brother, Uncle Nick. *Like a Crown Victoria, some old kinda grandpa kinda car. And he was a bad driver.*

Some of my parrain Danny's favorite memories of PawPaw, as well as Aunt Sandy's and Aunt Suzette's, are of the days he'd pick them up from preschool. *He would take us to buy ice cream at the stand across from the church. And then bring us over here for MawMaw to feed us lunch. And she would fuss at him every day, "Aubrey, I can't believe you bought them ice cream, I'm trying to feed them." But the next day, he'd do the same thing.*

For Uncle Jay, another of my dad's brothers, it's the watermelons. *Every year, when watermelon season came around, we'd hop in the car and drive to Sugartown to go buy watermelons. That was one of his favorite things. He would grow some in the garden. And one time Nick and I went. He walked in the yard and picked up a watermelon and broke it on his knee. And we sat in the grass and ate it just like that, with our hands and stuff.*

He jingled when he walked. Papa Wayne tells me a story of how when my dad was about a year old, he had been sick with encephalitis— practically comatose. When PawPaw Aubrey came to check on him, nervously rattling the coins in his pocket, Dad uttered his first words in days: *PawPaw, nickel!*

I collect these little portraits—hoping I'll gather enough to render my own, breathing, life-size version. The stories pour forth in patterns, in rhythms. A series of scenes blurred, sparkling by time and by grief. Tiny moments, really. Altogether ordinary but possessing elements of grandeur and idealism that make PawPaw Aubrey feel simultaneously familiar and alien, human and sainted.

His chair was the first chair as you walked in, Aunt Anne tells me. *I'd open the door, and PawPaw would be sitting right there, shelling pecans or peas, watching Lawrence Welk or Jimmy Swaggart. And he'd say, "Come here, baby." And I'd climb up in his lap and give him a hug and a kiss on his fat cheek. And he always always always had his little cigar. That smell, still today, reminds me of him.*

PawPaw Aubrey, says Uncle Richard, *he was the icon. He was the guy. His word was the word. Everybody depended on him, you know?*

I can picture my great-grandfather, just there. But even when I reach deep into the realm of possibility, folding time into creases upon which we might stand, facing each other as equals—he feels untouchable to me. When I imagine us together, I see us standing awkwardly, struggling to connect in the miracle of each other's company, only able to conjure the simplest of small talk.

When I was a kid, my papa Wayne remembers, *we'd get on the horses, and we'd go out to the old pastures. There were four or five hundred cows and calves out there. And we'd look at every single one, and sometimes we'd do this, and he would not say one word.*

Stepping into these homes, the landscapes of our history writ large— something shifts between me and my aunts and my uncles, my cousins and my grandparents, something that wasn't there before. Threads of our shared histories are retying themselves, the knots unwieldy and frayed at the ends. But they promise, perhaps, to hold.

By the time I return to Papa Wayne, I've worked myself into a nervous wreck, amplified by my father's insistence that Papa "will never say how he really feels." But I can't put it off any longer. I take a deep breath and turn down the oak-lined driveway.

Papa Wayne smiles and kisses me when I come in, but I can already feel the shadows of the gulf returning—that ancient silence. He is not cold toward me, but he is visibly tired. He answers my questions clearly, straightforwardly. Unlike most everyone else I've questioned, he reveals no residual questions, no fact unresolved in his mind. This is what happened: how it began, how it ended. A chapter in our history book, shut and saved on some corner shelf, not to be bothered with again. By way of his responses, he displays complete and absolute closure, betrayed only by his avoidance of eye contact, by the pauses in between question and response, the stray "I guess." That interview is over in under an hour. He still smiles at me when I leave, but this time I can see he is happy for me to go.

Day 7

ON WEDNESDAY, THE SEARCH FOR THE SILVER MAZDA—THE most viable lead of the entire investigation—came to a disappointing close. After interviewing the vehicle's owner and a series of witnesses, investigators found that when the car was sighted, the driver had been on his way to a sports car rally. The passenger explained he was wearing a bandanna over his nose and mouth because he was recovering from the flu.

In Longview, another agent from the Tyler office, George Kieny, came to see if Balfa would provide the written permission for the FBI to search his and his girlfriend's vehicles. Balfa agreed to the search, and then asked Kieny if he could be formally questioned again. "I talked to my attorney, and I want to clear a few things up."

He explained that he had told Agent Harrel the day before that he had left his house at 5 a.m. "It was actually sometime in between 5 a.m. and 6 a.m.," he said. Kieny nodded, wrote the change down in his notebook. "And if you need someone to attest to that, I had discussed the plans to leave early with my dad, Harry Balfa is his name, the night before."

"Okay."

"Also, I told the other guy I got my laundry done at Manuel's, but it was actually Aguillard's."

"Got it. Anything else?"

"Yeah, one more thing. I think I told him I met my girlfriend Debbie at one—after talking to her, I think it was closer to twelve thirty or twelve forty-five."

Kieny closed his notebook and thanked Balfa for his cooperation. On his way out, he asked the officials at the jail to take lineup photographs of Balfa and five other men who resembled him. "Have them forward those images to the New Orleans office, ASAP. Make a note about the mustache too. I'm pretty sure that's not consistent with the witness's description of the guy they're looking for."

That same day, the possibility of a new breakthrough in the case emerged when a private detective called the FBI's information line. He explained that, for reasons unrelated to the Aubrey LaHaye kidnapping, he had been hired to investigate a man who lived on the LaHaye property, whose parents, Alton and Ocelia Adams, worked for Glenn and Janie as a field hand and housekeeper. During his surveillance, the detective had used a shotgun microphone to listen in on conversations at the Adams household, during which he'd overheard someone in the house say something along the lines of "We gotta feed that old man, or he's gonna die."

In response, the agents deputized the young men who had accompanied them on the search parties, inviting them to join in on the raid. My father agreed; Richard loaded up his machine gun. The general consensus—powered by pent-up fear, fury, and an explosion of relief at the notion that Aubrey might still be alive—was "we're gonna get this motherfucker."

That night, the posse of two dozen cop cars roared into the Adamses' yard, sirens blaring and engines revved, skimping on no spectacle. They surrounded the house. Someone shone a spotlight, revealing its dilapidated, crumbling state and Mrs. Ocelia running out the door, wearing nothing but her underwear. She screamed as an agent threw her to the ground. Alton, tall and thin, walked outside with his hands up, palms glowing against the darkness and his own dark skin. Eyes wide, he looked at the armed men around him, locking eyes with my father, who turned away. Someone handcuffed him, and two other agents kicked down the screen door, rushing into the house, where they found their guy and cuffed him. They noticed an old man sleeping in the bedroom, and, after ensuring it wasn't Aubrey, they took him too. Grimsley sat with the suspect in the back seat of one of the cars, holding him in a choke hold, whispering something terrifying in the man's ear.

Back at the camper in Emily's yard, the FBI questioned each of the Adamses long into the night. As the hours wore on and the exhilaration wore off, the agents began to realize the deadening truth: these folks had no idea what was going on. The all-too-obvious fact that their suspect—

a short, stocky Black man—didn't match Emily's description in the slightest settled in. This was not their guy, not even close.

When Grimsley shared this with the family, the silence filled the room like poison. Richard and Jody kept their heads down. Glenn slammed his fist into the table. Janie excused herself. My dad didn't sleep that night. He couldn't stop seeing those trembling, white palms.

A Big-City Man
in a Small Town

WHEN I SEARCH "AUBREY LAHAYE" IN THE ONLINE NEWS-
paper archive, limiting the search to end in 1982—before the
influx of kidnapping coverage—almost fourteen hundred results come up.

The bulk of the coverage deals in my great-grandfather's public life,
which began in October of 1939, four days after his youngest child, my
grandfather Wayne, was born—when Aubrey announced his candidacy
for membership on the 1940 Evangeline Parish Police Jury (an elected
body that is the Louisiana equivalent to a county board of commission-
ers). From that year through 1970, Aubrey LaHaye is mentioned in the
local papers almost weekly in association with his various civic pursuits.
His appointment to the jury made him the youngest juror, at age twenty-
eight, in the short history of Evangeline Parish. He would remain a
member for twelve years, eleven of which he'd hold the title of vice president. In this capacity, Aubrey was part of, and often a leading figure for,
every major crisis and resolution and initiative to take place in the parish
through the early 1950s. This ranged from declaring states of emergency
for property owners during bad flooding years, to running an aluminum
drive for war efforts, to creating the Rural Housing Authority and initiating the parish's first food stamp plan. Beyond the jury, he helped to found
institutions and organizations that continue to impact Evangeline Parish
to this day, including the Evangeline Parish Farm Bureau Federation, the
Mamou Rotary Club, and Guaranty Bank. From within these entities
and others, he was an ever-present force in those heydays of Mamou's
development, and over the course of four decades, he worked his way
to the directorship or presidentship or chairmanship of virtually every
single public initiative he was involved in.

Aubrey knew that for the town to grow, to thrive, there needed to
be more jobs, and he became an outspoken proponent for fostering new
businesses within the parish. He invested in a new textile mill where local

farmers could process their product locally and a creosote plant funded by Kennedy's Area Redevelopment Administration. Governor Jimmie Davis, best remembered for his penning of the song "You Are My Sunshine," attended the plant's dedication on a 109-degree August day in 1962.

Aubrey's most prominent business investment, though, was the Mamou Rice Drier and Warehouse, which he opened with his brother Elvin and friend Leslie Ardoin in 1949. The warehouse served a growing need for rice storage in the area as more and more farmers switched from cotton to the less labor-intensive crop. When they opened, the LaHayes and Ardoin had a storage capacity of 50,000 barrels of rice. Over the next several years, the business expanded, and at its most profitable the drier's total capacity was 220,000 barrels. Local reporters described it as the "Cadillac" of all rice driers in Southwest Louisiana. Though the LaHaye family possesses only a small share of the business today, the driers remain, an imposing citadel defining the Mamou skyline.

Day 8

JANUARY 13, 1983

ONE WEEK AFTER THE STRANGER KNOCKED ON THE DOOR, there was little evidence Emily was sleeping, and she had to be reminded to eat something, anything, *please MawMaw*. At times she was resolute, hopeful, angry. At others, she was inconsolable. Most of the time, though, she sat, silent, in the living room with her daughter, her daughters-in-law, and her granddaughters. And, in an almost hallucinogenic state, she prayed.

While the FBI continued to make their way down the list of potential suspects, the Sheriff's Department set up roadblocks once again on LaHaye Road. "Perhaps we'll find someone who only passes here on Thursdays," said Sheriff Vidrine. "Someone who saw something."

Agent Grimsley asked the LaHayes if they had any friends who owned crop dusters. Glenn nodded and asked why. "Since we don't have the copters out there anymore, it would be good to have someone keeping an eye out from the sky," he told him. He didn't share that in the FBI's instructions to the pilots, they told them to pay special attention to any circling buzzards.

At the bank, the FBI started opening Aubrey's personal records, hoping to find some indication of motive or "confidential contacts." At the end of the day, in the teletype report Grimsley sent to his director, the account of each of these efforts ended with the words: *results negative.*

The Banker

ONE DAY, SOMETIME IN THE 1950S OR 1960S, A MAN NAMED Kronten visited Aubrey at the bank. He stepped into his office, closed the door behind him.

"How are you doing today, Kronten?" Aubrey asked, standing up to shake his hand.

"Well, Mr. Aubrey, I'm here to say goodbye."

"Goodbye?"

"Yeah, I just can't make it over here. I've got to do more than I'm doin'. So I wanted to tell you how much I've appreciated your help, but I'm gonna pull my stakes and we're gonna move out to someplace else."

"Kronten, you're a capable man. You've got great ideas! Good friends. What's your problem? What do you need?"

"It's about property, Mr. Aubrey. I need much more property than I've got to make a go at it like I want."

"Well, what about the piece of property you're living on?"

"It's not mine, and I can't afford it."

"Well, what would you do if you could afford it?"

"Well . . . I'd grow rice on it."

"And do you think it would be prosperous?"

"Oh yeah, I mean if I could afford to run it, I could make some money there."

Aubrey hopped into the car with him to go look at the property. Together, they calculated how much it was worth, how much Kronten could afford to pay. They estimated the potential profit a farm would produce.

And then Aubrey gave him the loan.

"So," my papa Wayne concludes his fable, "Kronten stayed. He built a beautiful home. He progressed, did all sorts of stuff. Every time his old lady comes into my office, she has to kiss me and tell me, 'Your daddy was so good to us.'"

\\\\\\

AT A ROTARY CLUB MEETING IN 1974, AUBREY TOLD THE STORY OF how he—a man with no college degree or banking experience—came to be the president of Mamou's first bank. His education had come from his father, he said, who schooled him in agriculture and economics. Aubrey claimed that in his twenty years of banking, he had made "no mistakes," and that he'd never had a single farmer fail to pay his dues.

"If someone came to ask him for a loan," recalls Greg Monier, who worked at the bank as a young man while Aubrey was president, "he asked who your parents were, who your grandparents were. And a very few times, 'Do you have a job? Do you have the ability to pay?' That wasn't as important."

Guaranty Bank opened in Mamou in August 1950, with plenty of fanfare and a capital stock of $100,000. Aubrey would hold his position as president for the next thirty-two years, developing a reputation as an especially liberal lender for area farmers.

"There were not a lot of laws at that time, and it didn't matter—he wouldn't have followed them," Aunt Gayle, Uncle Elvin's daughter, tells me. "Federal regulations, they didn't have all that. And when anybody came in the bank, he could tell by their facial expressions, by their eyes and all, that they were sincere and they would pay him back."

"Somehow or other he knew who to trust, or he'd trust them all. I don't know which," says Papa Wayne.

For almost thirty years, Aubrey managed almost every dollar coming in and out of Mamou, with little regulation. He was a handshake businessman, who held the whole town's finances in the vault of his own mind. Guaranty Bank's recordkeeping was sporadic at best, loans were doled out daily without a drop of ink spilled. To this day, I struggle to find a scrap of my great-grandfather's handwriting, any record of his work, of his thoughts—all of it lost to time and to that bayou.

It started in the late 1970s, the federal oversight. All of South Louisiana was undergoing a recession as the previous decade's oil boom came to a devastating collapse. People were starting to default on their loans. "People would come to the bank and say, 'Things are bad, can you help me?' And believe it or not, he would do one of two things: he would either extend the loan, or he would give them more money to try to get them out of it," says Greg Monier. "It was a horrible decision. But it was a decision he made for all the right reasons."

One of the bank's biggest customers was the Mamou Community Rice Mill, of which Aubrey was also president. "They began to fall on hard times," says Monier. "And Aubrey would loan them more money from the bank. It was feeding a dead dog."

Then, things got worse in 1980, when the Soviet Union invaded Afghanistan, and President Jimmy Carter issued an embargo on all grain shipments. In Evangeline Parish, this was devastating. "It was a rough time for this community," says Ted Smith, a board member at Guaranty Bank at the time. "You had all these bad farm loans, and you had some bad real estate loans because the houses people had, they paid the notes through farming."

All the while, the Community Rice Mill loan, "the albatross" as Smith describes it, was just getting bigger and bigger. Aubrey was doing everything he could to keep it afloat. Whatever Guaranty couldn't handle, he would convince his son-in-law, Sonny DeVillier, who was president of Acadiana Bank in Eunice, to take on. When that bank faced criticism from the FDIC, Guaranty had to take the loan back. Then, the FDIC came into Guaranty, took one look at the size of that loan and demanded the bank raise additional collateral, or they'd be shutting the whole thing down.

"Well, all these people [on the board] have been sitting on stock. Getting small dividends, never feeling that they would have to put money back up," explains Smith. Now, the bank's survival depended on the board members to reach into their own pockets and pay out thousands and thousands of dollars. "So they pointed to Mr. Aubrey, and said 'How could you let this happen?' He let it happen because he trusted people. He pulled for the underdog . . . Aubrey would have rode it all out. He would have brought the bank down riding it out with these people."

When the FDIC told Aubrey he had to get out, or they were going to close the bank, he reluctantly announced his retirement on the front page of the Opelousas *Daily World* in an article headlined "Give Me That Old Time Banking," published on December 17, 1982, weeks before his abduction. "Knowing people and lending money was what it was all about," he is quoted saying. "Today there are so many government strings to work around." He remained on the board and told the journalist he was looking forward to spending his retirement fishing.

Day 9

O N FRIDAY, THE FBI ASKED EMILY TO PARTICIPATE IN ONE last composite drawing. The artist's name was Johnny Donnels. He didn't use an identikit as the earlier ones had, drawing instead directly from Emily's oral descriptions. As he worked, asking her to rebuild this person who had blown her life to bits, he told her stories of his life in New Orleans. He owned a gallery by St. Louis Cathedral, he said, had lived in the Crescent City for most of his life. Had she ever seen the movie *A Streetcar Named Desire*? With Vivien Leigh? Well, he lived on Desire Street! Had been Tennessee Williams's neighbor back in the 1940s.

Donnels pulled Emily in and out of her hell, an experience both disorienting and rejuvenating against her monotonous despair. In the end, she agreed that Donnels's rendering looked most similar, of all the composites, to the man who had taken her husband. Small, squinty eyes, high cheekbones, a wideish nose, and a beret cap, clean-shaven. "That's the most like him," she said. "But I'm telling you, it's not what he really looked like."

That day, without any updates, there was only one article published on the Aubrey LaHaye kidnapping, a short piece on page four in the Alexandria, Louisiana paper, the *Town Talk*, titled: "No Progress Made in Kidnapping Case."

Prayers to MawMaw

OWARD THE END OF MY MAWMAW EMILY'S LIFE, WE DEVEL-
oped a routine every time we'd visit Papa Wayne's and Mommee
Susan's, barreling through the unlocked back door, past the kitchen
to Papa's blue leather armchair. We'd kiss him, and he'd smile, and then
we'd head straight to the back, through the hallway lined with portraits
of our grandparents, their parents, their parents, and their parents too.
At the end was the door to MawMaw's apartment, which—if it wasn't
already open—we'd knock on, wait two seconds, then enter, bombarded
by air thick and perfumed.

Most often, MawMaw would be sitting up in her bed, visiting with
her caretaker or some friend who'd stopped by, hair icy white cotton
candy, eyes sharp and quick, hands trembling, just a little. The lights were
dimmed, her silhouette bathed in the pinkish ambience of her bedside
lamp, glowing upon piles of antique quilts. There was something childish
about the bedroom. She had dolls propped up on her armoire, staring
unfocused in elaborate hand-stitched dresses. I remember thinking she
could have a room like this, such a "girly" room, because she didn't have to
share it with a husband.

We'd come over to the bedside, lined up one behind the other, and
press our lips against her soft, wrinkled cheek. She'd ask us about school,
about our teams, our friends. And then, having fulfilled our obligation, we
were allowed to run wild into the swimming pool or up the stairs, where
Mommee Susan kept chests of old prom dresses.

MawMaw's decline was perhaps my first real experience of irreversible
change. This routine had become a regular practice of my daily life, something I'd do forever. We kept going, week after week, month after month.
And then one day she got a new bed. A hospital bed. And gradually, her
sitting position widened its angle. Though I was growing ever taller, at
one point I had to tiptoe to get my upper body over the metal railing and
reach her face upon its pillow. I think I believed she would get better.

In February 2006, my youngest brother, Luke, was born. At this point, MawMaw Emily wasn't leaving her apartment often, but on "good days," her caregiver would help her into her wheelchair, push her down the hall, and set her up at the center of Mommee Susan and Papa Wayne's living room. So she was the day she met Luke, her thirty-fourth and last great-grandchild. I remember that she asked to hold him, and I was nervous she might drop my tiny new brother. My dad came beside her and settled the baby in her lap, his head resting in the crook of her right arm. Someone, maybe my dad, maybe Papa Wayne, kept a hand on him there. MawMaw spoke to Luke, told him things long lost to my memory and his too.

She died nine months later, at the age of ninety-two, twenty-three years after she lost her husband. She slipped out of life still lucid, though sleeping, surrounded by family, prepped and anointed for the afterlife.

I was ten years old, practicing backbends on my parents' bedroom floor, upside down when I heard the news. Even though I had been told it was coming, I never realized it would *actually* come. How unsettling, for someone to be simply, suddenly gone. I couldn't manage to cry and was angry at myself for it.

For years afterward, when I said my prayers before bed, I'd pray to MawMaw as I'd pray to God, imagining her as I had always imagined him—a massive, transparent, bodiless face in the stars and the clouds. God was there too, sometimes old and bearded, sometimes young and Jewish, but usually nothing more than a shadow. I'd tell her I loved her, and about whatever I had done that day. And at the end, I'd pray—less concerned she hadn't achieved heaven than in my unshakable fear that death *hurt*—that she was okay.

Day 10

SATURDAY MORNING, EVERYONE AT EMILY'S HOUSE GATHERED— as they had every morning for the past ten days—in the living room. Today it was the eldest granddaughter Smokey's turn to lead the group in prayer. Standing in front of the fireplace, Smokey had the rosary beads wrapped so tightly around her palm the white skin flared red each time she shifted them over. The room was less full than it had been a week ago, but a sense of claustrophobia prevailed in the spaces between Emily's family and the strangers in uniform, who now had become so much less like strangers.

In Emily's first language, Smokey began each decade, "*Notre Père qui es aux cieux*," the words blending into the air, for some a mindless refuge, for others background noise for deeper, more desperate prayers. Over and over, "*Je vous salue, Marie*"s proclaimed honor and glory for a woman who had lost everything, and over and over, they begged to be delivered from this evil.

St. Ann's

THESE DAYS, I DRIVE DOWN LAHAYE ROAD SLOWLY. I PASS Aunt Dusty's house—mostly unchanged since Uncle Glenn and Aunt Janie lived there, the oak trees only larger. Across the street is Aunt Sandy's. She and her husband bought the small, movable house in a rush after Uncle Glenn died, to be close to Aunt Janie. And they never left. Next is Parrain Danny's, the original LaHaye Road house—Aubrey and Emily's, where it all began. A fig orchard separates it from Aunt Suzette's—built to be close to MawMaw Emily in the years after PawPaw's death. Glenn's youngest son, Uncle Billy, lives directly across the street from Papa Wayne and Mommee Susan's white columned palace—which looks as if it were pulled straight from the antebellum era. Actually, my papa Wayne designed the whole thing himself in the 1960s. He had planted the oak trees with my grandmother on their very first date. A little farther is Uncle Jay's yellow colonial, where I spent most of my youth playing with my cousin Olivia.

One Sunday evening, I turn left onto Highway 13, which people still call "the new Highway 13," even though it was built in 1972. When my dad was growing up, every time they'd make this turn on the way to Mamou, MawMaw Emily would say, "This is your pawpaw Aubrey's highway. He's the one who made it happen."

I make my way to Sixth Street, the struggling-to-beat heart of downtown Mamou, a walkable half-mile stretch of daiquiri shops and bars whose rotating names we note each year when we return for Mardi Gras. It's all anchored by the constants of the iconic Fred's Lounge, "the Cajun Music Capital of the World," and the historic Hotel Cazan across the street. Before you get to all of that, though, there is St. Ann Catholic Church. It's one of the largest buildings in the little town, with rose-colored bricks and a single gable roof. This, too, has PawPaw Aubrey's handprints on it: he was chairman of the fundraising board, which raised the money to build the church in 1955.

I'm visiting late, giving myself a comfortable cushion after the 5 p.m. Mass lets out. There are still a few people lingering, but no one questions when I walk inside. Alone in the gaping, peaked nave, I genuflect and duck into the last pew, lean over to pull out the kneeler, and fall onto it, hands clasped and pressed into my forehead; a set of rituals forever embedded in my body, no matter how long it has been. I breathe deep and allow myself to soak in this mystic comfort, this familiar sense of quiet. Not all that long ago, when an altogether simpler and more certain faith guided my movements, I spent so much time like this, in places like this. They call it adoration, the opportunity to spend more intimate time with God outside of Mass, to "visit" Him outside of the public sacrament. It was once my favorite form of prayer.

Things have changed since then, my convictions fading in their devotion, my devotions fading in their conviction. But my eyes still lock straight onto the flickering red candle, the Eternal Flame, beside the tabernacle, signifying Christ's presence within it. I still feel at home here.

I recenter myself and consider this place as it was a lifetime ago, Paw-Paw Aubrey's church. What did he ask of his God in the quiet? It occurs to me how unlikely it is that he ever sat in these back pews. I fall back on my ankles, lift the kneeler, bend to genuflect. My footsteps echo down the aisle, and I feel only a little silly. The evening light pouring through the stained glass lends everything a reddish hue. I choose the second pew from the front, a spot reserved for a selection of Mamou's best-dressed old ladies. And then I think of MawMaw Emily.

I imagine her standing here, the church filling up around us, two thousand people standing shoulder to shoulder, every door open so those forced to stand outside in the wet chill can hear Father Nunez boom: "Aubrey was taken from his home, like a lamb to the slaughter." Then, all together, they pray God have mercy on the slaughterer.

I look to the sanctuary and imagine the spectacle of what was perhaps the church's highest attended service: Father Nunez, dressed in ceremonial white vestments meant to represent Aubrey's passage into heaven, flanked by an army of eleven other priests who had traveled from around the state to preside over the funeral. The coffin, sealed tight, held something dark and inconceivable—a body the Bayou Nezpique had ruined, stealing even the chance for his loved ones to say goodbye.

The funeral took place only two days after the search came to its end, and at the very same time that Uncle Sonny started delivering the eulogy, divers were searching the Nezpique for potential evidence. They wouldn't find any.

"Aubrey G. LaHaye," he began. "What would he have said this day to all of us here assembled, each with our personal thoughts and recollections?"

Aubrey might have offered a story, he said, a tale reflecting on how no one need despair, reminding that his seventy years of good work were not wasted because of "some coward who would take a good man from his bed in his own home."

He would tell us not to be afraid of life, suggested Sonny. "Can't you just hear him telling each of you to believe that life indeed is still worth living, and to hold fast to that belief?"

I sit in this feeling, this commingling of finality and eternity. Where the doors to Paradise open and those of Earth's violent hells claim to close. The before and the after.

I stay at St. Ann until it starts getting dark, the glow of the red flame taking up more and more space upon the altar, my thoughts merging into prayers. Before I go, I cross myself and recite an old favorite: "Oh my Jesus, forgive us our sins and save us from the fires of hell. Lead all souls to Heaven, especially those who most need of thy mercy."

I walk back down the aisle, imagining the way the organ's dissonant wail marked time as PawPaw Aubrey's five eldest grandsons, my father among them, carried his body out of the crowded church. MawMaw Emily came last—her children wrapped around her—taking their first steps into the new world.

On the Nezpique Bridge

JANUARY 20, 2018

I T SHOULD BE RIGHT ABOUT HERE . . ." MY DAD LEANS FORWARD in his seat as he turns off the highway, slowing down to accommodate the road as it shifts to gravel, darkening under the forest canopy. There is no one down here. No houses. No traffic. The gravel—for about fifteen seconds—shifts to concrete.

"Wait, Dad. Was that it? The bridge?"

"I think so." He's slowing down, starts turning the diesel truck around on the tight little lane. We idle our way back, to the middle of the con-crete, then open our doors together and step out.

On that eleventh day, Sunday, January 16, 1983, after the sharpshooter Kurt Vezinat sent his wife and son to report what they'd found to the Mamou police, Detective Guillory had rushed to the bayou to confirm what Vezinat had known to his core: the body floating in the Nezpique was, in fact, Aubrey LaHaye's. The road was cordoned off, and a dozen officers and agents arrived at the scene.

A local doctor who lived nearby, BJ Manuel, volunteered his boat for the retrieval of the body. Everyone on the bridge went silent as he and Sheriff Vidrine puttered out into the bayou's center. Once they reached that miserable mass, Dr. Manuel could see a tarp haphazardly wrapped around the body. A ragged, yellow towel covered what must have been Aubrey's face. Soaked into its folds were flecks of grime and dead leaves, and in one spot, a golf ball–size circle, pink. The doctor leaned over, holding his breath, to loop his rope around the body, try-ing his best not to touch it. Once the knot was tied, he turned back to the sheriff, who directed them toward the bank. The burden was heavy, heavier than a body should be, but it dragged behind the boat nonetheless, cradled by the bayou all the way.

At the bank, the two men stepped on land, grimaced, and pulled in on their ropes, dragging their cargo through the mud. Sheriff Vidrine reached down to unwrap the tarp, and in an instant, he revealed the dreaded outcome: the gray-skinned remnants of my great-grandfather.

Aubrey had a rope tied around his neck, coming down his back and holding back his left arm, and then tied again around his waist. Attached to another rope were two metal rims, apparently used as a sort of anchor. They sat strangely in the shallow water beside Aubrey's feet— still barefoot. Sheriff Vidrine looked up at the bridge to find Sonny, the designated family member assigned to officially identify the body as Aubrey's. Though everyone already knew.

None of the LaHayes came to the bridge. None of them would ever see their PawPaw, whose already-decaying body would be transferred immediately to the coroner, again. After hearing the news, they all remained at Aubrey and Emily's house, reduced to nothing. All my dad can remember of it is holding his father, and the uncanny way his own body felt that shallow mourning turn, so suddenly, visceral.

This is the first time Dad's been to this section of the Nezpique, which runs several miles southwest of our house. When I told him I wanted to see the place myself, he asked if he could join me.

"I don't think the bayou crosses the road anywhere else in this area . . . but"—Dad hesitates, running his hand over the waist-high concrete walls, disturbed—"but I think . . . I remember from the pictures that the bridge was wooden."

I know the photo he's talking about, published in the *Mamou Acadian Press* a few days after the body was discovered. Deputy Floyd Soileau and the Mamou chief of police stand on the bridge, pointing down to the bayou, to the body. My dad's right. The graffiti-strewn cement sides unnerve me too; they look wrong.

I walk up and down the length of the bridge, the width of the river, around ten feet. In rudimentary spray paint, curlicues and gashes are emblazoned "Brandon and Liz 4 Ever," and a bit farther down, brighter, "Fuck Brandon"; a series of names: "Duke Mew," "Pierrotti," "Chet." In one dark corner I make out a messy "Jordan." In another, I spot the word "Terror." Largest of all, flanked on one side by a swastika and on the other the Star of David, in huge angular script is written "SINISTER."

"Come see this," Dad calls from the other end of the bridge. There is a sign, revealing that this bridge was built in 2007, replacing the old wooden one before it. I nod. This young stone holds no memory of the body floating beneath it in 1983; its artists wouldn't have known any-thing of this particular violence. I turn to face the edge, confronting the muggy, slow-moving water below.

"Do you know which side he was on?" my dad asks, standing, lost, in the middle. I don't. Something draws me to the northeast side, where the water folds around the bottom of a cypress someone has cut down clean. Bone-white limbs reach out over the banks, hiding a portion of the bay-ou's trail from view. The water is shallow. You can see a line on the banks, a chromatic separation between dust and mud, with scattered trash along the edges, beer cans and a Kraft macaroni box.

The other side of the bridge presents a neat strip of bayou, framed on each end by trees leaning into each other, their reflections visible on the surface, a gothic silhouette against a bright gray sky.

We stand in silence, on opposite ends of the bridge, shivering. My father runs his hand over the top of his head, flattening the long dark wisps sprouting from his balding crown. He presses down on his eyes and drags his hands down his face, before returning them back together to dangle over the railing. He fingers his wedding band, plain and gold, engraved on the inside with his and my mother's initials, "ML + CE, 1992." Right beside it in identical, but faded script: "AL + ED, 1930." The ring, it too knew these waters.

Weeks before, when I'd sat down with Mommee Susan, she'd described PawPaw's murder as the opening lines of a drama for our family. "A pain-ful drama, that lasted a long time. It opened a door to dysfunction. To pain. Pain. Pain."

Leaning over the Nezpique Bridge, a memory emerges: my high school religion teacher telling us of evil, the way you can sense it in a place. The way your soul can feel darkness moving in spaces of sin. She'd used examples like the strip clubs or voodoo houses in New Orleans. Bourbon Street. I'd roll my eyes.

But now, I consider a place's capacity to remember. In this spot, where some all-consuming anger, desperation, jealousy, or greed possessed someone to beat an old man to death and discard him into these waters. I close my eyes and reach for the essence of evil, call to it.

The flora and fauna offer me no response. There is a legacy of silent tragedy in this bayou, of bodies sunk in her waters, nestled on her banks. Even the fish here are contaminated. Mercury, the authorities say, urging women of childbearing age to eat no more than one serving of Nezpique bass per month. I think of my childhood, of the hoop net bounties my brothers brought home. Of my fairy villages, abandoned without a trace of magic left behind. Of the tupelos and magnolias covering the bodies of the last of the Atakapas-Ishak people, whose distinctive presence gave this bayou its name: "tattooed nose." Of *Le cocodrie* sleeping for centuries, then viciously slaughtered, to be replaced forevermore with concrete and spray-painted over in profanities. Of the French spoken upon these banks, for over a century, doomed to be traded for something less lyrical, more economical. And on the day they pulled Aubrey LaHaye from the Nezpique's depths, the waters and the trees and the grass and its mud all sat still, resolutely tight-lipped about how he ended up there.

I soak in the truth that this may well be the place where my great-grandfather was bludgeoned to death. I look to my father, battling his own demons, and think to myself that if I were alone, I would scream. I would call out to PawPaw Aubrey's ghost, find out if he lingers. If I were alone, I'd scrape the banks clean, dig holes in the mud, and check behind each tree, hoping to find something missed all those years ago: a smear of blood, the murder weapon itself. I'd step out into the bayou and immerse myself in this baptism of pollution, water, blood, and decay; shiver against the Nezpique's cold January caress, and sink to its bottom, my eyes blinded and stinging. Unable to move. Tied there. Breathless. Heart beating slower, slower, slower.

PART II

The Aftermath

The Dark Decade

I N THE MONTHS AFTER PAWPAW AUBREY'S DEATH, MAWMAW Emily would wake most mornings on the couch, stiff and achy, buried beneath a mountain of blankets. She couldn't bring herself to sleep in that big, empty bed. But they weren't good for her bones, the couch cushions. Pushing herself into a sitting position, her joints cracked and rattled within her. But she was still, inconceivably, here.

She'd move toward the dusty sunbeams pouring out over the kitchen sink, losing herself in the trance of routine. She'd put the coffee brewing and then reach up into the cabinet for their cups—the white porcelain ones with a little green band around the lip, set them atop their matching saucers on the counter.

Then she'd see them, the two of them, side by side. And her breath would catch.

She'd open the cabinet, put one back.

"Things were different, after," says my aunt Dusty, sitting at her kitchen table, the same kitchen and the same table where her parents, Glenn and Janie, sat almost every evening of the eighties, smoking cigarette after cigarette. "Everybody was on edge. Everybody was scared. I remember we all got dead bolts on our doors—the same dead bolt at our house, MawMaw's house, and Uncle Wayne's house—all the same key."

"And alarms," remembers my uncle Nick, a few weeks later at his own kitchen table. "Everybody had alarms. We didn't know how to work them, and they'd go off. We'd never locked the doors before."

PawPaw was laid to rest. But the investigation stretched onward. There was still a killer on the loose.

That the sonofabitch was out there, free, reddened the world for the two eldest grandsons, my uncles Jody and Richard. Each tall, imposing twentysomethings with fearsome reputations for their tempers—the young men faced their new reality with fury. One family friend remembers the generalized sense of hostility. "Anybody that rolled down the road," he recalls, "they were ready to shoot and kill and say, 'Who are you and what the fuck are you doing here?' They didn't know who to trust."

As the leads dried up, MawMaw Emily's house emptied. The FBI agents disbanded to study the probe from a distance. The calls dwindled. The local media slowed in their coverage. And the relentless current of time resumed, pulling Evangeline Parish back into its previous patterns and habits and obligations. This was true for the LaHayes, too—despite the surreal, detached quality these motions of normalcy took on. But work had to be done, bills had to be paid, meals had to be eaten, the semester had already started. And as it does so incomprehensibly after each of its million daily tragedies, the world kept turning.

My papa Wayne escaped to long shifts at the hospital. Mommee Susan attended daily Mass. Aunt Tot and Uncle Sonny retreated home to Eunice with their girls, with Tot driving into Mamou at every opportunity and Sonny throwing himself back into his law practice and his bank. Aunt Janie buried herself in the project of her grandchildren. Uncle Glenn could be found at the rice dryer or at his mother's kitchen table. He'd go every single morning and every single evening, so she never ate alone.

They all felt it. The all-consuming, magnetic draw to that house. Wherever they were, part of them always remained with MawMaw Emily, a network of overwhelming concern, directed at her from a dozen different points.

My dad, who was supposed to return to Baton Rouge for the spring semester, decided he couldn't do it. He registered late at LSU-E and moved back into his childhood bedroom. When his study group needed a place to gather, he volunteered his grandmother's house. "We wanted people in there at all times," he remembers.

For the first several months, they developed a schedule, ensuring someone always slept in the house with MawMaw Emily, every single night. Because although no one would say it out loud, they all worried the kidnapper might come back for her, or for someone else.

In the months and then years following PawPaw's death, MawMaw Emily diminished into a shadow of her former self, wearing her husband's absence like a cloak. She wouldn't cook, so she'd hardly eat. Her chickens became a chore for the yardman. Her garden grew wild with weeds. "She aged ten to fifteen years, just like that," remembers Uncle Jay, who was in high school at the time. "She almost couldn't walk . . . She was on a downward spiral."

Despite it all, at first MawMaw Emily wouldn't hear of moving in with her children or, worse, into a home. She was terrified to be alone, but something kept her rooted in the house she and PawPaw Aubrey had built.

The family decided to set up a trailer home in MawMaw Emily's driveway, into which Uncle Richard and his wife, Cindy, agreed to move full time with their two-year-old. They installed an intercom system that connected the house to the trailer, so that if MawMaw ever needed anything, she didn't even need to call, but to simply ask aloud. "We cooked, we loved, we enjoyed her, we enjoyed her stories," says Aunt Cindy. But it wasn't always easy. "To see those vulnerable times in the middle of the day . . . I didn't know how to deal with her falling. She was like a leader. She was the matriarch. She had always had all the answers. And now, she came in with none. We didn't know how to deal with it."

On LaHaye Road, PawPaw Aubrey's death seemed to break open a dam of unimaginable miseries, one after another. "In town, they'd say, the 'charmed family' that were the LaHayes was now cursed," my aunt Michele, who had married my parrain, Danny, just six months before the kidnapping, remembers of this time. "And then came all the deaths, one after the other."

In September, eight months after PawPaw Aubrey's murder, his eldest granddaughter, Smokey, was discovered, seven months pregnant, at home with a bullet in her head, a hunting rifle on the ground beside her.

Smokey had been struggling for years, had become pregnant with her sister Sandy's ex-boyfriend, resulting in a scandalous shotgun wedding attended only by the same sister. Now, three years later she was pregnant again, working a job at Uncle Sonny's bank in Eunice, a job she didn't want. Most everyone knew she was abusing drugs. But that morning of her death, she'd been caught by Uncle Sonny embezzling from the bank. After confronting her, he told Smokey to go home and gather herself, and then to come back for a meeting with her dad.

She never returned.

She left behind a two-year-old daughter, my cousin Maggie.

"We'll never get all the answers to why she did what she did," Mommee Susan tells me. "But I think Aubrey's murder spurred these things that happened next, like dominoes." It was the misery, she says, the stress and the fear that overshadowed everything after that tragedy. Not everyone made it out.

A year after Smokey's death, her husband, Robert, took his life, too, standing in front of her grave at the St. Ann mausoleum. He had told his stepfather, not long before, that Smokey was calling him. "She wakes me up at night, hollering my name to come join her." He left Maggie an orphan, who would spend the next four years being passed between Robert's parents and Uncle Glenn and Aunt Janie, until Robert's parents died too.

In the end, Uncle Glenn and Aunt Janie raised Maggie as their own, never speaking of the tragedies that had befallen all of them. Growing up, the only proof Maggie had that her mother existed lived on the walls. On occasion she would stare at the portraits of that unknown, dark-eyed woman. But Maggie understood, as did everyone else, that Smokey was not to be spoken of. She tells me now, all these years later, "Jordan, I am forty-one years old, and I can count on one hand how many times someone has brought my mother up to me."

"We could never talk about Smokey," says Aunt Suzette of her older cousin. "Just like we could never talk about PawPaw. I feel like I learned to cope, to grieve, poorly from watching that hurt fester and fester and fester."

I came to know the story of Smokey and Robert in much the same way I came to know about PawPaw Aubrey. Some adult explained it to me once as a child, without any detail, heavy with secret I interpreted as lore. It became a ghost story my generation would whisper about together around the campfire—how our mysterious aunt Smokey had killed herself, and her husband had followed a year later, to the date, upon her grave. How our strange uncle Sonny had something to do with it, though we never understood what. I'd think of Smokey, on occasion, when I saw Maggie—my beautiful, oh-so-cool older cousin. But I understood I was never to ask her about it.

When I find the obituary the family listed in the newspaper for Smokey, it says that she died at her residence "following a short illness." Only when I visit their graves all these years later do I uncover the error at the heart of our myth. Smokey died on September 8, 1983; Robert on August 29, 1984. It is only when we start talking about PawPaw Aubrey that my father tells me Smokey was pregnant. A boy.

Aunt Dusty tells me that to this day, she still isn't sure she knows the whole story of what happened to her big sister, whom she idolized.

"I don't know if I ever asked . . . as I got older, you know, different people told me different things." Aunt Dusty never felt she could ask the questions out loud, "because . . . I didn't want to make my mama sad." A tear releases itself from the corner of her eye, falling straight onto her cheekbone. "Who wants to see their mama cry?" As we sit there in the kitchen, and she tells me this story, her eighteen-year-old daughter Ella sits in the corner, her face shining with tears. She's never heard her mom talk about this part of her life before. Realizing this as she prepared for the interview, Aunt Dusty invited her to sit in and listen—a fracture in the cycle of silence.

Meanwhile in Eunice, Aunt Tot, Aubrey and Emily's only daughter, was battling a breast cancer diagnosis. Her daughter, my aunt Anne, remembers going with her to shop for a prosthesis bra, and the way she sat in a chair in the living room, barely moving, for three years. It was shortly after Aunt Tot went into remission—after the family had begun to release themselves from the fear of losing her—that they lost Anne's sister, Kaye.

It was MawMaw Emily's seventy-fifth birthday, April 22, 1989. The family had planned to come together to cut cake and sing. Instead, once again, everyone gathered to weep. Uncle Sonny and Aunt Tot's oldest daughter, Kaye, was twenty-one, recently married with a one-year-old son. She'd been driving her husband, his brother, and his wife home from a Rod Stewart concert in Lafayette. And she'd fallen asleep. Both women in the car died instantly.

"I kept coming home for funerals," remembers my dad, who was at this point attending medical school in Shreveport. "It was relentless." Parrain Danny remembers asking for permission to see Kaye's body in the casket, which had not been opened to the public at Uncle Sonny's request. Danny had never seen PawPaw's, or Smokey's, and part of him had never managed to accept their absence, still clung to a particle of irrational hope: maybe it had all been a mistake. "I needed to see her," he tells me.

After Kaye's death, against an atmosphere still shuddering from grief after grief, Uncle Sonny stopped showing up for the big family to-dos on LaHaye Road.

Uncle Sonny, Aubrey's only son-in-law in a family where the two daughters-in-law were sisters, had always been an outsider in the family. Following in her mother's footsteps, Aunt Tot had married a man who shimmered in idealism and glowed in the gospel of capitalism. In many ways he was more like Aubrey than Aubrey's sons. He was even a banker, and a rich one at that. But unlike his father-in-law, Sonny operated from a position of political calculation and unsubtle self-interest that made him easy to dislike. The cynicism he carried scraped against the genteel sensibilities of his country in-laws. He talked about politics at the dinner table, rolled his eyes when it was time for prayer. And he took Aunt Tot and their children away from LaHaye Road, to live in a mansion in *his* hometown of Eunice.

After Smokey's suicide, Aunt Janie never could bring herself to stop blaming Uncle Sonny for what happened. Embezzlement or no, he was the last person to speak to Smokey. And whatever he said, in Aunt Janie's mind, led Smokey to pick up that gun. While mourning his own daughter's death six years later, Uncle Sonny felt he could no longer stand the propriety and falsity of it all, and Aunt Tot started coming to visit her mother and brothers on LaHaye Road without him.

The family could hardly contain their relief at his absence, at having to accommodate one less tension. Aunt Michele remembers an occasion where she stood next to Aunt Tot, washing dishes after lunch at Mommee Susan's. "I asked, 'How is Uncle Sonny?' and she looked at me and said, 'You are the only person who asks about him anymore.'"

Against this backdrop of loss, the LaHaye family was also losing PawPaw Aubrey's farm.

Around the same time as his death, the FDIC mandated Guaranty Bank get the Community Rice Mill loan off the books. Aubrey had pumped blood into the loan for almost a decade, and when the bank's lawyer discovered a personal continuing guaranty on a note, signed by Aubrey LaHaye, they came after the family. Uncle Glenn and Papa Wayne found themselves in court, fighting to save the family estate, and to interpret their father's intent. Their position held that the guaranty had been made only in regard to the original note on which it was listed—which was documented to have been paid. But the bank demanded the LaHaye estate be responsible for the Mill's entire remaining balance, plus all the interest it had accrued over the entire course of its existence.

The case pitted the bank Aubrey founded against his surviving family, unthinkable six months before. Uncle Glenn, who had been working there for years, the heir apparent, resigned. The case dragged on until

1987, working its way up to the Supreme Court of Louisiana, which ultimately ruled in favor of the bank. The LaHaye family had to pay the bill—which added up to what today would be the equivalent of over a million dollars.

"The wealth of the family was sacrificed to pay that," my mommee Susan tells me, with a bitterness that sounds unfamiliar in her voice. "Wayne expected some of these people from the bank to side with us, and they didn't, and it was awful. Heartbreaking. All these old friends."

Most of the LaHaye family believes today that the lawsuit would never have occurred had Aubrey been alive to explain himself. "Nobody could believe he could have left it all so undone," says my aunt Michele. "With something that big . . . it was really strange. It changed Papa's whole base of friendships. It was like [the leaders at the bank] just shook their heads, like they *had* to do it." Many of the LaHayes, still to this day, see the lawsuit as a betrayal by men who owed their success to Aubrey. "They took advantage. Took money, took the bank," says Parrain Danny.

Uncle Sonny, a banker himself, wrote in his journal at the time: "We all know it is a debt that never was—it was an effort on Mr. LaHaye's part to protect the bank—and the bank betrayed him, albeit after his death. Everyone's life will be impacted."

To cover the Mill's debt, Uncle Glenn and Papa Wayne had no choice but to start selling off pieces of the property their father had spent his life accumulating. And once again, they found themselves stunned by how quickly their father's old friends stepped up to take their slice, for pennies on the dollar.

"We sold everything," my dad remembers. "We had no more timber, no more oil, no more farm. They sold it all. And the accountants said, 'Y'all are gonna be out of debt forever now.' *Then* came the capital gains tax. And we had to freaking mortgage the damn thing again."

The debt to the IRS took longer to pay off. "My daddy had to go to work," my father says. Before the lawsuit, Papa Wayne had enjoyed the easy, stress-free wealth that comes with being a small-town doctor whose father owns everything. After 1987, money stopped being infinite. As Uncle Glenn and his sons' income waxed and waned with the fickleness of farming, it would fall on Papa Wayne and his doctor's salary more than once to save what little remained of the family estate.

The little that remained was the heart of it. The family homesteads. The property on LaHaye Road. They sold everything else they could come up with, all to save their homes—and just enough land that Uncle Glenn and his sons would have something to farm.

"When you think of the people that benefited from Aubrey's death, who got rich because of that lawsuit," my uncle Jay ponders, echoing an undercurrent of suspicion vibrating through the surviving LaHaye family, "well, you just have to wonder . . ."

In a cataclysmic end to the decade, on Ash Wednesday of 1990, Uncle Glenn was discovered in a ditch.

They found him about a mile and a half down a dirt road off LaHaye, stretching into the farm. In February, the fields on each side of the road would have been filled—lakes still and sleek as glass, the entire sky within them. Uncle Glenn's truck was pulled over to the left of the little road, the driver's door open, the seat bathed red—blood dripping through the dirt and grass, past the rifle on the ground, all the way to the bottom of the ditch. His body lay in about a foot of bloody water, a hole in his chest. Crawfish crawled on his face, his neck, his hands, his wound. He had one rubber boot on. The other lay sideways on the ground beside the truck.

My papa Wayne remembers how, at the scene, Detective Rudy Guillory wouldn't let anyone touch the body—"To make sure it wasn't . . ." he trailed off. But I know what he was trying to say. To make sure it wasn't another murder. Everyone's immediate thought, even seven years after PawPaw Aubrey's murder, was that this had to be related. They had come back for Uncle Glenn. Considering it a possible crime scene, Guillory had to ward off Elvin's son-in-law Dickie, who couldn't stand the sight of the crawfish picking off pieces of Uncle Glenn's skin. Guillory allowed him to stand beside the body, and to shoo the creatures off him.

Once again, one by one, the LaHayes—spread near and far—received their notices. *Something terrible has happened. Come home.* My father, now a medical resident in the University of Texas Medical Branch in Galveston, was making rounds on the general surgery urology floor, and his supervisor told him to sit down and call his dad.

Uncle Billy, Uncle Richard, and Parrain Danny all have memories of being the unfortunate one to tell Aunt Janie that her husband was gone. Likely, they all arrived right around the same time. But no one remembers the way she screamed like Aunt Dusty does. MawMaw Emily could hear the dreadful sound from her yard across the pasture, and Aunt Dusty remembers her yelling out, "What's wrong? What happened?"

"And I didn't want to tell her," Aunt Dusty recalls. "I just came in the house."

When PawPaw Aubrey died, Uncle Glenn had taken up the post of family patriarch, as head of the family farm. Quietly, Papa Wayne held him up where he could. But in 1990, the farm—stripped away to its barest bones—wasn't paying its own bills.

To keep the operation afloat, Uncle Glenn had defaulted again and again. When he died, he owed over $700,000 in farm loans. And so the story goes, he had come to that ditch from a meeting at the bank; they were going to seize his property to pay the debt.

The life insurance the family received after his death was enough to save it.

Officially, Uncle Glenn's death was ruled a terrible accident by the coroner, Sheriff's Office, DA's Office, and the Acadiana Crime Lab. He was out there to shoot coyotes, putting on his rubber boots, pulling his gun out from the back seat of his truck, when the trigger went off. But my dad tells me, "No one will say this out loud to you, but I think most people know it was a suicide."

My dad is wrong. Many, many people say it out loud. My uncle Jay remembers how, right after it happened, he was asking a lot of questions, and his mother, Mommee Susan, sat him down. "This stays between me and you," she said, "but I think he did this himself. Leave it alone." When I ask her, all these years later, she tells me—out of Papa Wayne's earshot—that she still believes this is what happened.

"Sure, it's a better storyline," Aunt Cindy argues, "that he killed himself." But she, and a few others, can't see it. Tearfully, Aunt Dusty tells me, "To this day . . . I know my dad would have never done that to my mom. Definitely not."

Asking my family members about this darkest day, I receive less resistance than I expect. Many of them recall the experience as though it were retrieved from a separate life, a version of themselves they hardly recognize, that they've tried to forget. Some of them, though, still carry the weight within them—only now do I finally recognize its source. My uncle Billy can hardly manage to get a single word out, though he tries. But speaking to all of them, I realize with wonder that my aunts and uncles and my grandparents have never, ever truly spoken about this to one another.

"I can't believe he told you that story," my dad says, shaking his head after we spend an afternoon with Papa Wayne, who despite his now failing memory described the day his brother died in more remarkable detail than almost anyone else. He is the one who remembered the crawfish crawling on Glenn's body. "He's always, always shut any discussion of that right down." Papa had even admitted, quietly, "Some people, they say he did it to himself."

Though Uncle Glenn and Kaye and Smokey and PawPaw Aubrey and the weight of so much loss were rarely spoken of, the families of La-Haye Road held the hearts of MawMaw Emily, Aunt Janie, and Aunt Tot in their rituals. Morning masses, weekly suppers. Sunday lunches, afternoon coffees. And somewhere right in the middle of all the tragedy, in the late '80s, MawMaw Emily found the will to live again. "Just like that," remembers Uncle Jay, "she's back in the yard. Doing this and planting this." "She was cooking again," says Aunt Suzette, "making her peanut pralines and back in her little ladies' card group."

She lived another twenty-three years after PawPaw Aubrey's death, another lifetime. The fact was—they needed her. Amid so much misery, she came to stand, for the family, as a bedrock of survival, of impossible faith. A beacon of simple joys: of candied peanut butter and homemade pound cake and coffee milk mornings, of impeccable style and dance parties in the living room, and stories told in the purest of Cajun accents, the dying sort that sings from those who spoke the real language first.

Years later, when Aunt Cindy asked how she did it, how she found the will to continue on, MawMaw Emily said it was about her children, her grandchildren. They were already suffering so much. She couldn't bear to bring them any more hurt.

"I didn't want . . . I had this feeling I didn't want them to feel sorry for me or to worry about me. I was going to take care of myself, good or bad . . . That was the purpose. That's what God gave me. That's how I got the help I got. God gave me the knowledge and the ability to protect myself from being a misery to my children. I knew it was hard enough without them having to worry about me."

When my dad calls this era of the LaHaye family history "the dark decade," he cannot help but draw it all back to PawPaw Aubrey—to ask the question: Would any of this misery have unfolded if he hadn't been taken? We imagine a world in which that January morning hadn't been so foggy, in which the community duck hunts hadn't been called off. Richard and Jody would have met in Uncle Glenn's kitchen, would have been sipping coffee before the hunt when the stranger knocked on the door. They would have seen the headlights turn into the driveway at PawPaw's next door, the windows light up from inside. They would have seen the truck. And maybe, just maybe, they would have caught him sooner, before PawPaw Aubrey was killed. And in a world in which PawPaw is saved, so is Smokey, perhaps. And then, so is Robert. Maggie grows up in Eunice, with two parents and a brother. PawPaw Aubrey intercepts the bank's lawsuit, or at least gets the chance to explain that he never meant to guarantee that whole loan. And no one questions him. The estate is saved. Parrain Danny goes to work at Guaranty Bank, starting on a path to becoming president someday. Uncle Glenn still has his father to advise him. He still has a daughter. And maybe, just maybe, it wasn't an accident. And he would still be here too. In this world, perhaps we even get to keep Kaye—in this world where tragedy becomes less likely, where things always work out for the LaHayes.

I wonder what it might have been like to have this great-grandfather for myself, to crawl into his lap in the recliner and know the scent of his cigars. I imagine my childhood at Mommee and Papa's extended through the pasture to Pawpaw and MawMaw's—where I'd have a face, a voice, for the legacy I'd supposedly inherited, an unbroken thread from my grandfather's childhood to my father's to my own. I imagine PawPaw beside MawMaw Emily on the couch, arm wrapped around her shoulders. How might it have changed me, to witness that generation in the fullness of their devotion to each other? To begin my life watching the two of them holding each other up as they walked to the end of theirs, hand in hand?

I wonder what he would have made of me.

The whole universe tilts, though, if PawPaw Aubrey had survived 1983. If the kidnapping had never happened, Dad realizes, he would have returned to LSU at Baton Rouge for the spring semester, instead of moving home and enrolling at LSU-E. He was studying to be a veterinarian at that time, and without the encouragement and inspiration of the premed students at the community college—perhaps he would have stayed the course. He wouldn't have decided to instead follow in his father's footsteps, to become a doctor. He would have had no reason to move to Galveston, Texas, for a urology residency. And he would have never met my mom.

"If PawPaw Aubrey hadn't been killed," he tells me, "I'm not sure you would exist."

"Hot, Cold"

ONTHS AFTER FILING A FREEDOM OF INFORMATION ACT request for "any and all FBI records regarding the murder of Aubrey LaHaye," I receive the records in the mail: a manila envelope with two CD-ROMs inside. Uploading the files to my computer, I am instantly overwhelmed by their sheer messiness. In no particular order, with indecipherable chicken scratches and redactions throughout, the records consist of almost two hundred pages of FBI correspondence regarding PawPaw Aubrey's murder. Before I'm halfway through it, I'm wondering where the rest is.

There are no handwritten notes from interviews with MawMaw Emily, no copies of the composite drawing. No mention at all of the many phone calls my family remembers the FBI intercepting over those ten days. I know potential suspects were interviewed but can find no transcripts or notes regarding those conversations. Not even names. Almost every mention of a suspect is redacted.

Frustrated, I track down the investigators themselves. I've had the obituaries for many of them, including Detective Rudy Guillory, in my notes since the beginning. But maybe some of the others were still around. Maybe they still remember.

I send an email, with a list of names, to the Society of Former Special Agents of the FBI and am surprised at their quick response. Two of the agents are still alive, the society's executive director tells me. And one of them is Agent Ed Grimsley.

When I get him on the phone, he starts out, "Now, are you Wayne's granddaughter, or Glenn's?" He doesn't remember everything, he tells me. But he remembers, vividly, all of *them*. The LaHayes, the people of Evangeline Parish, whose houses they milled about, whose couches they slept on for a time. "We developed a relationship with those people that doesn't typically happen that way. They were just wonderful."

\\\\\

Back in January 1983, after the discovery of Aubrey's body, investigators gathered a slew of new evidence from the Bayou Nezpique crime scene: Aubrey's eyeglasses, discovered on the bank; the two tire rims that had weighed down his body; the rope he'd been tied with; and the bloodied, yellow towel that had been wrapped around his head. This had been the site of the fatal blow, according to the autopsy—not a bullet, but a blow. Perhaps two. In the wounds, the coroner found a dark, greasy material and a fragment of amber-colored glass. PawPaw Aubrey had been beaten to death. By what? We still, to this day, do not know. A murder weapon was never recovered.

Two knives were turned in, found within a mile or so of Aubrey's home. They were sent, with everything else, to the bureau's lab in Washington, DC, for testing. When the results came back, there was only a single viable fingerprint to work with, found on one of the tire rims—but it didn't match any in the existing database. And on one of the ropes, a blond hair. The lab assured investigators the print and the hair would be preserved for future testing.

Locally, investigators published photographs of the tire rims in the newspaper, one of them "distinctively" light blue and belonging to a "1978 or 1979 Nova or a 1978 to 1981 Camaro," hoping someone might recognize it.

On January 19, 1983, three days after Aubrey's body was found, the FBI arranged for Emily to view a photographic and in-person lineup, overseen by Special Agent Owen Odom and Detective Guillory. They had identified a suspect. Taylor Strother had been named by two separate citizens as someone who looked like the composites. A known criminal in the area, Strother's activities ranged from burning down his own family home to simple battery to shooting a man with a .12 gauge after an argument. Notably, though, in 1971, he robbed a hired chauffeur, forcing him to drive down a rural back road before taking $320. At knifepoint.

According to the FBI reports, Emily "tentatively identified" Strother in one of these lineups. The report says he consented to a search of his home, as well as a polygraph examination. From his home, the FBI collected three pairs of blue jeans with what appeared to be bloodstains, a yellow washcloth "dissimilar in color but similar in weave, wear, and appearance" to the towel found on the body, and two tire tools—one covered in something that looked like blood.

Despite how damning this evidence appeared at the outset, the FBI

Headquarters Laboratory results didn't turn up anything that could actually be used to charge Strother. They confirmed that there was blood on one pair of the blue jeans submitted, but comparisons made against Aubrey's blood were "inconclusive." When I read this in the correspondence, I wonder why they wouldn't use the word *negative*. The material observed on the tire tools was not, in fact, blood at all. And the washcloth wasn't a match for the towel found on the body. Regarding fingerprints, the report reads "no fingerprint records were located here for Taylor Strother." But why wouldn't they obtain his fingerprint for comparison?

From there, Strother disappears from the record. Without any conclusive indication otherwise, I can only assume that because they had no hard evidence on him, the investigators had to move on. When I try to find out what happened to Strother after 1983, all I can gather is that he was in a devastating wreck in 1995, was arrested for a DWI in 1996, and died at age forty-nine in Franklin, Louisiana, in 1997. With nothing else to grasp at, I, like the investigators, force myself to move forward—storing his name away, for now.

In one FBI report written that January, the agent states:

> On January 24, 1983, meeting held of all agents and law enforcement officials involved in instant investigation and list of 30 names of "look alike" and possible suspects were compiled. These individuals being systematically evaluated and will be interviewed prior to being eliminated as suspect. Most names obtained from private citizens responding to wide dissipation of composite sketch of unsub.

It is unclear if, at this point, John Brady Balfa had already been eliminated from the pool of suspects—or if he was ever officially eliminated at all. In the FBI records, I can see that sometime after Balfa's second interrogation, an agent took the time to write down that he had a thick mustache, "which would indicate he was not the individual who entered victim's home" based on MawMaw Emily's description of a "clean-shaven" man. Other correspondence suggests they were working on confirming his alibi and had acquired documentation from the Best Western in Atlanta, Texas, that proved Balfa had checked in between 9 a.m. and noon. Beyond that, it appears that the Balfa probe was dropped. No one questioned him for the remainder of his time in the Gregg County Jail. His rape trial took place in February 1983; he'd come out of it with a conviction and the lenient sentence of ten years' probation and a $10,000 fine. By March 1983, he was walking free.

When I ask Grimsley about it, he tells me that the real reason the FBI moved on from Balfa, was, in fact, the mustache.

"When we first interviewed Mrs. Emily, she was very insistent that the culprit who came in was clean-shaven," he said. In the half-dozen composites they worked on with her, she had always described a man with no facial hair. "That was the thing that just kind of eliminated him at that point. It seemed very significant. I mean, she just kept insisting . . ."

On February 7, 1983, the *Daily World* published an update on the investigation with the headline, "Murder Trail Turns Hot, Cold." On February 17: "FBI Not Giving Up on Murder but Moves Command Post from LaHaye Property." On March 20, they conducted another search of the Nezpique, dragging a magnet along the bottom of the bayou in hopes of drawing up evidence. Again, nothing. On March 23: "LaHaye Riddle Remains."

For the next six months, there was virtually no progress on the Aubrey LaHaye case. All the FBI agents except for one, Agent Owen Odom, left Evangeline Parish to pursue other investigations. Sheriff Ramson Vidrine continued to tell the newspapers he was sure the murderer was Calvin Ware, who was still on the loose. He was also promoting a theory that the murder was a contract killing, disguised as a ransom demand. "If they wanted money, it doesn't make sense," he said to a journalist. It didn't make sense that they never called, that they killed him. This was something bigger, he was sure.

Recalling Vidrine's contract killing theory today, Grimsley explains why the FBI agents disagreed. "Our experience has always been that a contract killing is usually done to send a message. So, people want it to be *known* that it's a contract killing . . . A contract killer would never want to try to disguise that message by making it appear that it was a kidnapping. If it were a contract killing, the kidnapper would have never asked for ransom. And a contract killer would never hide a body in a bayou. They'd put it somewhere it could be easily found—part of his message to the world, of saying 'This guy wronged me.'"

On July 12, 1983, Sheriff Vidrine got the call he'd been waiting on. "We got him. We got Ware."

The sheriff was practically in the car, headed to Douglas, Texas, before the FBI intervened. "We think it's a good idea if you stay behind for this," Agent Grimsley told him over the phone. "With all due respect, he's no doubt heard what you're accusing him of, Sheriff. If it is him, we have to do this right."

When wind made its way to the local reporters, though, it was Vidrine's door they came knocking on. He told them he and the FBI officials didn't agree on what should be made known to the public. "I think the more publicity you get, the better off you are," he said. "Sooner or later, the facts will come out and you'll solve the case and get your man."

The FBI's philosophy won out. For weeks, there were only sparse updates on Ware. There was an interrogation, the FBI reported, never confirming if there had been significant findings. Still, Ware continued to be named as a "potential suspect."

Months passed. Then, in September, after a miscommunication between the Evangeline Parish District Attorney's Office and Texas officials, Ware was allowed to post a $2,000 bond. Unsurprisingly, he failed to appear at his extradition hearing and was again considered at large.

It took five months to apprehend him again, this time in Nacogdoches, Texas, on charges of attempted murder. He had shot a man seven times with a .22 rifle. Authorities posted his bond at $10,000, and he was forced to sit through more questioning by the FBI. For three days, he would not say a single word. On February 9, 1984, over a year after Aubrey LaHaye's murder, the investigation's only viable suspect was transferred back to Evangeline Parish in handcuffs and feet shackles. Only then did FBI agents make an official comment on their findings. In the *Daily World*, Agent Grimsley stated, "After an extensive interrogation, we feel he is not a suspect." Just like that. A report published a month later quoted Agent Cliff Anderson clarifying that Ware wasn't "definitely" disqualified as a suspect, but that he would not be charged because of the results of a polygraph examination.

Reading through the papers alongside Evangeline Parish past, I feel the anticlimax of it in my throat. *A polygraph test?* I call Grimsley.

"Yeah, it was all pretty straightforward, honestly," he tells me. As he remembers it, Ware had an alibi. "I wish I could remember what it was, but it was pretty tight." I wonder why they wouldn't have put that in the newspaper, why they instead would attribute the elimination of their biggest suspect to a polygraph. And why there were no records of any of this in my FOIA file.

But the fact of the matter was: investigators likely didn't have a single piece of physical evidence to connect Ware to the murder. They were going solely off speculation and rumor. Without a weapon or a witness, something to connect him to that pile of rope and rims—they had no way to charge him for the crime. MawMaw Emily had even said, when she saw his picture, that she was sure it wasn't him.

My family members don't have recollections of this development at all—though I find it difficult to imagine they weren't privy to updates on the investigation, or at the very least following it in the news. "I just remember it didn't pan out," says Dad. "Ware didn't have anything to do with it."

Later that March of 1984, Grimsley offered the public a grim update on the status of the Aubrey LaHaye case: "We really aren't any closer today than we were when we first started. All I can tell you is we know a lot of people who are not suspects."

That summer, Sheriff Ramson Vidrine announced he would not run again for office. In an editorial, he named his department's failure to solve the Aubrey LaHaye case as one of his biggest regrets. He said he believed it would have been solved if he'd had cooperation from the federal agents involved.

Shortly after, Vidrine admitted to his wife and his doctor that he had cancer, self-diagnosed. Stomach cancer, which had already spread into his brain. By October 4, 1984, he was dead.

That's Him

E XCUSE ME, MA'AM, I HAD A LITTLE ACCIDENT DOWN THE ROAD. *I was hoping I could use your telephone to call a wrecker.*
Emily stood in the St. Landry Parish Jail. She wore a white collared shirt, buttoned all the way to the top, tucked into a pair of electric blue linen pants, cinched just below her waist. Her hair was impeccably coiffed, lips painted dark red, her hands folded at the waist, shoulders pin straight. The pants, purchased years before, hung on her hips looser than they once had, but their color absorbed all the attention in that gray room. She stared at this man from behind one-way glass. He was tall, slim, white—holding a sign with a chest-sized number 5. He walked out of the room. Then another came forward.

Emily rubbed her thumbs together, her brows furrowed, trying to ignore the officers staring at her so expectantly.

"Can I see just number 3 . . . and number 4 too?" she asked St. Landry Parish detective Roy Mallet. He nodded and called it in over the radio. The officers on the other side sent the two men back in.

"Could I get a chair? To stand on, perhaps? I want to get a better look at his arms."

"Yep, of course, Mrs. Emily." Detective Rudy Guillory reached into a closet nearby and pulled out a plastic office chair, then held out his hand as she climbed on top of it.

Detective Guillory and Agent Owen Odom had visited Emily's house that morning, joining her, Glenn, and Wayne for morning coffee, as they had so many times over the last year. It had now been twenty months since they'd found Aubrey's body.

There was a spark in Guillory's eye, something hungry, that alerted her. He wouldn't say much, only that they had gotten a tip. He asked if she would look at another photo lineup. Her heart sank into the carpet.

"Rudy . . . I can't tell anything from a piece of paper. Everyone always looks the same."

He tilted his head to the side. "Mrs. Emily, you don't think you'd know it if you saw him?"

"I . . . I just don't know, Rudy. After all of it, I don't trust my own mind much anymore."

Guillory put his hands in his pockets, turned to Odom, who gripped his briefcase, which held the lineup inside, in his hands.

Guillory asked Emily, "What if you saw him in person?"

And so here she was, in the St. Landry Parish Sheriff's Office, staring at him. The longer she looked, the more she was sure. Yes. She gave a single, curt nod. "May God forgive me, it's number 3. That's him."

John Brady Balfa.

Things I Know About John Brady Balfa

THE FIRST THING I EVER KNEW ABOUT JOHN BRADY BALFA was in his name. It was in his people. Across Acadiana, everyone knows the name Balfa, even now.

It was July 24, 1964—the day Dewey Balfa took the stage at the Newport Folk Festival and introduced Cajun music to the rest of America. He and the Eunice Playboys played on a lineup that included Joan Baez, Johnny Cash, and Bob Dylan. They were billed as "Cajun Band."

The first song they performed was an ode to their home, a melancholy waltz led by the fiddle, a song called "Grand Mamou":

O, chère bébé, j'suis parti,
J'suis parti pour m'en aller-z-à Grand Mamou.
O, 'tit monde, ô, ma chère petite
Moi, je connais, je mérite pas ça, toi, t'(es) a-près faire.[1]

The musicians were confused at the way that the audience of almost 20,000 sat still throughout the entire song. How they didn't dance, only listened. They imagined themselves failures until the end, when the crowd roared in applause.

After seeing the rest of the world react to the music of his ancestors, Dewey's fate was sealed as the fiercest advocate of Louisiana French heritage of his time, the spark behind the folk revival of the old sound. After the festival, he returned to Evangeline Parish, filled with purpose. He started pushing for local recording studios to make traditional Cajun music records, and he set about searching for opportunities for his family band, the Balfa Brothers, to bring the music of their father and their grandfather and their great-grandfather to the wider world.

---

1 Because Cajun music is mostly orally transmitted, there are a lot of different versions of the same song, especially lyrically. This is the one Dewey Balfa is said to have typically played.

There were five brothers in the band. Dewey and Will each played the fiddle. Rodney had guitar, harmonica, and vocals. Burkeman played the triangle and the spoons. And Harry, John Brady Balfa's father, held the prized spot as accordionist. Their childhood would have been similar to Emily's a generation before; their father, Charles, was a sharecropper and a multi-instrumentalist, as his father had been. Family life was centered around the evenings when they'd all come together to practice the traditional Acadian folk songs in their living room. As teenagers, they started playing at the local dance halls under the name "The Musical Brothers."

By the time Dewey returned from Newport, though, talking of traveling the world and spreading the gospel of Cajun music, Harry had purchased a little piece of land and begun working as a carpenter. He was raising his boys in the way his father had: in a quiet, stationary lifestyle on the prairies of Duralde, a small community on the outskirts of Mamou. He had little interest in becoming a touring musician. When Dewey returned to the Newport Folk Festival in 1967, this time as the fiddler for the Balfa Brothers, Harry stayed behind. The band went on to perform at dozens of other folk festivals across the country and to make several records of traditional Cajun music. They were the first Cajun musicians to perform in Europe and were even on the lineup at the 1968 Summer Olympics in Mexico City.

To this day, the Balfa Brothers are some of the best-known names in the history of recorded Cajun music, their records considered classics, carrying those centuries-old songs into the future. When I was growing up, these songs served as background noise in most of the restaurants our family visited. They bounced from my uncles' guitars against the walls of Papa Wayne and Mommee Susan's living room. Today, whenever I tell people from home the name of my great-grandfather's accused murderer, they ask, "Is he related to *the* Balfas?"

A journalist once asked Harry Balfa about his sons' lack of interest in music. He responded: "When they were growing up, they had television and radio and other distractions. When we were young, there wasn't anything else but our music." And after four generations of the Acadian sound ringing through the family, a branch of the Balfa legacy ended with Harry.

John Brady Balfa was just a few years older than my dad and his cousins, his family a sort of blue-collar foil to the LaHaye family. The Balfas, like the LaHayes, have deeply entrenched roots in the area, cousins everywhere you look, and a lineage that has existed in Evangeline Parish since the Acadians first arrived. John Brady would have possessed an intimate connection to the community born of his uncles' musical legacy, as well as his parents' professions. People in Mamou went to see Dr. Wayne LaHaye when they were sick, and they visited John Brady's mother, Mildred, whenever they needed their hair done. They negotiated their mortgages with Aubrey LaHaye at Guaranty Bank, and then called Harry Balfa to install their kitchen cabinets. Both families would have attended Mass at St. Ann's on Sundays.

John Brady, by all accounts, hoped to surpass the working-class lifestyle he'd grown up in. In 1977, he enrolled in the political science program at LSU-Eunice, with plans to complete his degree at LSU in Baton Rouge, before going on to law school. At the time, the charismatic, controversial Cajun governor Edwin Edwards was kicking off his second term in office.

"The governor was his *hee-row*," emphasizes Doug Pucheu,[1] a classmate of John Brady's at LSU-E, and later at LSU. "John wanted to be like that. That's why he was goin' to law school. He always talked about it."

"He was incredibly ambitious," echoes Brian LaHaye, a distant cousin of ours who went to college at LSU with John Brady. "Wanted to be like Edwin Edwards. That was his idol."

Edwards, the four-term populist icon, is remembered today as much for his ability to speak Cajun French and his dedication to the working class as his jail time in the late '90s, following a conviction of seventeen counts of racketeering, extortion, money laundering, and fraud.

But in the late 1970s when John Brady Balfa was in college, Edwards was still sitting pretty at the height of the state's oil boom. A native of the Acadiana town of Crowley, he developed a passionate following among the Cajun rural communities. They had been paid little attention by politicians in the past and were ecstatic to claim the guy in the big seat as one of their own. Gearing up for his next campaign, he'd visit his constituents in Acadiana, and they'd break out the red carpet. The fattest pigs were slaughtered, the biggest houses cleaned and prepped, the seediest bars stocked, and the prettiest ladies lined up, all for Edwards's arrival. Mamou's Holiday Lounge famously hung a life-sized cutout of the governor

---

1 Pronounced "Pee-shoo."

above its front door with a sign reading "Bienvenu à Grand Mamou Governor Edwards." The cutout and sign remained there for decades after Edwards's time in office, even after he was incarcerated.

"John craved that kind of power," says Doug. "He wanted to be able to do whatever he wanted."

In the fall of 1978, the LSU-E Student Government Association announced John Brady Balfa as its new president. In a photo published in LSU-E's *Bayou Bengal*, he sits at the center with six other elected officers around him. He is thin, with the characteristically dark Balfa hair and a light mustache, neatly dressed, a pen in his shirt's front pocket. He's twenty years old, his future gleaming in all its promise.

And like a true Louisiana politician, John Brady knew how to work the system. Around the same time, my aunt Michele was dating the last boy she'd love before my uncle Danny. She was a high school senior, but her boyfriend was a student at LSU-E. Just under the drinking age of eighteen, Michele and her friends needed fake IDs to get into the local bars with their older boyfriends. And so the story goes, John Brady Balfa was where you got them. A student ID from LSU-E indicated you were over eighteen years old. "He had this little machine in that office, for making student IDs you know," she tells me. "So all of us at Sacred Heart High had them, fake LSU-E IDs from John Brady Balfa."

John Brady arrived in Baton Rouge in the fall of 1979 ready to conquer the world. He immediately put his name on the 1980 ballot for student body president at LSU, a university with a student population of over 27,000, in comparison to LSU-E's 1,300.

Greg Bergeron, an LSU-E friend who became John Brady's roommate in Baton Rouge, remembers being impressed by his ambition. He even helped with the campaign. "He was charming. He was the first guy I ever met who pressed his jeans. All his stuff was dry-cleaned. Very polite."

Doug was less inspired. When John Brady asked him to be his campaign manager, he declined. "I thought he was crazy for even trying to run," he tells me. This was not Mamou, this was not Eunice. John Brady had no idea what a little fish he was. "A lot of the time it's the big-city fraternity dudes that run." Mike Futrell would win that election by a landslide, and John Brady was far from second place. (After his term and graduation from LSU, and then LSU Law, Futrell went on to serve two tours of duty as an officer in the US Navy, two terms in the Louisiana

House of Representatives, and currently holds the position of city man-ager in Riverside, California.)

Doug, who went on to become an attorney himself, remembers meet-ing Futrell in law school at LSU years later, after John Brady had already been convicted. As Doug recalls it, they got to talking about that election, and Futrell told him, "You know, that guy threatened to kill me while we were running." Doug responded, "You should have believed him."

When John Brady arrived at LSU, he moved into an apartment complex on Alvin Dark Avenue, in the neighborhood just behind the university's rowdy conglomerate of bars known as Tigerland. Most of the Evange-line Parish folks attending LSU lived there, taking turns hosting Monday night football screenings and gumbos and pregames for wild nights out. Everyone was drinking. But John Brady had a problem.

"John drank in a way that was pathological," remembers Brian, who was John Brady's other roommate at the time. "He'd schedule his classes on Tuesdays and Thursdays to maximize his drinking. We're talking go through a fifth of whiskey on a Friday night. Another one on Saturday. On Sunday, he'd start on a third one to calm his nerves, get ready for the week."

Doug was living around the corner from John Brady and had a pre-law class with him. "We both hated it. We'd bring a quart of Jack Daniel's and promise we'd only have a few swigs." They'd leave the class with the bottle empty, almost every time.

Greg was a partier. And it wasn't just alcohol, he says. The drugs were everywhere. "But John frowned on that," he says. "He would never. Alco-hol was legal, you know. And John was a *raging* alcoholic. He outdrank anyone I ever knew. Damn, though, drugs probably would have at least calmed him down, instead of firing him all up."

The alcohol fueled a fury that none of its witnesses have forgotten. Stories abound of John Brady bowing up to guys ten times bigger than him over one disproportionate offense or another. "He had the abil-ity to switch his personality so fast. But when the manners and charm didn't work anymore, he would revert to this irrational anger or passive-aggressiveness," remembers Greg. There was an insecurity to him, he says, that lost all logic. They'd be with a group of friends, and something would strike a nerve. "The pouting! He would go in his room and stay away from us, or he'd sit in his chair, and you could feel it. And these guys all fell off. They didn't want to deal with somebody that fragile."

"I was getting real fed up with him," says Doug. "He was real polite when we first met him, then after a while he just got to be a real dick."

On one morning Greg will never forget, he was sleeping on the sofa, recovering from a party they'd hosted the night before. John Brady was awake and had started cleaning up the detritus. "He'd drink the leftover beer, warm," recalls Greg. "I wouldn't help him clean, like 'Just because you're cleaning right now doesn't mean I have to.'" This set something off in John Brady. "He took a long-necked bottle, broke it on the coffee table, and held it to my neck."

Still, Greg stuck around, and even supported John Brady dating his sister for a time. "He could be so gracious and accommodating . . ." Besides, the qualities that made John Brady difficult to be around were things people in college typically grew out of: immaturity, insecurity, drinking too much. Someone who could put himself together so well, who had such charm and manners and ambition—well, most anyone would have believed there was a future there. "Like my dad said once," remembered Greg, "he was the kind of guy you wanted your daughter to marry."

This is what attracted Greg's sister to John Brady in the first place. "That all appealed to me," she tells me. "It looked like a good thing." Today, Colleen Jackson is a trim, confident-looking woman, exuding a highly professional aura not unlike her brother's. With some difficulty, I try to imagine her sitting at a countertop in a dingy Alvin Dark apartment, drinking beers with John Brady. "We immediately kind of hit it off," she says. She dated him for a little over a year during the time he was a student at LSU, around 1980 to 1981. "He had Cajun roots, I had Cajun roots. We had a lot in common." He'd share his uncles' music with her, driving her to Henderson to eat at Pat's, where they had a giant dance floor and the Balfa Brothers' albums playing on repeat.

John Brady was a generous boyfriend. He would shower her with gifts, bought her a dog, would even buy her clothes. "He was all about impressing," says Greg. "There was a while I tried to keep up with him, the dry cleaning and all that, but I couldn't afford it. I didn't have the bankroll he had."

"John was a regular old guy like us," says Brian. "He didn't come from a family with any kind of money. We figured there was something up that no one knew."

At one point, Greg purportedly got the story from John Brady, who said he'd made an agreement with a businessman and family friend back home, Eddie Soileau.[1] So long as he stayed in school, Soileau would send John Brady a $1,000 check each month.

Eddie Soileau is today recognized as one of Acadiana's most successful entrepreneurs. He began his pipeline business, Sunland Construction, in Eunice in 1974. Through years of growth and strategic acquisitions, Soileau has built a portfolio, encapsulated by the holding company Sunland Capital, that includes various energy, industrial, and infrastructure businesses across the country. Sunland Construction, where it all started, is still operating its corporate office out of Eunice, with Soileau, now in his eighties, as its figurehead.

When I visit Soileau in his office at Sunland, I ask about this money. "If I did [give it to him], I don't remember, I don't recall," he says, simply. Whether or not he sent monthly payments to John Brady while he was in school, in 1985 Soileau testified in court that he did issue loans to John Brady later, loans meant to help pay off gambling debts.

The gambling Soileau does remember.

"He was bright," he tells me. "He was well-liked, and he would have made a terrific attorney. Tall, nice-looking guy. Very personable. Real politician kind of guy. The one bad flaw . . . he loved to gamble. I couldn't believe the dollars he got involved in."

"I remember back then he'd wake up, pour a Jack and Coke," says Doug, expertly pouring air into an invisible tumbler, then putting his hand—thumb and pinkie extending out of his fist—to his ear, "and he'd call his bookie."

It was the manager of their apartment complex that turned them onto the sports gambling. "John got way in deep," Doug remembers. "And he didn't know a damn thing about sports."

Even after John Brady and Colleen had broken up, creditors would call her house phone trying to reach him. "I had no idea the amount of money he was betting," she says, "and later found out he was actually betting on his losses."

Things started to escalate, remembers Brian. John Brady would come in late almost every night, often with bad company—people easily ten years older than him—occasionally with black eyes and bloody noses. "We knew something bad was gonna come out of that."

---

1   Eddie Soileau is of no relevant relation to the Sheriff's Deputy Floyd Soileau.

\\\\\\

BY 1982, JOHN BRADY BALFA AND GREG BERGERON HAD BOTH dropped out of LSU. Thanks to his relationship with Eddie Soileau, John Brady was able to land them both jobs at Sunland. The work came one assignment at a time—constructing pipelines to run oil, gas, and other substances where they were needed. The jobs often lasted for a few months and could be located anywhere from Tennessee to Texas. Though the hours were brutal, the pay was good, and Sunland ended up being a holdover for many of the area's young, unmarried men. Brian LaHaye was already there when John Brady and Greg arrived.

It was at this point that Greg and John Brady's friendship started to unravel. On one occasion, in between jobs, Greg made the trip to Eunice to pick up a paycheck. The office manager told him John Brady had already come to pick it up for him. "I said, 'That is absolutely not true.'" Greg reported the theft to his manager and was reimbursed, but John Brady wasn't fired. "The next time we worked on the same job, we weren't on speaking terms because he had shown his true colors."

When I mention to Colleen that Greg wasn't surprised to learn John Brady had been convicted of murder, she shakes her head in disagreement. "No. It was shocking to me. There were many moments when I told myself they had to have gotten it wrong. But I guess you don't want to admit you could have been such a misjudge of character for such a long time . . ."

In my aunt Michele's kitchen, the very kitchen from which MawMaw Emily started the coffee that dreadful morning, she pours another glass of wine and leans in close.

"Years passed. We lost track of John. He went to LSU," she sets it up. "Then one day, my friend Gigi calls me. She says, 'You know John Balfa? From LSU-E? Well, he totally flipped out.'"

The story going around at the time, likely in 1982, was that John Brady had burned down his apartment complex, and he had done it "on the anniversary of the day he raped his wife." "He had a thing with anniversaries," she tells me. "And on the day of that conviction, he burned down the apartment complex she was living in."

In this story, I recognize the aura of rumor, likely exacerbated by the years since John Brady has acquired a murder conviction.

What I know is this: On February 19, 1982, at around 7:20 p.m., fires were started in a downstairs hallway and two bathrooms in Midway Apartments on Alvin Dark Avenue in Baton Rouge, where John Brady Balfa was living, causing about $5,000 in damages. John Brady was named a suspect because a witness saw him in the stairwell, acting suspicious, while the fires were just starting to burn; and because the apartment managers noted they had recently seized John Brady's stereo equipment as collateral for back rent owed. If what Doug Pucheu said about the apartment managers acting as bookies is true, it's possible John Brady owed them gambling money.

I know that on this day, John Brady was wearing an LSU baseball cap, blue jeans, and a printed T-shirt. A few days later, fingerprints lifted from the cans of lighter fluid found at the scene came back as a match for John Brady's, and he was arrested on a count of aggravated arson on March 3, 1982. I know he denied all charges. And that, for some reason the record does not show, he never had to go to court.

I also know that at this time in his life, John Brady was not married, and he had no formal convictions of rape. Yet.

"They called him the honeybun rapist," the former assistant district attorney Richard Vidrine[1] tells me. It's the fall of 2017, and I'm sitting in the Evangeline Parish courthouse, across the table from one-third of the prosecutorial team from the Aubrey LaHaye murder trial. Between us are two boxes of files and a stack of paper: the DA file from the John Brady Balfa case. Though Vidrine is retired, he's gotten me access to all this. He declines to be recorded, so for the next four hours, I fill my notebook with half-baked quotes and observations, including: *This was the biggest trial we had in Ev* and *We were convinced beyond a doubt.*

As he speaks, Vidrine carefully reviews each packet of papers before showing them to me. I take photos of everything I can. Much of what I hoped to find in the FBI file is here, though not all of it. Detective Rudy Guillory's account of the St. Landry Parish lineup where MawMaw Emily identified John Brady, Uncle Glenn's January 6 statement, the Sheriff's Department action report. My eyes quiver over the stacks of records Vidrine's skipping over, the stuff he's not letting me see.

He does, though, pass me the file holding records from John Brady's rape trial in Longview, Texas.

---

1 Richard Vidrine is of no relevant relation to Ramson Vidrine.

From the first time I heard Aunt Michele's story of John Brady and his anniversary arson, the rumors of rape have swirled around my research. Brian said he heard John Brady had raped someone. Greg had heard he raped at least two women. Doug had heard of three.

Up until this moment, something has kept me from digging into the rape accusations, perhaps a skeptical reaction to the mythic origin story Aunt Michele had delivered. Perhaps because I am trying not to cloud my perceptions, limiting my concerns to PawPaw Aubrey's murder, imitating the spirit of our justice system in which one crime does not necessarily beget another. Just because he is a rapist does not mean he is a murderer. Perhaps I am hoping that the world isn't so ugly as its rumors.

I do know, however, that John Brady was convicted of rape once, in Longview. I've seen the newspaper articles. I've read that the incident took place around 2 a.m. on September 13, 1982. That she was a clerk at a 7-Eleven. A customer came in the door, heard a noise, realized what was going on, and called the police. John Brady ran, but the cops caught up with him, identifying his truck by the "Edwards '83" sticker on the back.

When I get home from the courthouse, I start reading through the records from that night. The police report. The witnesses' statements. The victim's statement. It's all here, right in front of me. What he did to this woman, in her own words, in her own handwriting. The honeybun he bought from the counter. The handprint-shaped bruise he left on her neck. The way she fought, and resisted, the whole time. The way she told him, "My life is messed up enough, please let me go." The way he smiled at the other customers on his way out, while she sobbed and pulled up her pants.

This. This is monstrous, I think to myself. These are not the actions of someone damaged, the consequences of poor choices, the mistakes of youth, the illness of addiction. *This is evil.* Pure, unabashed evil.

The disgust slithering over my skin smolders when I read about the trial, uniting with a global rage burning bright that fall of 2017, when the sexual-abuse accusations against Harvey Weinstein were spurring the beginnings of the #MeToo movement.

The trial, which took place in February 1983, was agonizing—a litany of praises for John Brady by members of his family, giving character witness testimony to his potential, his intelligence, his good, kind heart. To the fact that he was going through a rough patch. His defense attorney pleaded with the jury in that familiar refrain: "Don't give up on this man totally. Please don't take away this man's hope for the rest of his life."

This was the second attorney posted to John Brady's trial. His first had withdrawn as counsel sometime before in a letter I find loose in the DA file. He writes: "It has become clear to counsel that the defendant refused in cooperating and persists in so refusing to cooperate openly and honestly about the offense for which he stands indicted." I store this away in my memory, this evidence that John Brady is, in fact, a liar.

When he took the stand, he told his side of the story: it had all been her idea. She had initiated all of it. He had not done *anything* wrong. He told of how he was nine beers deep when he arrived at the 7-Eleven, lost, on his way back to his apartment. "When someone is propositioned, and nobody is around, not too many people would refuse," he told the jury. When asked, he was unable to explain his victim's bruises, or why he ran. Greg tells me he thinks it's possible John Brady truly entertained this delusion to avoid taking responsibility. "John could have made anything in his head to be justifiable," he says.

The jury, mostly, was unmoved. They had seen the photos. They knew he was full of shit. Eleven of the twelve did, at least. One man, and only one, would not stand down. He would not send John Brady to prison. To avoid a mistrial—which would force the victim to relive the whole thing—the jury members agreed to a guilty conviction, with a lenient sentence of ten years' probation.[1] They sent her rapist back into the world, free.

Two years and two more criminal trials later, when the judgment against John Brady in the Aubrey LaHaye case came back unanimously guilty, my aunt Michele tells me she remembers being unsure, beyond a reasonable doubt, that he had done it. "If I had been on the jury, it was questionable to me," she says. "But I remember thinking that I knew he had done some really, really bad things. And that even if we were wrong, he needs to be in jail anyway. He's terrible."

---

1 To this day, Texas is one of a handful of states that still allows jury sentencing.

Deborah Kinney

SHORTLY AFTER JOHN BRADY BALFA'S RAPE TRIAL ENDED IN March of 1983, he married Deborah Kinney, the woman he'd named as his alibi in the Aubrey LaHaye case. Brian remembers when they started dating, during a Sunland job in Atlanta, Texas, in 1982. Her mother owned the Kentucky Fried Chicken franchise in Atlanta, and it was where she and her sisters worked. KFC, she would later testify, is where they met.

John Brady and Deborah got engaged in December of 1982, imagining an October wedding. They'd later change their minds, opting for the spring of 1983. At the time of their engagement, John Brady was out on bail, awaiting his trial for the rape case in Longview. I can't help but wonder how a woman accepts a proposal from a man awaiting trial for rape. What did she know? Could he have manipulated her into believing he was innocent?

The couple married on April 17, 1983, at John Brady's childhood home. "It was a simple little ceremony," remembers Brian. "I remember it got real emotional. John Brady started crying, and he hugged his daddy, and all this. They were obviously a close family."

The marriage was short-lived. By September 1984, Debbie had moved out and gone back to Texas. Their divorce was finalized by November.

I think often about Debbie, about her vantage point on January 6, 1983. And I imagine three parallel universes. In the first, John Brady arrives in Atlanta, Texas, a murderer, and it is imperceptible. He puts on his fiancé face and plays the part—brushes Debbie's hair behind her ear with the same hand that bludgeoned Aubrey LaHaye to death only hours before. They talk of *Tootsie*, of his upcoming job assignments, of her mother, of their wedding. She notices he's acting a little off, asks him about it. He hugs her tight, tells her not to worry so much, and she buries her face in his neck.

In the second, he did it, and Debbie knows. She is his confidante. She spends the day telling him to act normal, to be sure people see him all over Atlanta. Her heart sits in her throat. She's worried for him. She loves him, no matter what. He can't get caught. She squeezes his hand and barely registers the movie. He passes the popcorn to her sister. Safe inside his hotel room, he tells her everything. Maybe he cries. Maybe he's scared. She definitely cries. She's definitely scared. They hold each other tight, until outside the window, the sky shifts from black to blue.

In the third, it is as John Brady and Debbie have always said. A normal day. A wonderful day, two lovers reuniting after some time apart. Pizza, cigarettes, and arms wrapped around each other. Neither with any idea that two hundred and forty miles away, a body sinks into the Nezpique. Neither with any idea of all that is to come.

The Case of Terry DeVillier

SEPTEMBER 18, 1984

A FEW DAYS BEFORE EMILY PICKED JOHN BRADY OUT OF A lineup, he had taken off work to meet with his probation officer. First, though, he made a trip to Eunice, to his bookie's house off Highway 13, about a mile south of the Nezpique.

At the time, John Brady was placing bets with Terry DeVillier[1] just about every weekend.

Terry answered the door, shirtless. "Come on in, John."

Here's where the story splits in two, per John Brady's and Terry's testimonies in the trial that would take place six months later. John Brady would claim Terry owed him money. Terry would claim John Brady owed *him* money. In John Brady's version, Terry pulled the gun first. In Terry's, John Brady did. Terry would claim that John Brady demanded Terry tie himself up, throwing him a coil of rope.

The rope wouldn't factor into John Brady's story.

Both told of how they wrestled on the floor, how Terry bit John Brady on the arm, grabbed a gun off a side table, and shot at the wall. Both told of how John Brady stabbed Terry in the back, the blood spilling everywhere. John Brady claimed it was self-defense.

The incident ended with Terry at the hospital getting stitches, and John Brady at the police station, covered in Terry's blood. Each gave their statements, and an investigation was opened at the DeVillier house, which officers found in disarray, blood all over the hallway and the bedroom. The spool of rope on the floor in the living room.

In the evening, the detective asked if John Brady would accompany him there. He arrived on the scene in the passenger seat of the officer's car, uncuffed, having sufficiently convinced the officers at the station that he'd been attacked, that it had been self-defense. After he arrived, though,

---

1 Terry DeVillier is of no relevant relation to Sonny DeVillier.

and those officers convened with the ones who had processed the scene, they came back to the car, cuffed him, and moved him to the back seat. He was then taken to the St. Landry Parish Jail. He wouldn't leave for almost six months, and he would never be a free man again.

At around 9:30 p.m. that night, St. Landry Parish detective Roy Mallet gave Detective Guillory a phone call. "Hey, Rudy, sorry to be calling so late. I wanted to let you know, today our officers brought us a case of attempted burglary and attempted murder here in Eunice. The guy came in looking for money, carrying rope and a knife. If I'm not mistaken, that MO sounds a lot like the big LaHaye case y'all have been investigating, am I right?"

"Who's the guy?"

"His name is John Brady Balfa. He's a Mamou fella. Ring any bells?"

At Harry Balfa's House

SEPTEMBER 20, 1984

"A NYTHING YOU WANT, YOU'RE WELCOME TO IT," HARRY Balfa told Agent Owen Odom as he guided him and Detective Roy Mallet around his property. "We don't got nothin' to hide out here."

Located at the dead end of a long, windy, wooded gravel road in Duralde, the "Balfa compound" was centered by the house Harry had raised his kids in. Five hundred yards down the road, Timmy had recently finished building his new house. Charles had taken over his older brother Harry Jr.'s trailer a few years back. And John Brady was still living in the outdoor kitchen.

"Can we look in here?" Detective Mallet asked Harry, gesturing toward what looked like a toolshed behind the outdoor kitchen. They hadn't had time to work up a warrant, but Harry had been cooperative, had signed a consent form. He knew his son had been in trouble, though he didn't yet know what these officers were investigating. He nodded, opened the door, and switched on the single light bulb—which illuminated some dusty shelves housing tools and paint cans, a table at the center. On top of it was a pile of rope, two types: the hemp all knotted up in the nylon. "Okay if we take a sample of this?" Odom asked Harry, who nodded. "What about this?" Mallet picked up an open can of bright orange paint, and looking at it, said, "I guess we don't need the whole thing . . ." He searched around for a swab. Harry bumbled over, "Look, how about this?" He pulled out a pocketknife from his jeans, wiped it on his sleeve, then sliced a sliver of the dried paint from the lid. "Will that work for you?" Odom opened an envelope for him to drop it in. "Thank you, sir."

They stepped back out into the yard and started walking toward the barn. When Mallet looked up, he scanned the building's periphery and noticed a tire. "Odom," he said, walking over to it. "Does this look anything like the ones you've got back at the station?" Odom put his hand on it, rolled it over. Harry stood back, hands in his pockets. "Is the rim painted?" asked Odom.

"Oh, yep," said Harry.

He explained that about five years before, John Brady and two of his brothers, Timmy and Charles, had bought some tires at a flea market while visiting their mother in Houston. While they were in a restaurant, someone had stolen the tires off Charles's new Firebird. A flea market was next door, and a set of mismatched junk tires—which they spray-painted black—had gotten them home. After the insurance money came through and Charles was able to replace his tires, the flea market set was tossed in the junk pile.

"Are all four tires still on the property?" Odom asked.

"Umm, yeah, I believe so. They should be somewhere around here," answered Harry, wary of the sudden intensity with which the agent was eyeing the tire at their feet.

"Can you help us find them?" Mallet asked.

"Of course."

They found one under a livestock trailer nearby. Another one in the junk pile. But after searching the barn, Charles's workshop, and every nook and cranny Harry could think of, they still only had three tires.

"We're gonna be takin' this," Odom said, hefting up the first one, the Chevrolet. "And we'll probably be back."

Gathering Evidence

O N THE MORNING OF SEPTEMBER 21, 1984, AGENT OWEN Odom pulled John Brady Balfa into the Sheriff's Office at the St. Landry Parish jail and handed him an Advice of Rights and Waiver form.

The day before, after their visit to the Balfa property, Odom and Mallet had removed the tire from the rim they'd brought back to the Evangeline Parish DA's Office. When they set it beside the Camaro rim that had been attached to Aubrey's body, they looked at each other and nodded. The rims looked alike. They went back to gather the other two, and to make absolutely sure the fourth one wasn't on the property. They had plans to return that afternoon for a third search, but first Odom wanted to get John Brady's side of the story.

John Brady explained that he had already been interrogated about the Aubrey LaHaye murder. He repeated the account of his whereabouts, citing this time that he had left his dad's house between 5:30 a.m. and 6 a.m. before driving to Eunice to pick up his laundry at around 6:45, and then heading out to Atlanta, Texas, to visit his girlfriend. He said he arrived in Atlanta around noon. The report closes with: "Balfa denied having anything to do with the kidnapping and murder of Aubrey LaHaye."

At the end of the interview, Odom brought out the Camaro rim that was attached to Aubrey's body and showed it to John Brady. "What is that?" he asked. "I've never seen that before."

Odom asked if he'd be willing to take a polygraph test. As he had when he was first interviewed about the LaHaye case, John Brady refused.

That same day, they brought Emily in for the lineup.

A few days later, on September 24, after the FBI and local law enforcement had made four trips in total to the Balfa residence, their findings were packaged up in two boxes and sent off to the FBI Laboratories in

Washington, DC. Inside the first box were three mobile home trailer rims, a brown ski vest, a blue-and-silver ski jacket, two Chevrolet Camaro wheel hubs, the paint sample, two sets of fence pliers, a plastic bag containing three types of rope, a length of hemp rope, a ten-inch pipe wrench, and an amber-colored bottle. The other box contained the three Chevrolet Camaro wheel rims. The DA's Office instructed the lab to perform a series of tests, comparing the ropes and rims from the Balfa property to those attached to Aubrey's body. They requested that comparative tests also be conducted on the rope used to tie up Emily, and the paint splatters found on it, against samples of rope and paint from the Balfa workshop. All the clothing, the wrench, and the pliers were to be tested for blood, hair, fiber, and tissue; and the amber bottle was to be compared against the glass fragment removed from Aubrey's head wound.

And, finally, any known fingerprints from John Brady Balfa were to be tested against the one the FBI lifted from the rim attached to Aubrey's body.

That same afternoon, Detective Roy Mallet and Chief Deputy Billy Frilot were interrogating John Brady about the Terry DeVillier assault. In the middle of the interview, John Brady asked them why the FBI had been at his house and why he was still being investigated in the LaHaye case. He said he thought he had already been eliminated as a suspect. In a report of the account, Mallet writes: "When asked how he had been cleared, he said Emily had been shown a picture of him and said it could not be him because he had a mustache at the time. When asked how he knew this, he said he had been told by someone."

I wonder who could have told him that he'd been eliminated from the investigation. For him to accurately (per Grimsley's account) identify the reason as the mustache, he had to have heard the information from someone at the center of it all.

John Brady repeated his statement about traveling to Atlanta, Texas, on January 6, 1983. This time he cited 5 a.m. as the time he left his father's house.

"So how long did it take you to get there? To Atlanta?" asked Frilot.

"Oh, I'd say about six hours or so. I arrived at the motel at 12:30 p.m."

The next day, on September 25, 1984, Mallet and Guillory got in the car to drive to Atlanta, Texas.

The Case Against
John Brady Balfa

T HROUGHOUT THE END OF 1984, JOHN BRADY SAT IN THE ST. Landry Parish jail, and he waited. The probation director at Gregg County had placed a hold on him, preventing him from making bond until he could be brought to Longview for a possible re- vocation hearing. In October, a grand jury indicted John Brady Balfa for attempted robbery and attempted second-degree murder in the case of Terry DeVillier. His trial was set for the following March.

But these were the least of his problems. The Evangeline Parish Dis- trict Attorney's Office was building a case against him for the highest- profile murder his hometown had seen in a generation.

The DA, William "Billy" Pucheu, had just been reelected to his third six-year term. A native of Ville Platte, Pucheu was a World War II vet- eran about a decade older than Glenn and Wayne LaHaye. He had a handsome, movie star–politician face and a talent for public speaking that made him the town's frequent choice as master of ceremonies for various community events. He and Aubrey LaHaye would have crossed paths at several of the many Catholic men's gatherings Pucheu organized as the parish's retreat director. He and Glenn were close friends; his wife, Gay, and Janie were members of the Magnolia Garden Club together. My dad dated his daughter Pam for years. His daughter-in-law Kim taught me sixth-grade science.

In 1984 Pucheu's office had tried over 21,000 cases. This was more than double what had been tried in the entire history of the District Attorney's Office prior to his appointment, reflecting—among other things—a marked increase in "not guilty" pleas by defendants. Pucheu had prosecuted cases on everything from card-games-gone-wrong knif- ings to goat theft, LSD distribution to out-of-season squirrel hunting. So, so many DWIs. He knew the grisly details of every single assault and rape and murder that had occurred in Evangeline over the past decade, all weighing upon his memory, forever tainting the lens through which he saw his hometown. But the Aubrey LaHaye kidnapping-murder case, he must have known, would be at the height of his legacy. Over the last few months of 1984, he and Rudy Guillory pored over the evidence they had on John Brady Balfa.

The alibi had its problems. When Guillory and Mallet got to Atlanta, Texas, they visited the Best Western Hotel and were given documentation that confirmed John Brady had indeed checked in on January 6—though there was no check-in time listed. (There was, however, a separate FBI report from January 1983 that confirmed John Brady had checked in between 9 a.m. and noon. Whether it is because they did not know it existed, or because it gave him just enough time for the alibi to possibly work, and therefore didn't support their case—this record never made its way into the State's official case.)

While they waited for the evidence from the FBI labs to come back, Guillory and Pucheu started looking into John Brady's finances. What they found was a history of serious financial straits culminating in not one, but three attempts to secure a loan from Aubrey LaHaye at Guaranty Bank. Because of John Brady's history of dishonored checks, each application had been denied.

In January 1983, John Brady was about to have his truck repossessed after failing to make a single payment on the note in the three months since he bought it. He had just received his first bill for student loan payments for a degree he never got. He owed $7,200 in dishonored checks to various entities, including payments to his lawyers and bondsmen in relation to the Longview rape case. And a portion of his paycheck was being taken out to pay the $5,000 personal loan his boss, Eddie Soileau, had granted him. John Brady needed money, badly.

A motive. And a reason to hate Aubrey LaHaye, too.

Guillory, Pucheu, and Odom felt they were getting somewhere. All they needed was physical evidence to tie it all together.

Meanwhile, in Washington, DC, Special Agent Allen T. Robillard, of the FBI's microscopic analysis unit, sat with ten sections of rope in front of him. Two were taken from Aubrey's body; one was a synthetic rope, which had been tied around his waist and knotted around his right hand; the other was a knotted mess of two separate ropes—one of natural fibers and the other synthetic—used to attach the tire rims to his body, tied around his neck. There was also the rope used to tie Emily to the bed, made of natural fibers.

In the other pile, there were four pieces of synthetic rope and two natural fiber ropes—all taken from Harry Balfa's toolshed.

Robillard's job was to find the connections, if they existed. It was a process of elimination. Right off the bat, by basic physical appearance alone, he could tell the two natural fiber ropes taken from the Balfa yard had nothing in common with the natural fiber ropes found on Aubrey's body or on Emily's bed. He pushed them aside.

Now with four synthetic ropes suitable for comparison, he started to investigate their construction. Which direction were the fibers twisted together? How many plies is the rope made of? How many plies are within the ply? He kept going and going, until he got to the rope's very core. Using a compound microscope, he measured the diameter of the fibers, noted their shape, their chemical composition. When compared to the synthetic ropes tied to Aubrey's waist and to his neck, he found the Balfa ropes matched in physical characteristics, composition, and construction and "could have originated from the same source." What the records do not show, though, is how the analysts defined "source." They *could have* come from the same manufacturer, then, but it remains unclear whether they came from the same spool or were ever attached at all.

Somewhere in the same building, the J. Edgar Hoover FBI Headquarters, Special Agent David Nichols of the instrumental analysis unit had the rims. Using a microscope, he studied the makeup of the paint finish on the Camaro rim that had been tied to Aubrey's body. He found three layers of paint: black enamel paint, blue metallic paint, and another layer of black enamel paint under that.

Conducting the same tests on the three rims discovered on the Balfa property, Nichols found a different layer structure. These rims also had three layers of paint, but from the outside in, they were: black enamel paint, silver color paint, and dark gray paint. He took a sample of the top layer, the black enamel, from all four rims. Microscopically, he could see that the color was the same in all four instances. When he added chemicals to the paint specimens, none had a reaction. Next, he performed an instrumental examination, using first a gas chromatograph—which burns the paint, causing gases to be released characteristic of the paint's organic nature, which the machine records via a chart for comparison. Then he performed an x-ray analysis using a scanning electron microscope. In both instances, he found the results to be consistent across all four rims. He concluded that while the rims themselves were not identical, and the paint structures were different—the outer layer of paint on all four rims could have originated from the same paint source. Such as spray paint. This supported the State's theory that the rim had been one of the four mismatched, thrifted rims that the Balfa boys had spray-painted, then thrown in the family junk pile.

Nichols then turned to the paint samples. Orange paint was found on the rope tied to Aubrey's neck and the rope used to tie Emily to the bed. It was also found on some segments of the synthetic rope found on the Balfa property. Using the same methodology of paint testing he conducted on the tires, Nichols compared the samples on each of the ropes to the paint sample scraped from the can in Harry Balfa's shed. He found that in all four cases, the paint was the same in physical, microchemical, and instrumental properties. And could have originated from the same source.

All this was submitted to Billy Pucheu and Rudy Guillory in a report filed on December 14, 1984. The analysts also reported that blood was found on the ski vest and jacket, though in an amount too small to be matched, or to even be certainly determined human blood. Upon learning this, Guillory called the lab and asked about the pattern of the splatter. "Yes," they told him. "It is consistent with someone receiving a hard blow to the head." No blood was found on the fence pliers or the pipe wrench. They found, also, no relationship between the glass shard found in Aubrey's head and the amber bottle taken from the Balfa house.

Still, they had the rims. They had the rope. They had a financial motive. John Brady Balfa knew Aubrey LaHaye and had negative interactions with him. They had a criminal history with a similar MO. John Brady had been in Mamou on the morning of January 6, 1983, awake before the sun rose. He had left before the day was over, putting miles and miles between him and Evangeline Parish. And his alibi, as far as the investigators could see, wasn't watertight.

They scheduled the grand jury hearing for February 1985.

Hindsight

'M TURNING ONTO HIGHWAY 190, POINTED EAST TO BATON Rouge after a long weekend interviewing folks across Evangeline Parish. Normally, I'd just spend the night at my parents, but homework is calling me home. Dad still wants a recap, though, and our phone call—as it so often does—will carry me through the entire hour-and-a-half drive.

"Did you know Mrs. Lori went on a date with him, with John Brady?" I tell him of my most recent revelation—that my best friend's mom had spent her nineteenth birthday with my great-grandfather's accused killer.

"Lori Parks?"

"Yes!"

He laughs. "Wow. Just wow."

The connection is just one more in the remarkable web of intertwined worlds, emphasizing every day just how small Evangeline Parish actually is.

"You know, I worked in that office," Dad ponders. He's talking about the LSU-E Student Body President Office. Four years after John Brady held the position, after PawPaw Aubrey had already been killed, my dad followed in John Brady's footsteps in student government, earning an election as Vice President.

"I can't believe your aunt Michele knew him," he says.

As the void between my dad and the stranger who killed his grandfather folds around such uncanny familiarity, I hear something shift in his voice. "You know, I think I've told you this before, but there are a lot of people in this town to this day who don't believe they got the right guy." He has told me. But for the first time, I decide to push him.

"Well, Dad, what do you think?"

"I'll tell you this," he tells me. And to the windshield, I nod to the familiar, nebulous refrain. "I don't think we have the whole story."

JOHN BRADY'S STORY, AS TOLD BY HIS ROOMMATES AND OLD girlfriends and acquaintances and college buddies, is soaked in foreshadowing.

But despite the telltale signs of his deterioration, despite the timing—the alcoholism, the gambling, the violence, and the failing out of school all reaching their climax right at the end of 1982—a pall of doubt lingers for me. I don't know that I believe anyone ever truly worried about John Brady murdering anyone until he had been convicted of murder, despite what they say.

"I knew he was crazy, but I didn't know how crazy," says Doug Pucheu. "When they told me he murdered someone, I didn't have a problem believing he could murder somebody."

"He didn't consider the consequences of when he did something," recalls Greg Bergeron. "Like who is gonna gamble $3,000 on three or four games? When you got no money to pay for it? The consequences never clicked. He never looked at it from a standpoint of, 'What happens if I get caught?' I could see him doing all this just because of his impulsive nature and not considering the consequences. . . .'"

"You know what's funny?" Brian LaHaye asks me. "Back then there were people I knew that said, 'There's no way John did that,' even with the evidence and everything else. They were like 'ahhh, nahh.' And there are still people today who will say that. As for me? I believe he did it. It's been through the court system. I don't have a reason to doubt it."

"I have no doubt in my mind that it was him," says Eddie Soileau, sitting behind his desk at Sunland.

John Brady Balfa has maintained his innocence for forty years now. I decide to stop sneaking around in the bushes of old roommates and ex-girlfriends, and to knock on the door. In October of 2017, I write a letter to John Brady, imagining him leaping at the chance to tell his story, even if he can't tell me all of it. Even if what he tells me is a lie. I imagine a sort of friendship forming between us, or at least a dialogue. I so badly want to hear his side of the story, the way he'd tell it now.

In my letter, I introduce myself as the daughter of Dr. Marcel LaHaye, the granddaughter of Dr. Wayne and Susan LaHaye, the great-granddaughter of Aubrey and Emily LaHaye. I tell him I was born in 1996, thirteen years after Aubrey's death, and that for most of my life, I knew virtually nothing about the case at all. I ask if he would share his story with me—any story at all, about Aubrey or not. "I am writing without any assumption that I know anything about the kind of man you are," I put down, in all earnestness.

I place it in the mail, addressed to John Brady Balfa, Louisiana State Penitentiary at Angola.

How Do You Plead?

COMING UP LATER TONIGHT ON TV 10 EYEWITNESS NEWS:
In January of 1983 Evangeline Parish banker Aubrey LaHaye was
kidnapped from his home at knifepoint. His body was found a week
later floating in a nearby bayou. For nearly two years, the investigation
into LaHaye's kidnapping and killing has had no major breakthroughs.
But Justine Weeks reports there may be new light shed on the case. . . .

Across Louisiana news organizations, the secret was out: John Brady Balfa was to face charges for the murder of Aubrey LaHaye. But per the request of District Attorney Billy Pucheu, local media were awaiting the results of the grand jury hearing before releasing his name. All local media, that is, except for KLFY-Channel 10 in Lafayette, whose January 15, 1985, report named John Brady Balfa as the long-awaited suspect to the highly publicized case, alongside a photograph of him.

Pucheu was furious. In a press release issued by his office, he emphasized the issue: "The reporting was done without regard to its effects on the outcome of the case and without concern for the victim's family or the defendant's rights." At this point, Pucheu did reveal that a grand jury would be impaneled in February, and that—in the absence of evidence that extortion took place involving Guaranty Bank—the FBI had turned the case over to the DA's Office. No federal charges would be involved. Despite the increasingly hungry audience, he refused to give the media any more details about evidence, the accused, or the case.

He did answer the phone, though, when his son called. Doug Pucheu—John Brady's old college buddy. He was the district attorney's son.

"So you really think Brady did this, Dad?"

"Wild, right? It's shaping up to look like it, son . . . Shit, I remember him hanging around the house while y'all were at E . . ."

"I mean, Dad, if you think he's guilty, you've gotta prosecute him. You've always said you don't prosecute unless you're sure they're guilty. If you think he did it, well . . . shit. I believe you."

On February 15, 1985, after four days of deliberation, the grand jury indicted John Brady Balfa for the armed robbery, aggravated kidnapping, and first-degree murder of Aubrey LaHaye—the last a crime punishable by death in Louisiana.

As Pucheu walked out of the courthouse, he kept his lips locked. His phone rang for a week straight, but he refused to make a single comment on the case.

On February 17, the headline "LaHaye Indictment: Grand Jurors Link Balfa to Banker's Murder" ran across the top of the *Daily World*'s front page. And right beside it: one of the earliest stories regarding Edwin Edwards's first indictment on charges of mail fraud, obstruction of justice, and bribery. John Brady had found himself right in step with the man he so admired. Side by side, deteriorating on the front page, their indictments in hand.

Edwards would be acquitted of his charges, this time. John Brady would not.

On March 10, 1985, John Brady Balfa was back on the front page of the *Daily World*, this time photographed. Outside of the parish jail, in between two police cars and with a cowboy-hatted officer right behind him—he is pictured looking right at the camera. He is handcuffed, wearing a white button-down shirt, blue jeans, and cowboy boots, and he has a thick, thick mustache.

Though the entire town had its eyes on John Brady, in Judge Joseph Emile Coreil's courtroom the previous Friday he was just one of thirty-five defendants getting arraigned. All in all, the whole thing took about five minutes.

"Be informed," Coreil recited, "that John Brady Balfa at the Parish of Evangeline, State of Louisiana, on or about the sixth day of January 1983, committed first-degree murder of Aubrey LaHaye. How do you plead?"

"Not guilty."

"That John Brady Balfa at the Parish of Evangeline, State of Louisiana, on or about the sixth day of January 1983, committed aggravated kidnapping of Aubrey LaHaye. How do you plead?"

"Not guilty."

"That John Brady Balfa at the Parish of Evangeline, State of Louisiana, on or about the sixth day of January 1983, while armed with a dangerous weapon, robbed Aubrey LaHaye. How do you plead?"

"Not guilty."

Merry Christmas to You and Your Family

ON DECEMBER 13, 2017, I RECEIVE A RED ENVELOPE IN MY mailbox in Baton Rouge, stamped with the Purple Heart. Handwritten in the corner, the return address reads: John Balfa.

I stare at it, locked in a stalemate with the potential of what it could hold. I call my roommate to come look at it. I lay it on the counter, and, stalling, I call my dad.

"Open it," they say.

A Christmas card. In tacky sparkling pink, red, and green, with a little bird, some polka dots, leaves, and Christmas ornaments hanging from their limbs, the words *faith hope peace* adorn the front.

Opened, in printed script: "Christmas wishes from the heart."

In John Brady Balfa's handwriting:

> *Jordan,*
> *Merry Christmas to you and your family.*
> *John Brady*

This is the only direct communication I'll ever receive from him, the only words he'll ever offer me.

Naomi

WRITE ANOTHER LETTER TO JOHN BRADY, AND ANOTHER. BUT
I never hear from him again. In the absence of his voice, I turn to his
family, most of whom still live mere miles from LaHaye Road. His
brothers, his sisters, his cousins. I track down cell phone numbers from
mutual friends, find them on Facebook. But I am met with almost total
radio silence, with the exception of one sister who texts me, asking that I
never contact her again.

One morning, I am sitting around a fire pit at our family camp with
the longtime Evangeline Parish sheriff and my dad. My dad had invited
Sheriff Eddie Soileau[1] over after a recent conversation they'd had outside
his office. Sheriff Soileau told Dad he was there the day PawPaw Aubrey
was kidnapped, one of the many law enforcement officers who'd flocked
to the LaHaye house. He also told him he didn't believe they'd gotten the
right guy.

This theory was derived from the sheriff's long friendship with a
woman named Naomi Nero, who had once worked for Sheriff Soileau in
his office. Naomi, he explains, is John Brady's little sister, almost twenty
years younger than him, the product of his mother Mildred's second
marriage. As they got to know each other, Naomi began to share with
Sheriff Soileau her own suspicions around the case. And she'd convinced
him that John Brady was innocent.

A few weeks later, I pull into Naomi's driveway and realize I've passed this
house almost every single day of my life prior to leaving for college—to
get anywhere at all. The charming white cottage is half a mile from my
parents' house. A single pasture separates us.

Naomi's partner, Mary Beth, greets me at the door, four miniature
schnauzers yapping at her feet and their toddler sleeping in her arms.

---

1   This is not the same Eddie Soileau from Sunland, nor does he have any relevant relation to
him or the Sheriff's Deputy from the crime scene, Floyd Soileau.

It hits me that I know these people. They have been attending the same Catholic church as my family throughout my entire childhood, watching me grow up one Sunday at a time. "Come on in, Jordan. How is every-body? Naomi's comin'."

The house is decked out in pink balloons and posters. Their daughter celebrated her first birthday the day before. Naomi, somewhat harried, rushes into the kitchen, swiping her dark hair behind her ear. "Oh, hey, Jordan, how are you? Would you like something to drink?"

Within minutes, we are sitting each on one end of the couch with a cup of tea in our hands, Mary Beth rocking the baby across the room. Studying Naomi, I'm struck by her beauty. Deep, dark eyes and an olive complexion. When her teenage daughter comes out from a back room, I am surprised she is old enough to have a teenage daughter.

The tension dissipates as I describe my project, both women listening intently. "Mr. Eddie said you weren't totally convinced John did it?" Naomi jumps right in. "That you weren't settled on him being the man who killed your grandfather? I'm sorry . . . your great-grandfather?"

I tell her I've heard from more than one person that John Brady might not have done it. "I mean, I just know something doesn't feel quite right about the whole thing . . ." I explain, as noncommittally as I can manage. "I'm trying to get to the truth, if I can."

She nods, takes a deep breath. "I'll tell you then, Jordan . . . You know our mother just died?"

I had heard. It had happened a few months before. I'd wondered about John Brady in his cell—unable to attend the funeral, unable to say good-bye. "Yes, yes, I'm so sorry."

She turns away from me, her eyes shining. It's still fresh. "That was the hardest part of all of this, you know . . . I'm so sorry . . ." She takes a deep breath, presses her fingers to her eyes. "Seeing my mama . . . what she went through with John getting sent over there . . . She'd have breakdowns in front of me, as much as she tried to hide them. That was her *child*. That was her baby. And she just had so much faith and hope because she felt, we all honestly feel—we don't know for a fact—but we feel my brother could never . . . have done this. He could have never done this."

I'm nodding, trying desperately to maintain eye contact despite all my instincts to look away. I shift gears. "Naomi, can you tell me what he was like? Tell me about John as you knew him, before he went to prison?"

This gives her the chance to gather herself. Taking another deep breath, she shakes away the glass, and smiles. She was nine years old when he was put away, she explains, and doesn't remember a whole lot. "But I was always up his butt."

She recalls how he'd come home from college and let her tag along wherever he went. Even as a child, she had an awareness of his gambling addiction. "I remember he'd take me to the racetrack. I was this little girl and he'd tote me around to watch the races."

John Brady is now a trusty in the prison, she tells me, has a garden and a cat. "This cat that showed up at his door one day, and he started feeding it," she says. "It's a big thing for him, the simple stuff like that." He suffers from Bell's palsy—a symptom, she says, of the high levels of stress he's carried living at Angola. "He used to be so handsome," she says. "He was tall, dark, and handsome. And you know what? Now he's unrecognizable. His nerves were bad for so long. The whole side of his face has fallen. And he's vain, so he's embarrassed, hides his face when he's talking to you, *hides his face*. It's terrible."

When she was young, Naomi says she and her mother would visit John Brady in prison once a week. Now it's less, but as often as she can. "We email back and forth a lot," she says. "But I did want to go see him last Sunday . . ."

She looks down at her hands. "I wanted to know for sure how he felt about me talking with you . . . I couldn't do this without sitting down with him, and really seeing."

He gave her his blessing, she says, but she begged him to talk to me himself. "I said, 'John this might be your chance to get your story out there.'"

But he wouldn't. And it was because of my last name. "I'll tell you something he's said numerous times, Jordan. He'll look at me, and he'll say, 'The LaHayes know I didn't do this. They know I didn't do this. They know.'"

Poker-faced, I ask, "But what makes him think that?"

She shakes her head. "I wish I had more information," she says. "He's so guarded."

He doesn't trust the LaHayes. He doesn't trust me. Naomi says she tried to explain to him that I was born long after all of this, that I was distanced from it. He'd shake his head and say, "They took enough away from me." *He blames us.*

At this point, Naomi's eyes start to fill again. She gets quiet and almost whispers, looking at her feet, "He's been having a really hard time." Taking a deep breath, then turning back to me, her voice cracks.

"He broke down," when she went to see him. He told her, "Every decade that passes of my life, I mourn. I grieve. I grieve for the life I don't have. I grieve for the children I'll never have. I grieve for every decade of this life."

Naomi points at me, "You and I will never know how that feels. Because we . . . even though things happen in our lives, we are still living them. We go on and every day is a new day for us. And with him, *every* day is a loss. And it's hard on him, it really is . . . It's hard for him, and it's hard for *me*." She gets up to find a tissue, "I'm so sorry, I just . . . I feel so hopeless. You wanna fix it, and you can't."

Before I leave, Naomi tells me that, on better days, she and John Brady imagine life once he gets out. "He'll say, 'Where am I gonna go? What am I gonna do if I get out?' And I tell him, '*You're gonna live!*'" She tells him he would come live with her—wouldn't even need to worry about getting a job. "He can have a little farmer's market, grow some vegetables. I guess it's just a dream . . . But maybe it's not. Maybe it's not."

Turning out of her driveway back toward home, back toward the Bayou Nezpique, LaHaye Road at my back, I layer Naomi's dream over the landscape. I imagine John Brady Balfa here, walking distance from my parents' house, observing the same sunrise as my dad each morning. The Nezpique cradles them both, curling out wide and dark around the entire parish, remembering the dent of Aubrey LaHaye's body. I see the fertile prairie it feeds, the one all our ancestors farmed, holding John Brady Balfa's garden within it. The whispers of forty years bubble up around a man the land and all its people haven't seen, haven't known, since he was twenty-seven, lost, convicted of murder. The truth is tempted to boil over, screaming, into the air. But will more likely sink back to the bottom. This is a man who, for many, will always be a murderer.

PART III

The Trial

Notes of Evidence

THE 1985 TRIAL OF JOHN BRADY BALFA WAS ONE OF THE biggest spectacles in the collective Evangeline Parish memory. People from across the region attended, the LaHaye family sitting right up front. Some of them were absorbed by the process, retaining every detail, even after all these years. Others only recall the legalese and vague anxieties of the courtroom.

"I remember wondering if I should go," my aunt Michele tells me. "And Mommee Susan was like 'Oh, we all need to be there.'"

Michele attended most days of the trial, even the preliminary hearings. She remembers everything, even down to what she was wearing—a peach linen smock and high heels.

My uncles Richard and Jody were building levees on the farm and would argue over who would go and who would stay to work. Their brother Billy's wife, my aunt Kristy, was working as the secretary to Assistant DA Bruce Rozas at the time and accompanied him to the trial. "I went with him," she tells me, "literally, in his car." But she doesn't remember anything, not one single thing.

Aunt Sandy, who attended every day, remembers MawMaw Emily's testimony as impressive. "She was stern," she says. "She was good." The rest of it seemed to stretch on forever and ever, she recalls. "Just, the rims. Just *days* of talking about that, it seemed. The *details* they had."

My dad, home on break from his first semester in medical school, was there every day too—in absolute awe at the way the case was built. Still to this day, when I raise questions about the evidence, he insists: "It was all there. The rims. The paint. Laid out so clear."

The younger, school-age grandchildren attended, too. Aunt Anne, who was a teenager at the time, recalls, "They told us we all had to be there like a show of force. It was for journalists, it was for TV, for the court. To show we all believed he was guilty."

My mommee Susan recalls how John Brady sat in the courtroom, expressionless. "That kid in his tie and his sports coat, listening to all this. No emotions."

Papa Wayne, when I ask him about the trial, only says: "I think I remember most of it. I never talk about it. I don't remember ever discussing it with anybody. Except maybe Glenn and Susan." Later, I realize that for most of the trial, he, Uncle Glenn, and MawMaw Emily wouldn't have even been in the courtroom—each of them sequestered witnesses, spending those weeks in a quiet room somewhere else, waiting for it all to be over.

Memories could only get me so far. Eventually, the undulating tapestry of oral accounts I've collected begins to feel all so heavy in its lack. I'm desperate for something solid. Primary sources. Records. I want to know exactly what was said, by whom.

But the court transcript for the *State of Louisiana vs. John Brady Balfa* isn't in the DA file, and the Evangeline Parish clerk of court has no idea where it might be. Neither does the Third Circuit Court of Appeals, or the State Supreme Court. I'm told again and again that cases this old simply "get lost in the shuffle" sometimes—an increasingly maddening dismissal. At a loss, I mention my struggle to a journalism professor, and he tells me that the LSU Law Library maintains holdings of duplicate records and briefs from the state's higher level courts, going all the way back to 1912. Skeptically, I submit a request.

A couple of weeks later, even after the ten six-inch-thick files are delivered to me at the law library on a cart labeled *Jordan LaHaye, John B. Balfa vs. The State of Louisiana*, I am reluctant to consider that I'll find the actual transcript inside. I'm so ready to be disappointed that I refuse to peek ahead, and I spend the next month visiting the library daily, meticulously taking notes on thousands of pages of pretrial motions in Files 1 and 2—propelled by a self-consciousness about my inexperience in criminal law, hypervigilant in my fear of missing something important.

Then, right smack in the middle of File 3: NOTE OF EVIDENCE (November 18, 1985) TRIAL BY JURY—FIRST DAY. I've got it.

Emboldened, I flip my way through. Past the entire jury selection, which took four days and all of Files 3, 4, 5, 6, 7, and half of 8, which is where I find her. MawMaw. She is the prosecution's first witness. The district attorney's first question for her, after her name, is how long she and her husband were married.

We would have celebrated our 55th anniversary this year.

Suddenly, finally, I'm there. Bent over the library table, my eyes a centimeter from the even, typewritten words, eating them. I'm in the aisle of that 1985 courtroom, the most sterile of wooden-wrapped spaces. MawMaw Emily's steely green eyes are fixed right on the young mustached man at the defense table. He doesn't meet them, leans back in his chair, picking at his fingernails. It's just the two of them, the rest of that crowded courtroom and the world beyond listening invisibly, Billy Pucheu's voice booming through the ether.

The only time emotion betrays her, the only sob that breaks forth, is in answer to Pucheu's question: *Did you ever see your husband alive again?*

No, she says. *When he turned his back in the bedroom and left me tied to the post, that's the last time I saw my husband alive.*

"I Know I'll Be Cleared of This"

JULIE CULLEN, ONE OF ST. LANDRY PARISH'S FIRST FEMALE lawyers, was announced as John Brady's attorney just before his arraignment in March 1985. She came in swinging, filing four motions right off the bat. The trial was originally scheduled for June 24.

A New Orleans native and 1977 Loyola Law School alum, Cullen had kicked off her early career as a criminal prosecutor for the Louisiana Attorney General's Office, working on some of the state's highest-profile cases. She was in the middle of such a widely publicized proceeding, charging the Ruston police chief with malfeasance, when she announced she was starting her own practice and turned the case over to the attorney general himself. Her boyfriend, the attorney David Miller, had taken a job with the District Attorney's Office in the small town of Opelousas in St. Landry Parish. In the summer of 1983, Cullen made the leap and followed him, switching over to defense. A year later, she was working for the St. Landry Indigent Defender Board. In this capacity, she handled some of the parish's biggest cases for indigent defendants—frequently putting herself on the opposite side of the courtroom from her lover, Miller. Her early success as an indigent defender made her enormously popular with the St. Landry jailhouse gang, who all knew her by name and clamored to have her represent them.

In Acadiana in the 1980s, a female attorney was still an anomaly. Cullen spoke to this in an interview published in the *Daily World*, describing a certain uneasiness whenever she prosecuted cases in smaller towns for the Attorney General's Office. "I was an outsider and a female, but once people realize you're competent, there's no problem," she said. Such hostility awaited her in Evangeline Parish, a place famously distrustful of outsiders, of city folk, and of change.

In September of 1984, Cullen was assigned to represent the indigent John Brady Balfa in the case of the DeVillier stabbing. David Miller was the prosecutor. In the March 1985 trial, the jury ruled in DeVillier's, and Miller's, favor, convicting John Brady of aggravated battery. In May, District Judge Robert Brinkman sentenced him to eight years of hard labor in state prison.

While working on the DeVillier case, Cullen learned about the charges against John Brady in Evangeline Parish and started gathering information. She had five pending capital cases at the time, but something about John's must have inspired her—she agreed to represent him outside of indigent appointments, pro bono. She even hired an investigator to assist her in preparing for John Brady's trial, using her own money pending the court's ruling on whether it would provide one for her (it wouldn't). With her experience in criminal law, it's unlikely this would have been the first time Cullen came across a client who she believed had been wrongly accused. Greg Bergeron's words echo in my mind—the stories about John Brady's charm, how when it benefited him, he could be so damn likable. Inspiring, even.

John Brady's Evangeline Parish trial would be heard by Judge Joseph Emile Coreil, a born and bred Ville Platte politician, who had served two terms as a state representative before becoming a city judge in 1974, then a district judge in 1977. An old-school Democrat in an ultraconservative parish, his persona in the courtroom was no nonsense, all business. For months, he listened, long-faced and serious, as Cullen and Pucheu battled it out in pretrial hearings.

The trial was rescheduled three times—first as a result of a motion by Cullen, then twice more because of scheduling conflicts. All the while, John Brady was ferried back and forth to jailhouses in St. Landry, Evangeline, and Gregg County, Texas, where his probation for the rape conviction had been revoked.

From the outset, it was apparent that Pucheu did not take Cullen seriously. His tone toward her was condescending, his posture dismissive. They feuded for months over various issues of discovery, that is, over each side's obligation to share copies of evidence with the other. The prosecution, especially, has a legal obligation to provide any evidence that might be considered exculpatory to the defendant.

At a hearing on April 12, 1985, Cullen claimed that she had yet to receive any information whatsoever from the State. "My only knowledge about this case and the evidence that the State has is rumor, speculation,

and things that may have been carried in the news media," she told Judge
Coreil, who ordered Pucheu to deliver the information to her within two
weeks' time.

On May 3, 1985, she still hadn't seen the LaHaye autopsy report. Assistant DA Bruce Rozas claimed the State didn't consider it important to
the case and had no intent of using it. Therefore, they had no obligation
to provide it to Cullen. "Obviously, cause of death is an issue in this case,"
she argued. "The *time of death* is an issue in this case . . ." If Aubrey died
mid to late morning or later on January 6, 1983, John Brady's alibi placed
him on the road to, or already in, Texas. If he died after January 6—John
Brady, who was booked into the Gregg County Jail on January 7, could
not have been the killer. The judge agreed with Cullen that she was entitled to the information, but also that it wasn't the State's responsibility
to provide it. He issued a court order directly to the coroner, Dr. George
McCormick, giving him fifteen days to get Cullen the autopsy.

She did not receive it until July—over two months later. On the report, though, the blank beside "Date of Death" was filled in as "unknown."
Over the course of her not-quite-decade-long career, dealing with dozens
of murder cases, Cullen had never handled one in which the pathologist
could not offer a date of death. When she called McCormick, he told her,
"I could go back and do it right now," but that the only way he'd provide
an estimated date and time of death to her was if the District Attorney's
Office requested it.

So Cullen filed a motion ordering the DA's Office to make the request.
Pucheu protested, once again claiming this was not his responsibility.
"Miss Cullen thinks she can order me to do all kinds of things," he said
in an October 1985 hearing. "I will go all the way to the Supreme Court
before I bend to her whims and her pettiness because that is not my job."

Cullen turned to Judge Coreil and reiterated: all she was asking of the
DA was to make a phone call. "When a man's life is on the line, I think
that is not too much to ask," she said. "This is crucial evidence . . . He
is prohibiting me from being able to investigate my client's case." Judge
Coreil denied her motion.

Cullen's difficulties in gathering information regarding John Brady's
case echo my own. I think back to Richard Vidrine and the way he carefully selected certain sections of the file to share with me; how none of the
courts could provide me with the public record of the trial. There's a pattern here, and it goes back to the beginning. To my read, it seems Pucheu

had convinced McCormick to deliberately withhold the autopsy information, a basic and fundamental piece of evidence, from the defense. *Why?*

More roadblocks plagued Cullen's path to building a case for John Brady. "The FBI will not talk to me without approval from the district attorney," she told the judge. "The district attorney will not give me the approval, and the district attorney won't ask them the questions I need." In response, Pucheu said "this little lady" was demanding the State do all the work for her.

Finally, on November 5, 1985, just two weeks before the trial was to begin, Pucheu provided Cullen with a report estimating time *since* death as "ten to twelve days prior to the examination of Aubrey's body," indicating Aubrey had to have died, at latest, on January 7, 1983. The report came from Dr. William C. Rodriguez, III, a forensic anthropologist working with McCormick. At the time, the field of forensic anthropology—the study of skeletal remains to aid in law enforcement efforts—was still new in courtrooms. Cullen was immediately skeptical.

Besides the issues with the autopsy, Cullen was on a crusade to get the trial moved out of Evangeline Parish entirely. She argued that because of the regional prominence of both families involved, the shocking nature of the crime, and the extensive media attention given to the case over a two-year period, John Brady Balfa could not get a fair trial in Evangeline Parish.

In a two-day hearing held on September 4 and 5, 1985, she presented her evidence. Over the course of the proceedings, Judge Coreil heard testimony from representatives of local media, who brought forth, per court order, every newspaper article published and documentation of every broadcast aired in or near Evangeline Parish over the previous year that tied John Brady Balfa to the Aubrey LaHaye case. All in all, there were twenty-nine newspaper stories and thirty-five television news broadcasts, many on the front page and in prime-time spots. These did not include the dozens more news items covering the investigation before John Brady was named, nor the ones covering his other criminal charges.

Pucheu emphasized that many of these stories were repetitious follow-ups, in the back of the paper, alongside several much more significant stories. He also pointed out that none of the articles or reports had shown any actual prejudice toward John Brady. He even went so far as to ask Ben Reed, the editor at the *Ville Platte Gazette*: "Did you ever hear any word of John Balfa being at risk of being lynched?" Reed, shocked, said he had not.

Each media representative, though, did say they expected the story to continue to be high priority. Many of them would report on the results of that very day's hearing.

After the media testimony, the hearing's second phase proceeded. Judge Coreil subpoenaed fifty potential jurors to determine whether enough unbiased, acceptable jurors could plausibly be found to serve in John Brady's trial. Immediately, two-thirds of the group were released for health reasons. Of the remaining nineteen, only one said they were unfamiliar with the case; everyone else had at least heard about it around town or seen it in the news.

In addition, over half were connected in some way to either the Balfas or the LaHayes. Among them were schoolmates of John Brady's brothers, patients of Aubrey's son Wayne, the owner of the car lot where the LaHayes bought their vehicles. One woman said she had kept up with the case closely because her daughter was dating Calvin Ware's stepson. She had also banked with Aubrey LaHaye for years and was friendly with John Brady's dad and brothers. Her daughter had gone to school with John Brady, and she said she didn't believe he could possibly be involved because "he was too much of a kind person." The body had been found two miles from her house.

Several people spoke to the way John Brady was being discussed around the parish. "It was all over town," one man said. "You couldn't escape it."

"I heard a lot of people say they didn't think he was guilty," said a woman. Another said she'd heard people go both ways. A third said the same thing, but that she'd heard more people say he didn't do it. Only one man said everyone he'd heard speak about the case believed John Brady was guilty, and that he didn't believe he could get a fair trial.

At the end of the day, Judge Coreil denied Julie Cullen's motion for a change of venue, stating: "It was the court's opinion that the matter did not seem to occupy a prominent place in their minds and most remembered very little about it. Most testified that they had no fixed opinion as to the guilt or innocence of the defendant." The trial would take place in Evangeline Parish, and it would begin on November 18, 1985.

On the same day as the change of venue hearing, the *Daily World* published an exclusive interview with John Brady Balfa.

"My feelings are mixed about a lot of things," John Brady told reporter Monte Williams while sipping on iced tea, sitting on the edge of his jail cell's twin-size bed. A bucket of fried chicken rested on a three-legged stool in between him and Williams, who sat in a chair provided by the guard. "But I know I'll be cleared of this."

Sitting in the cell, Williams described the man before him as "deliberate" and "pensive." John Brady wanted to discuss the nasty things his family had been hearing around town. "People are talking like I've been bad all my life . . . it disturbs me the way they're acting like I have to prove myself innocent." He told Williams he had "no doubt" a jury will find him innocent. "I didn't do it," he said. "And I believe a jury will back me up."

Williams, referring to the confluence of legal troubles John Brady was facing besides this case, asked him if he had any regrets. John Brady said he was sorry for his family, for the ways this had affected them. "They're good people," he said. "They work hard." Then he added one more thing: "What I do regret in life is not having a kid. Even with all this mess, I miss that."

Second-Degree Murder

NOVEMBER 19, 1985

GOOD MORNING, LADIES AND GENTLEMEN," JUDGE COREIL boomed to a room bursting with the clamoring crowd of potential jurors, journalists, curious locals, LaHayes, and Balfas. It was the first official day of the John Brady Balfa murder trial. "Let's proceed."

Immediately, District Attorney Billy Pucheu announced he had a preliminary matter that needed to be taken up outside of the earshot of prospective jurors. Coreil asked all two hundred of them to step outside.

"If Your Honor pleases, the State would like to amend the Bill of Indictment by changing it from first-degree murder to second-degree murder."

The night before, Pucheu had gathered the LaHayes in Wayne's living room—Emily, Wayne, Susan, Sonny, Tot, Glenn, and Janie, and whichever grandkids happened to be around. He wanted to get the family's blessing to reduce the charges.

To win a first-degree murder conviction, which came with the possibility of a death sentence, the State would have to prove that John Brady had a specific intention of killing or seriously harming Aubrey. For second-degree, they only had to prove that he had an intention of committing another serious crime—such as kidnapping or armed robbery—which had directly resulted in Aubrey's death. And the fact was, the State's case was made up almost entirely of circumstantial evidence.

They would have a better shot at getting a jury to vote in favor of convicting John Brady if they weren't weighing the cost of his life. The intensity of the media coverage, also, would be dimmed. My dad was there and remembers Pucheu saying, "If he gets the death penalty, the amount of press that is going to come to y'all . . . it's gonna be ugly. You don't wanna do that."

So the LaHayes decided John Brady Balfa should be sentenced to die in prison—just not in the electric chair.

Voir Dire

OING INTO THE TRIAL, THERE SEEMED TO BE A COMMUNITY-wide understanding that there were sides to be taken. That the State was an absolute stand-in for the victims, for the LaHayes. That collectively the LaHayes were wholly convinced, already, of John Brady Balfa's guilt. For many in Evangeline Parish, this trial was less an effort to parse out truth than a battle between the two incompatible realities. The LaHayes knew John Brady was guilty. The Balfas knew he wasn't.

Whether this was a fundamental misinterpretation of "innocent until proven guilty" or a result of the family's close relationship with the DA—it is unclear. But it raised yet another obstacle in an already difficult path to jury selection in this small town. People held an allegiance to one family or the other or, knowing both, feared having to vote on a verdict that would forever alienate them from the family they had "failed."

Of the first two hundred people subpoenaed for voir dire, one hundred and thirty-five were deceased, had never received their subpoena, were ill or elderly, or only spoke French. The remaining sixty-five were interviewed over the next three days, before another one hundred subpoenas had to be issued. One went to the mayor of Ville Platte. In all, it took four days and eighty-six interviews for Pucheu and Cullen to assemble a full jury with two alternates.

The potential jurors each took their turn being scrupulously evaluated by Pucheu, and then by Cullen. Pucheu asked about the candidate's address, job, family situation. To every woman considered, he asked what their husband's name was, and whether they worked in or out of the house. He asked them, "Can you stand to see a woman cry and remain unaffected, unswayed?" At first, this question seemed to be referencing potential witness testimony—MawMaw Emily's in particular. Then he got more specific: "I have heard Miss Cullen sometimes cries during her closing arguments. Would that affect you or could you put that aside and decide—base it solely on the facts and the evidence, or would you be swayed by the tears of Miss Cullen?"

More standard questions dealt with the law, ensuring potential jurors fully understood John Brady was considered innocent until the State showed enough evidence to prove him guilty. Pucheu asked whether they had ever been the victim of a violent crime, whether they had ever testified in court before, whether they had relatives or close friends in law enforcement. Whether their obligations at work or home would occupy their minds so much that they could not focus on the trial itself.

Cullen had her own, more specific, line of questioning. "Do you know where the Bayou Nezpique is?" "Have you done any banking with Guaranty Bank?" "Have you ever been in a crowd of people, where you think you recognize someone, only to find it's not them?"

One of the most pressing issues referred back to the change of venue hearing. "What have you heard about this case?" Most people had at least read about the murder, if not about John Brady, in the papers or seen it reported on television. This wasn't considered problematic on its own; the jurors' knowledge of the case was only an issue if they were aware of John Brady's crimes outside of the Aubrey LaHaye murder, which might induce prejudice toward him.

The most likely reason for a person to be excused, though—whether by the judge or by one of the attorneys—was their relationship to either the LaHayes, the Balfas, or the DA's Office itself. Among the eighty-six people interviewed over the course of those four days, eight of them were a friend, relative, neighbor, or employee of Pucheu's. Another's son had been prosecuted and convicted by him. Nine were patients of Papa Wayne's—including three women whose children he delivered. Three farmers said they knew Uncle Glenn professionally. Ten people said they banked with Aubrey LaHaye before he died. Jane Fontenot, a shop owner in town, said she frequently sold the LaHayes, and some of the Balfas, their shoes. Ronald Lebleu, who worked at an auto shop, said he drank coffee just about every morning with Mr. Dewey Balfa. He had spoken to Dewey the very morning of jury selection, explaining why he wasn't dressed for work. "Oh, you're probably going in for my nephew's trial," Dewey had responded. Three people were close friends of Aubrey's. Five said they had gone to school with John Brady, either at Mamou Elementary, Mamou High School, LSU-E, or LSU. Seventeen people claimed to be close friends with members of the LaHaye family. Eighteen people said they were close to the Balfas. Of these, ten people said they had close associations with members of both families.

When the jury was finally assembled on the afternoon of Friday, November 22, its members included a single mother with a master's degree, whose kids rode the school bus driven by Dewey Balfa each day, and a commercial pilot who had served on a jury before, but for a civil case. There was the truck driver with a tenth-grade education who had once been the victim of an armed robbery; and the nurse who had only lived in the parish for six years but had once chaperoned a Sacred Heart High School band trip to Mexico with Papa Wayne and Mommee Susan. There were two nursing home workers, one of whom had a brother who had been convicted of rape a decade ago in Evangeline Parish; she couldn't remember if it was Billy Pucheu who prosecuted or not. There was a retired fourth-grade teacher who admitted she didn't want to serve, a housewife, and an employee of the Dixie Glass company who had one brother who was charged with manslaughter about twenty years before and another who worked as a sheriff's deputy. The local Winn-Dixie's dairy manager was on the jury, despite admitting that he was related to the sheriff's deputy who ran the Evangeline Parish Jail and had a relative charged with rape in this parish. And there was also a fabric shop manager, who said she never read or watched the news and whose grandfather was a third or fourth cousin of Aubrey LaHaye—though she'd never met any of the LaHayes before. The last juror selected was a man who used to work for Sunland and thought he might have worked on a pipeline with John Brady in March of 1983.

These twelve, pulled from the furthermost reaches of Evangeline Parish's tightly wound LaHaye-Balfa spectrum, would decide John Brady's future. Relatively early in the selection, the pursuit of the gold-standard unbiased juror was abandoned as the small town folded in on itself, the interrelations of family trees, schoolyard memories, and business dealings distilled into a question of proximity. "Are you close enough to be affected by your role in this man's future?" "Can you step back enough to locate truth, or something resembling it, beneath the bloody mess of connective tissue?" "Are the bonds that connect you to this place and all its tangled roots loose enough that you might free yourself from them, just long enough to decide whether *this* man killed *that* one?" And these twelve, with their various problematic associations—well, this was as close as they could get.

May It Please the Court

O N MONDAY MORNING, MOST OF THE MAIN CHARACTERS IN the case against John Brady Balfa sat not in the crowded court-room, but just outside of it. Wearing their Sunday best, the sequestered witnesses settled on benches in the hallway, leaned against the wall, maybe paced beneath the oak trees outside. Emily, Glenn, and Wayne would have found a corner—someplace Emily could sit down. John Brady's father and his brothers would have settled somewhere on the opposite side of the room. Detective Rudy Guillory I imagine pacing the hallway, taking stock of the cast. Various other members of local law enforcement and the FBI lined the walls. There was the coroner. The local doctor who pulled the body from the Nezpique. John Brady's bonds-man. Employees from Guaranty Bank. John Brady's ex-wife. Her mother.

Looking at that initial list of witnesses roll-called on the first day of trial, I notice a few who never testified. Terry DeVillier, for one. John Brady's rape victim, for another. I assume that they were subpoenaed in case Cullen decided to put John Brady on the stand—giving Pucheu full access to his colorful criminal record.

But I also remember something my aunt Michele told me, when she was talking about the "wife that John had raped." I had initially dismissed it as part of that apocrypha. But it arises now, vile and clear. "She was brought in to sit in the courtroom and upset him while he was on trial. And she would just cry. I remember watching her, and she would cry and cry and cry."

On the other side of the door, Billy Pucheu began his opening statements.

"May it please the court. Good morning."

He started with boilerplate explanations of the jury's role within the American criminal justice system and gave the legal definitions of the crimes John Brady was being charged with—armed robbery, aggravated kidnapping, and second-degree murder.

Then he told the jury the terrible tale of Aubrey LaHaye's kidnapping—the knock, the car trouble, the knife. His description of January 6, 1983, follows Emily's official accounts, with one subtle, but significant, divergence. As Pucheu told it, when the stranger said his name was "Vidrine," Aubrey had responded: "I don't think you are a Vidrine, but I know you." Whether it was a strategic edit on Pucheu's part, or a detail Emily had resurrected on her own at some point during their (unrecorded) conversations, the interaction introduces a new tension to Aubrey's relationship with the stranger in those few moments before his kidnapping. Had he said, "I know you"? Or "I think I know you"? Had he traced that lie right away, known something wasn't right?

Pucheu went on to tell of the ransom call, the search, the investigation. He told the jury they'd hear from Kurt Vezinat, the man who—while target practicing with his wife and young son on the bridge at the Bayou Nezpique on a Sunday afternoon—discovered Aubrey's body. They'd hear from Dr. George McCormick, who would testify that the banker died of multiple blows to the head. "Dr. McCormick will establish the time of death, which he will establish by hypothetical questions—hypothetical questions based on what is in evidence."

At this moment, Julie Cullen's head likely snapped up from her notes, her grip on her pen tightened, her brow furrowed.

"He will tell you," Pucheu went on, "that Aubrey LaHaye was killed shortly after being taken from his home at knifepoint that morning. He will tell you he believes Aubrey LaHaye was dead when that 7:10 phone call was made, which explains why no further 9:00 call came."

Pucheu warned the jury that much would be made about the mustache. He admitted that in almost every description Emily gave of the perpetrator's appearance, she said he had been "clean-shaven." Photographic evidence would be introduced to prove John Brady had been sporting a heavy mustache at the time of the crime. "That is of no significance," insisted Pucheu. Even without the mustache, he pointed out, the composite created during the early investigation looked enough like John Brady that multiple people working at Guaranty Bank had recognized him in it.

This sets up Pucheu's transition to the motive. Yes, John Brady Balfa was a customer at Guaranty Bank, he told the jury. In fact, Aubrey had turned John Brady down for loans on three instances over the previous year. "He knew him."

So why kill him? "Why, you ask, if he got him out and wanted half a million dollars—why, you ask, didn't he keep him alive? I've just told you the answer. Aubrey LaHaye knew him. He knew he could identify him. Like he said, 'You're not a Vidrine, but I know you.' So, what does he have to do? He has to kill him."

This logic is faulty, to my reading, full of leaps. Pucheu was essentially saying that John Brady assumed Aubrey, his banker, wouldn't recognize him or know him, didn't bother to wear a mask, and then was surprised that Aubrey *did* know him? And thus, had to kill him?

Pucheu closed his arguments by saying that in addition to all of this, the State would prove the murder was premeditated, based on testimony that the perpetrator had gone into the house with a knife and rope and the tires were removed from the rims. "It was a planned, premeditated, cold-blooded, unjustified, heinous crime, and it is defined in our laws as being illegal. We submit that when all the evidence is in, you will be convinced beyond any doubt, not only a reasonable doubt, but beyond any doubt, that John Brady Balfa, the man seated right there, should be found guilty of all three charges and particularly murdering Aubrey LaHaye on January 6, 1983. Thank you."

Julie Cullen stood, but instead of turning to address the jury as Pucheu had done, she faced the judge. "At this time, I would request the jury be excused."

Once they had filed into the jury room across the hall, Cullen announced: "Your Honor, at this time I would make a motion for mistrial."

Pucheu had just announced to the jury that Dr. McCormick's time of death estimate would be a key tenet of his arguments—that the coroner would testify that Aubrey had been killed almost immediately after he was taken from his home. This was the very information Cullen had spent months trying to get her hands on, that Pucheu had outright refused to give her.

This, Cullen argued, was evidence that the State had violated its discovery obligations to the defendant.

Pucheu responded by emphasizing that Dr. McCormick's testimony would be "based on hypothetical questions" rather than evidence in the record. "Until there is evidence in the record, then he cannot give us an opinion. Based on the evidence that we are going to put in—and that is what I have told the jury!—based on hypothetical questions on evidence that will be put in concerning when Mr. LaHaye ate, when he went to bed, did he have any alcohol, so forth and so on, he will give us an opinion."

This, of course, was a tactic. Pucheu had obviously arranged with McCormick to reveal this information within parameters that legally allowed him to withhold it from Cullen, knocking her off guard right at the start of the trial.

Cullen turned to the judge in exasperation. "Your Honor, obviously the State is in possession of this information. Whether the hypothetical questioning has been asked on the record or not is of no moment to this motion. The question has to have been asked because the answers have already been told to the jury."

The trial had hardly begun, and John Brady's case, which depended so heavily on his alibi, was already falling apart. Cullen's plan rested on placing John Brady in Texas by, at latest, the early afternoon of January 6. This left a window of only about two hours during which John Brady could have possibly entered the LaHaye home, killed Aubrey, tied him to two tire rims, and tossed him in the Nezpique.

Going in, Cullen's defensive strategy had been to discredit the State's evidence. She'd argue that Emily's identification was unreliable, would point out how the FBI analysts used the words *could be a match* and *similar* when comparing the items found at the Balfa house to those found on the body. And she'd emphasize how teeny, tiny the window of time was that allowed John Brady to be the killer. "The State can't prove when he died," she'd tell the jury. "Tell me, out of all of those hours—what are the chances Aubrey LaHaye died exactly during the couple in which John Brady was in Evangeline Parish?" Even with the forensic anthropologist's narrower "time *since* death" estimate of ten to twelve days from the January 17 autopsy, the percentage was still small—and *what* was this new-fangled field of forensic anthropology anyway?

Pucheu's opening statement, though, ground this theory into the dirt. If Dr. McCormick testified that Aubrey LaHaye had died immediately after the kidnapping, then the time of death lined up *exactly* with the window in which John Brady could have still been in Evangeline Parish.

After hearing arguments from both sides, Judge Coreil denied Cullen's motion.

"Mr. Sheriff, bring the jury back, please."

\\\\\\

IN HER OPENING STATEMENTS, JULIE CULLEN MINCED NO WORDS. "I'm not going to make any attempt at this time to argue the case, because you have no evidence. You've heard statements from Mr. Pucheu concerning what he expects the evidence to prove. That's not evidence. That's his hope."

Yes, she said. The State can probably prove that someone came into the LaHaye house on January 6, abducted Aubrey at knifepoint, and killed him. "But the evidence is not going to show you that that person is John Balfa."

Cullen encouraged the jury to listen carefully to the evidence as it was presented, but to listen closer to the evidence not presented.

She asked them to listen for two words that would run throughout the forensic testimony: "*consistent* and *similar*." "At the conclusion of the trial, you might feel that 'well, there is a lot of similarity there—maybe so. But you advised me on jury selection that 'maybe' was not going to be good enough for you. Possibly a little bit of suspicion is not proof. We're talking proof beyond a reasonable doubt."

Yes, Emily LaHaye is going to identify John Brady as the man who entered her house, she told them. But that testimony doesn't match her original description of the perpetrator, the one she gave on January 6. Cullen turned at this point to John Brady. When I look at this man, she said, I see someone "tall and slim, about six feet, dark hair, rather prominent nose, mustache." And John Brady *did* indeed have a mustache on January 6, 1983, she emphasized. There is a photo to prove it.

Yes, John Brady was in financial straits at the time of Aubrey's murder. "Who isn't?" Cullen asked. "People in debt don't go out and kill people. I mean you can't take leaps." And besides. Motive, she pointed out, is not evidence of a crime. "I'm asking that you don't convict John Balfa because he needed money."

Then she got to McCormick. "I suggest if Dr. McCormick makes an estimate of the time of death, it is strictly that. And that the basics— whether even an estimate can be made—is subject to question. I ask that when Dr. McCormick testifies, you listen very carefully."

The Widow

ILLY PUCHEU STARTED WITH HIS MOST COMPELLING, MOST sympathetic witness, the seventy-one-year-old widow of Aubrey LaHaye.

MawMaw Emily took this role seriously. I imagine her kneeling before her bed the night before, the same bed she'd been tied to the last time she'd seen her husband, the same gesture—hands in fists, clasped together. She prayed that whatever else God might give her in this life, he might infuse her bones, her voice, her demeanor with strength upon the stand—that she might play her part in the execution of justice. Aubrey, she knew, would be standing right behind her, gently grasping her elbow like he used to. *My Emily, tell them your story.*

She was well-prepared. It is obvious in reading the transcript that she and Pucheu had rehearsed—many of her responses to his questions echoing, almost word for word, the descriptions he used in his opening statements, which she had not been in the room for.

Nevertheless, she commanded the room. The LaHayes—except for Wayne and Glenn, sequestered as they were—were a force united, each projecting confidence toward their matriarch, holding back tears as they listened to her recount that terrible day. Journalists and the local curious leaned forward in their seats, absorbing every yet-unheard detail of a story they'd heard so many different versions of, the tragedy of it all now embodied in this little old woman.

"I woke up at five o'clock," Emily began, then walked Pucheu and the jury through the details of the knock on the door, the man standing behind it. When she got to the question of "Vidrine," her account mirrored something closer to the original than Pucheu's earlier description of the interaction: "'I'm a Vidrine, Mr. LaHaye,' he says, 'I live around the corner.' And Aubrey said, 'Oh yeah, surely I know you. Come right in.' He came in."

Emily told of how, while she was flipping through the phone book, she'd heard her husband say, "Oh no, no." "When I turned around, I saw the knife blade. He was holding the knife blade against him." When Pucheu asked her about the rope she'd been tied with, she said she did not know where it came from, and that she and Aubrey didn't keep anything like that in the house.

She told the jury how, while the stranger was walking her husband through the house, to the front door, she'd sat frozen, trying not to breathe. "I was afraid he would hear me move and maybe he would come back to me. So, I stayed quiet until I heard the door hit. When I heard him hit the door, then I knew he was going with him."

The Identification

MAWMAW EMILY'S IDENTIFICATION OF JOHN BRADY BALFA as the man who killed her husband was the emotional center of Billy Pucheu's case. Elderly, poised, sensible—she was the perfect witness. Her pain simmering, she had just told the jury a story of loss unimaginable. Hearing her, it was impossible not to empathize, to imagine one's grandmother, one's mother, oneself, in her place. It was hard not to admire her, such confidence, such grace. It would be difficult to doubt anything she said.

Regarding the day she'd gone to the St. Landry Jail in September of 1984, Pucheu asked, "Did you go to Opelousas and go to a lineup? Did you in fact pick the defendant John Brady Balfa out of that lineup on September 21, 1984?"

"I did," she responded.

Pucheu produced a photograph, which he explained depicted the in-person lineup shown to her on September 21, 1984. He asked her to draw a check mark above the man who she had identified. She correctly marked John Brady Balfa as the second one from the right, and Pucheu had the jury examine the photo.

"Mrs. LaHaye, do you see Mr. Balfa in this courtroom today? Will you point him out to the jury?"

"This is the man right here."

"I'll ask the man that she is pointing at to stand."

At first, John Brady wouldn't budge, just kept looking at his hands. Judge Coreil repeated Pucheu's request, "Please stand up, Mr. Balfa."

Balfa looked at Julie Cullen, who closed her eyes and nodded, and he slowly, reluctantly, stood from his seat at the front of the courtroom.

"Is that the man?" Pucheu asked.

Emily nodded. "That is the man that walked away with my husband at knifepoint on the sixth."

Throughout the extended proceedings of this trial—the months of pretrial hearings, the four days of jury selection, the opening statements—through it all, John Brady had sat silent, expressionless. Bored.

Now, though, standing in front of a full courtroom, facing my great-grandmother's stern pointer finger, he lost all composure. He pointed back at Emily and practically growled, "Be sure, lady! You better make sure."

With a smack of the gavel, Judge Coreil shouted, "Mr. Balfa, control yourself!"

In the gallery, my uncle Richard stood up.

He'd been unable to sleep for weeks leading up to the trial's start, imagining sitting behind the man who had killed his pawpaw, looking at the back of his head. He was terrified Balfa would get off free, pissed that the electric chair had been taken off the table. On his way out the door that first day of testimony, he grabbed his pistol, stuffed it in his back pocket. Coming in with the crowds, he'd managed to avoid attention from security, who easily recognized him as one of Uncle Glenn's boys. If things started to go south, he was going to kill that motherfucker himself. Now, forty years later, he remembers how he'd thought he was ready, had reacted the instant Balfa yelled at his mawmaw, put his hand to his pocket. ". . . and I couldn't do it," he tells me. "I sat back down. And thank God, I didn't do it . . . but I was just so full of fury."

Relaying the moment in the local paper, a journalist wrote that members of the Balfa family, overcome, ran out of the courtroom, sobbing.

In 1985, research on the reliability of eyewitness testimony was only just creeping its way into the American judicial system. Once considered the gold standard of evidence—for their ability to convince as well as their perceived proximity to truth—eyewitness accounts were now being poked and prodded by psychologists, whose studies were revealing a far frailer psyche than we imagined for ourselves. How dependable is the memory, really? How tightly does it hold on to a scene, an image, a face? Is it susceptible to influence, to bending? To breaking? How much can we depend on it to maintain law and order?

While a certain dedicated few, mainly defense attorneys, started shouting about reform, day-to-day courtrooms proceeded as usual. In 1982, when advocates began fighting to bring psychologists before juries to testify to the scientific unreliability of eyewitness testimony, the Louisiana Supreme

Court responded with two decisions barring such testimony from all criminal trials, citing other courts' claims that the "prejudicial effect" of such testimony outweighed its value. That precedent was overruled only as recently as 2019.

While Louisiana clung to the primacy of eyewitness testimony, though, new technologies emerged. Two years after John Brady's trial came the first convictions using DNA profiling.

The lights turned on—trillions of once-invisible traces ignited, glowing bright. Troves of exonerations followed. Of the first 250 people exonerated in the United States from crimes using DNA evidence, 190 had been convicted using eyewitness testimony. It was there, plain as day— our very genes the whistleblower. The memory can lie.

If an eyewitness expert were to have been allowed in that Evangeline Parish courtroom in 1985, they would have likely explained that eyewitness accounts like Emily's *should* be included and heard when considering a case like this one. But they would also explain to the jury how to effectively evaluate the accuracy of those accounts.

They might have suggested the jurors consider the high levels of stress Emily was under during the twenty or so minutes the stranger was in her home, holding a knife to her husband. They might have spoken about the studies that show victims are overwhelmingly likely to forget details, even big ones, about a traumatic event when a weapon is involved. Emily's age would have undoubtedly been raised as a factor, as well as the state of shock and exhaustion she sustained over the next several days, during which she was subject to countless interrogations, repeating the same story over and over, with small adjustments here and there. The expert would ask questions about the extensive amount of information she had absorbed around the investigation, with the FBI headquarters in her backyard and many of the key investigators being close family friends.

And then there was time. There were twenty months in between the kidnapping and Emily's identification of John Brady, allowing for infinite opportunities for the memory to have been loosened, or corrupted.

None of this would have been her fault. Our memories tell us our own story, and, to a degree, we craft them ourselves. They are everything we know. If we cannot trust them, our entire reality comes into question. This moment, when the stranger came through the door, had come to define so much of Emily's identity. This memory, it was paramount. What she remembered was what she knew. What she knew was what she believed she saw. And she believed she saw him. She saw John Brady Balfa.

It's unclear if Billy Pucheu, in 1985, knew or cared much about the burgeoning criticisms of eyewitness testimony. Likely, he was more concerned with its effect. Even today, with over two thousand studies pointing to memory's fallibility, juries tend to overwhelmingly believe eyewitnesses, especially when they convey certainty, as Emily did.

Julie Cullen knew all this. In her pretrial motions, she had tried to get the identification thrown out, working from an assumption that the lineup had been conducted in such a way that might have influenced Emily's identification of John Brady. Perhaps his name had been mentioned to her ahead of time, perhaps the officers involved had made some small suggestive comment, perhaps she had been in some way pressured to make the call. John Brady, after all, had been a suspect at the outset. Surely, in those frenzied days following Aubrey's abduction, the Balfa name was mentioned in Emily's house.

Cullen had no solid proof of this, though—besides any claims John Brady might have made about how the lineup was conducted. And she couldn't get that testimony into the record without putting him on the stand. Prior to the trial, when she tried to get more information from witnesses present at the lineup, from Rudy Guillory or Emily or other officers present, they refused to speak to her without the DA's blessing, which he wouldn't give.

So it was left to Cullen to discredit Emily LaHaye, on the stand, all on her own. It was a necessary plan of action, to dismantle the prosecution's most provoking piece of evidence. But in her cross-examination, Cullen misjudged the emotional power Emily had claimed over the room, over the entire community. Cullen's interrogation of the old woman was tinged in accusation and lacking any gentleness. Emily—who already saw Cullen as an enemy, protecting the man she was certain killed her husband—responded defensively, and with resolution. In the theater of that small courtroom, her performance had already won the audience's favor. Cullen, in confronting the victim with a battle stance, cast herself up as the antagonist.

Cullen targeted Emily's most vulnerable spot first: her initial description of the man who came into her home on January 6, 1983. Per the sheriff's deputy's testimony and police report, this description was of a white male in his early thirties, dark-skinned, round face, clean-shaven, five foot ten, 165 to 170 pounds, slim build, wearing gloves, a dark, lightweight jacket, a dark-colored tam-type cap—tightly fitted over his head.

During his questioning, Pucheu asked Emily to recall her initial impressions as she'd told them to the officers that day. "I told them he was tall and slim, very lean. He was not rude. He was not rough with me, handled me pleasantly, and he was about the size of my youngest son, which is six or a little more, and slim, narrow shoulders, lean."

"What about his voice?" Pucheu asked. "What kind of voice did he have, and what kind of accent did he have?" Emily responded that he had an accent "like we talk at home," pronouncing "Vidrine" correctly as "Vee-dreen" and "Pierotti" as "Pear-uh-tee." "He was pleasant, he was not harsh. He did not talk loud to me. He didn't handle us roughly," she said. "It was just like a Vidrine man from Vidrine would talk."

When Cullen got her turn, she scrutinized this testimony, pointing out the subtle ways the description differed from the one she'd given on January 6, 1983. For instance, Emily originally said the man was five foot ten, and now she was saying he was six feet or taller. And every time Cullen asked Emily to repeat her original description of the abductor, she just pointed at John Brady. "The description was exactly like this man sitting down."

Cullen pressed on. "Do you remember telling the police officers that the man was about thirty years old?"

"I think he was younger than that," Emily replied, haltingly.

Though it's difficult to know if the jury was picking up on it, Cullen was unveiling a troubling symptom embedded in Emily's testimony. On the stand, she wasn't trying to describe the man who entered her home. She was trying to describe John Brady, the man sitting right in front of her. She wasn't even entertaining any distinction, legal or otherwise, between "the perpetrator" and the defendant. To her, they were already one and the same.

"Now," Cullen asked her, "it is your testimony that you described the person as being tall and slim from the very beginning. This is what you are testifying today in court that you told the police officers that the man was tall and slim. Is that right?"

"Right," said Emily.

"If that is not reflected in any of the information or description the police officers took down, it would be a mistake on the police officer's report. Is that correct?"

"Is *he* not tall and slim?"

"Mrs. LaHaye, that is not my question. My question was—"

"—I want to know why you are saying it could be the police's mistake if I say he is tall and slim, and they say he is not tall and slim. Is *he* not tall and slim?"

She pointed at John Brady.

Cullen drew out shades of this same problem during Glenn's and Wayne's testimonies, relaying the details of the ransom call. She challenged "new" adjectives being used to describe the abductor's voice, adjectives that especially applied to John Brady, words like *educated*.

On the stand, Wayne elaborated on what he meant. "He spoke very clearly, and he seemed somewhat eloquent on the phone. He was not troubled for words. He didn't initially seem to be speaking from a prepared statement."

"But," argued Cullen, "I mean, the whole conversation took three minutes, and the gist of the conversation was a person telling you there were four people and that he was in charge and he was going to tell you what to do. I mean, you didn't have a lengthy detailed discussion about anything, did you?"

"No, we did not."

Besides all this, the detail from Emily's initial description that Julie Cullen was *most* interested in was the description, "clean-shaven."

The first piece of evidence Cullen introduced for the defense was the photograph taken on January 12, 1983, at the Gregg County Jail. In it, John Brady wears what Rudy Guillory, in testimony, described as "a two-week mustache . . . a good mustache."

My aunt Michele tells me the mustache issue has always bothered her: "Emily didn't like whiskers. Everyone knew how much she didn't like whiskers. Aubrey, Glenn, and Wayne never wore facial hair. For her to say he was very clean-shaven . . . that was something she would have noticed. That was weird."

When Pucheu questioned her about the issue, Emily, in a manner that reads a little rehearsed, responded by saying: "I always said he was a pleasant-looking man, and he was a clean-shaved man. So, I don't deny that he could have had a mustache. But he did not have a beard."

In cross-examination, Cullen addressed the tidy statement directly, asking if Emily had discussed the testimony with Pucheu before coming to court. She replied that she had, many times, as recently as the previous Friday. How many times, Cullen asked, did she discuss the possibility of a mustache over the course of the investigation—with Pucheu, police officers, the FBI? To each inquiry, Emily insisted, "I'm not sure. I don't know."

"So," Cullen asked, "this time in court, while you're here for the trial, is the first time you are making any statement about a mustache at all, and this thing happened almost three years ago? Is that right?"

"I'm not sure," Emily said, stiff and resolute. "I'm not sure I did not."

Cullen pointed out to the jury that none of the composite images made during the weeks following the abduction included a mustache. When one of the composite artists, a state trooper, was called to the stand, he testified that Emily had never given any description of facial hair whatsoever, only using the words *clean-shaven*.

He added the caveat, too, that in his experience it is not uncommon for these composite images to be unsuccessful in depicting an unknown subject. "A composite," he said, "is only as good as what the witness can do. As in any process, there are possible breakdowns between what the person remembers and what they can tell you. What I hear from them and what I put down." Billy Pucheu asked him if it was unusual for someone to forget some more "outstanding" feature, such as a mustache. "No, sir," he said. "It's not."

Sitting with the DA file, I hold these original composites in my hands, the carbon smearing across the page, staining my fingers. The four composites shown to the jury were labeled A through D. "A" is the state trooper's. It features a rectangular face with small eyebrows and wide eyes, a beanie sort of hat obscuring the hairline. Emily told the officers the hat was too big, so in "B" they removed it. This character appears gruffer, thicker, meaner than the first—his lips thinner and his chin broader. "C" appears to be a version of "A" with a different hairline, a floppy, somewhat goofy-looking middle part. And "D"—the one most widely used—was Johnny Donnels's piece. I also find, among these, a copy of "A" upon which someone drew, in ballpoint pen, a thick mustache over the subject's face.

When Pucheu questioned Emily about whether she found the composites satisfactory, she told him, "I did the best I could. I said he had a pleasant face, but I was never satisfied. I never told the man that made the composite I was positive and happy with his work. I always said, 'Well, you do have a little resemblance, but it is not like him.'"

When Cullen held each composite, "A" through "D," up to Emily, asking her to explain to the jury which parts specifically resembled John Brady, she admitted, "There are no similarities. If I said they were similar, it was to satisfy the man who was working hard to make it, and I guess I was ready to come to an end of it."

Cullen persisted, relentless, displaying each composite again, trying to get Emily to explain what features in the images reflected the person who had entered her home. "I am not satisfied with any of these," she repeated, increasingly distraught. "They don't look like him and I am sorry I was not capable of describing the face of the man who left with my husband."

Despite all of Pucheu's and Emily's insistence that the clean-shaven composites were useless and looked nothing like the abductor, the State went on to present testimony from the Guaranty Bank employees who had recognized Balfa in the images back in 1983. In Pucheu's mind, the contradictions of the composite's likeness must have been outweighed by the impact of having yet another thread connecting John Brady to the crime.

On the stand, Ramona Johnson said, "I could not pinpoint anything about it, but something about the composite did remind me of him."

Her coworker Joyce Reed had agreed with her. Johnson's father, who also worked at the bank, informed an FBI agent, who asked Johnson if she had any photographs of John Brady. The next day she brought in her Mamou High School yearbook and turned it in. She never saw it again.

Pucheu questioned Reed, taking the opportunity to reinforce the apparent insignificance of the mustache. She recognized John Brady in a composite image without facial hair, she confirmed. And no, she had no trouble recognizing Mr. Balfa in court today, with his facial hair.

But in cross-examination, when Cullen asked Reed to identify which of the composites was the one she thought looked like John Brady, she couldn't remember.

Cullen repeated the exercise with Johnson and asked her to explain what specific features in the composites reminded her of John Brady's appearance. "I'm not sure," said Johnson. "Maybe the eyes . . . I don't know. It's something about it. I can't exactly pinpoint it."

While cross-examining Emily, Cullen hoped to use the bank staff's testimonies to her advantage, suggesting the possibility that this talk about John Brady in January of 1983 might have somehow reached the widow. Perhaps even the yearbook had been shown to her—his name and face entering her consciousness amid the chaos so that when he stood before her in the lineup in 1984, he was familiar.

Emily admitted that she knew some of the employees thought the composite looked like John Brady, but Cullen could not get her to say when she had heard this—whether it was in the initial investigation or more recently in the context of the trial. As for the yearbook, Emily said she had never heard anything of that either, not until Cullen brought it up.

But what about the January 12, 1983, photograph of John Brady Balfa at Gregg County Jail?

After his interrogation of John Brady, Agent Kieny had sent the photo, along with six photographs of other Texas inmates, to the FBI office in New Orleans. Agent Owen Odom testified that he came into possession of these photos shortly after they were taken. "They were never shown to Mrs. LaHaye," he told the jury.

But why wouldn't the photograph have been shown to Emily? Wasn't that precisely why it had been taken?

During his two-day testimony, Detective Rudy Guillory responded to Pucheu's questions regarding other photo lineups Emily had been shown. I don't catch it the first time I read through the transcript, but later I'll come back to this testimony again and again—the simple "No, sir, she did not," Guillory utters in response to Pucheu's question regarding a January 19, 1983, lineup: "Did she, in fact, pick out anyone in that lineup as the suspect?"

What he says is not true. It directly contradicts the FBI correspondence records in my possession, which refer to a January 20, 1983, telecall between the New Orleans bureau and Houston's, stating that "a white male, age thirty-five, has been tentatively identified" by Emily via photographic and physical lineup. The record reads, "Emily LaHaye stated she thinks Taylor Strother is the individual who entered her home and kidnapped victim."

Guillory's claim that Emily made no identification of any suspect prior to John Brady Balfa was either a mistake or a lie. In fact, she had already identified someone, and investigators had deemed the evidence not significant enough to charge him with the crime.

But without access to the FBI files, Cullen had no way of knowing this or arguing it in court.

Finally granted access to witnesses of the September 21, 1984, lineup, here was Cullen's chance to unveil any mistakes that might have been made, any improper protocol that may have occurred to contaminate Emily's identification of John Brady. Reading through the transcript, though, it seems as though she was going in blind, untethered to any specific incident, just hoping to snag something.

Guillory, Odom, and Emily each recounted how the two investigators went to the LaHaye home on the morning of September 21, 1984. Odom had a photographic lineup prepared in his briefcase. All three testified that Emily requested an in-person lineup instead of a photo lineup. Guillory had made the arrangements with Detective Roy Mallet in St. Landry Parish, where John Brady was being held.

Cullen drilled down into the scene that followed, "Did you know the name of the person that was going to be in the lineup?"

"Of course not," Emily replied, offended by the implication.

"When," Cullen asked, "was the first time you found out John Balfa's name?"

To this, Emily hesitated, then offered, "When he was . . . uh . . . arrested."

This can't be quite right, as John Brady was never officially "arrested" for the Aubrey LaHaye murder; he was already in custody. It's possible Emily had meant to refer to his indictment, which would be the "correct" and "proper" answer—though I find it difficult to believe that between September 1984 and John Brady's indictment in February 1985, Detective Guillory did not inform her or his friend Glenn of the results of her identification.

"You did not know his name back in January of 1983?"

"I don't think so."

"During—"

"—I didn't know anything about John Balfa at all." Emily's posture was becoming increasingly defensive. She was shutting down.

Turning back to the details of the St. Landry Parish lineup, Cullen asked Emily if it was true that she had requested to see John Brady and one other subject again. "Yes, I did that," she replied. "But I knew who he was the first time I saw him . . . my decision was made. It was for the satisfaction of the officers who were with me."

Cullen looked at her quizzically. "Is it your testimony that the only reason you asked to have two of the individuals brought back was to satisfy the police officers?"

Emily's wall of certainty was shuddering, just a little, as its people-pleasing foundations betrayed her. "Yes," she said. "I was not, uh, strong enough to say, 'Look, that is the man.' I wanted to give them another chance to test me—to see."

But then, she doubled down. "I knew from the beginning it was him. This one." She pointed at John Brady. "This man right here."

The Body in the Bayou

EYOND EMILY'S IDENTIFICATION, THE DISTRICT ATTORNEY'S
case rested on the connections between the objects of the crime
and the objects found on the Balfa property. Most of this evidence
came directly from Aubrey's body.

Kurt Vezinat set the scene at the Bayou Nezpique on that all-important
Sunday morning of January 16, 1983. A slight, simple man with a thick
Cajun accent, he wrung his hat in his hands and spoke almost too quietly
for the jury to hear. He told of how he and his family had been driving
out in the country, "sightseeing." "I brought my rifle so we could shoot in
the water," he said. They arrived at the Bayou Nezpique bridge around
11:30 a.m. He told of how they started shooting bullets at the curiosity
in the water. Noticing a taut rope tied to one end, Kurt aimed, shot, and
snapped it—a precise shot. "And that's when I saw the back side of the
left arm, and the back side of a head, and the body come up."

Kurt told of how he instructed his wife, Beulah, to go with their son to
the police station in Mamou, then waited—alone with the body. When
they returned, they came with Agent Ellis Blount, Detective Guillory,
and the police chief. At one point there were about fifteen officers at the
scene, who collected as evidence some two thousand empty rifle shells
from the bridge—left behind by dozens of other leisurely sharpshooters
like Vezinat.

In cross-examination, Julie Cullen asked him if he had been aware
that Aubrey LaHaye was missing at the time. "Yes, ma'am," he told her.
He had known Mr. Aubrey "all his life," he said.

While law enforcement started investigating the scene, Dr. BJ Manuel
was watching football at his camp a couple hundred yards away. Aubrey's
body had technically been discovered within the confines of his property. When Sheriff Vidrine came knocking on his door, Manuel not only
volunteered his boat for the body's recovery but got in the vessel to help.
During his witness testimony, Manuel affirmed that he was able to iden-

tify the body while it was still in the bayou. "There was no question about it, when the body was pulled on the bank, it was Mr. Aubrey," he said. "In fact, [before] we got it up to the bank, when he was floating in the water, when I saw the back of his neck and shoulders, I felt it was him, even at that point."

One by one, Pucheu exhibited a series of photographs, entering each into evidence as Manuel confirmed "Yes, that is what the bayou looked like that day," "Yes, that is me in the boat," "Yes, that is Aubrey LaHaye's body as it looked when we pulled it from the bayou."

The photos: a square of smooth, brown water laced over by the forest's shadows, glimmering with sunlight—disrupted by a barely distinguishable, bloody bundle. Dr. BJ Manuel, Sheriff Vidrine, and two other men climbing into the boat. A pair of glasses, resting pristine beneath a cypress tree. Three men on the bank, pulling on ropes, something dark and fleshy emerging from the Nezpique. A banker's body lying on the dirt, blue pajamas clinging, rope tied around the neck and waist, attached at the end to the two metal rims. His head obscured by a yellow towel. His feet, bare. The body, again, this time lying on its side. A close-up of the rims, the Chevrolet emblem grinning.

While the sheriff and Dr. Manuel worked to retrieve the body, Detective Guillory and Agent Blount searched the area—walking the entire bank, on top of the bridge, beneath the bridge. They walked fifty yards on each side of the road. Guillory testified that he returned several times over the next few weeks to search, walking farther and farther down the road each time. The only piece of evidence they found, besides all that was connected to the body, were Aubrey's glasses on the bank. These were brought out in court, as well as the pajamas and the yellow, bloodstained towel, which had been wrapped around his head.

Guillory told of how he accompanied the body, muddy and still tied up, to Bossier City on January 17 for analysis, and he observed as Dr. George McCormick removed the ropes and conducted the autopsy.

Each time a new item of evidence was introduced, the courtroom went quiet—the twelve members of the jury each taking their turn to hold these relics, encased in plastic, in their hands. They could feel the ridges of the rope, see the paint flecks in its fibers. They could, if only it weren't for the entire courtroom's eyes upon them, hold Aubrey's glasses up to their face—imagine the things he had seen, scenes now obscured by the blur of the labeled plastic. They could see the dirt and something darker encrusted over the pajamas. Expensive pajamas. As my aunt Michele once described them, "the most beautiful old man pajamas you had ever seen."

The rims were too heavy to pass around. The jury walked to the front of the courtroom to see them up close, each taking their turn standing before those two ungainly halos, resting so conspicuously against the wall.

February 5, 2021

"This is the first time this box has been opened since the trial," says Patrice—the member of the Evangeline Parish Clerk of Court's Office assigned to chaperone me to the warehouse where the parish's oldest records are stored. The space is discombobulating, reeking of dust—mountainous with towers of cardboard storage. The information contained here is overwhelming in its abundance and its loneliness. Most of these boxes will never be opened again. I follow Patrice to a back corner, and I see the box I'm looking for long before she points it out. Coffin-size, hammered plywood, an altar in a room of white bankers' boxes.

My dad had heard the rims remained at the courthouse, in a box people had walked past for years and spoke about in whispers—*The rims they sank Aubrey LaHaye with.* The clerk of court confirms the rumor years later, when I ask if any of the evidence from the trial has been preserved.

This is it, he says. This is all he inherited. No one knows where the rest of it ended up—the pajamas, the rope, the glasses, the paint. The yellow towel that had been wrapped around PawPaw Aubrey's head. The piece of glass found in his wound. All gone, along with any potential remnants of DNA that may have clung on through the decades. The previous clerk of court had his own way of doing things, Patrice tells me. "It was a total mess. But no one comes back for cases this old anyway." *It hasn't even been forty years yet,* I think to myself, imagining John Brady Balfa, still locked in his cell, just a little older than my father. It's not as though an entire lifetime has even passed. There's a nonchalance about the whole thing that rings strange to me, as though it were par for the course to simply misplace items of such consequential weight.

But here are the rims, stored in this house of secrets across the street from the courthouse. "No one has ever tried to look at these since then?" I ask.

"Nope, you would be the first."

She's brought a screwdriver and takes her time working on the lid. While I wait, my eyes focus in on a mummified rat, curled in the corner.

Once she gets the box open, I follow her lead, and we work together to lift out each metal ring. We're in the middle of it before I wonder if we should be wearing gloves. There are eight rims in total: the two that had been attached to PawPaw Aubrey's body, the six taken from the Balfa yard. Four vehicle rims, four trailer house rims. It's not immediately clear to me which is which. I stare at each one, turn them over, feel their weight. All are covered in rust. One is encrusted with what I assume is Nezpique mud. Handwritten shorthand signatures and initials identify each investigator who put his hands on them. One of the rims appears to be painted blue, another yellow, another black. The rest, only metal. Then, I see. Two are tagged, marked as the dead man's weights. The muddy blue automobile rim. A silver trailer rim.

The room tilts. I turn my face back toward the rat.

I remember from the FBI records that all four vehicle rims had shared the same top layer of black enamel paint—this was the evidence so much of the case rested on. But I could see no black paint here on the two tagged rims. Had it chipped away, faded into the dust over the course of these forty years?

So much of the question—Did John Brady do it?—came to be entangled in these hunks of metal. In whether this metal matches that metal; this paint, that paint. Whether these obscure objects came from "the same source." Was the blue rim dragging PawPaw Aubrey into the Nezpique the missing piece of *this* set? Did it once hold the tire that rolled the Firebird, with the Balfa boys in it, from Houston to Evangeline in 1979? To me, they all look the same, and they all look different. To me, they are incomprehensible. I see yellow. I see blue. I see black. I see Chevrolet. I see rust and weight and holes. Eight circles turning, turning, turning.

A Tale of Tires

THE STORY BILLY PUCHEU SET UP IN THE COURTROOM THAT day was a story of missing puzzle pieces.

Once upon a time there were eight tires lying loose around the Balfa property. Four were the mismatched, spray-painted thrift shop tires from the brothers' trip to Houston. Four had once been attached to Charles Balfa's trailer home. The family used them for spares when needed, or as weights in their fishing boat, to keep it from bouncing as it gained speed. In the meantime, these tires rolled under cattle trailers, leaned against the barn, were tossed in the junk pile.

But when Detective Roy Mallet and Agent Owen Odom, and later Detective Rudy Guillory, went to search the Balfa property on September 20, 1984, they found only six tires. Three for a car, three for a mobile home. These were all taken in for evidence, described by Odom as looking "exactly like" the rims—the automobile rim and the trailer rim—attached to Aubrey's body. The missing pieces. A complete puzzle. *The end.*

To the investigators, Pucheu posed the question: "Did Harry Balfa appear surprised that there were only three automobile tires? Only three mobile home tires?" Guillory, Odom, and Mallet each responded that he had.

Julie Cullen tried to discredit Pucheu's theory in a twofold manner. First, she fixated on the Balfa junk pile, asking the officers and the Balfas whether it was fenced in, if the family kept close track of what went in and what came out of it. It was not, and of course they didn't.

She laid the groundwork to suggest that *if* the materials did come from the Balfa yard, who is to say that someone other than John Brady might have gone onto the property and taken them? Why does evidence coming from the yard have to lead to him?

And as far as Cullen was concerned, the *if* was still pretty big. She aimed to discredit the forensic testimony, to denounce the claim that the rims attached to the body were connected to the rims on the Balfa property at all.

The Same Source

R EPORTING ON THE SECOND DAY OF TRIAL, A JOURNALIST from the *Eunice News* described the way the Evangeline Parish courtroom had emptied over the previous forty-eight hours. Beneath the headline, "Interest Falls in Balfa's Murder Trial," the article reads: "A mob of people crushed through the door to Judge Joseph E. Coreil's courtroom on Monday after lunch to hear the continuation of the John Brady Balfa trial, but by end of the court session, many had voluntarily given up their seats and gone home." Interest dwindled even more, he said, on Tuesday, when FBI analysts took the stand, and Billy Pucheu and Julie Cullen "tediously" questioned them on their analysis of the evidence.

Sorting through this testimony as someone untrained in scientific analysis is, in fact, tedious. I have studied the transcript like I used to study for tests in college, rewriting the thing in various arrangements of bullet points, again and again until it lodges itself in my brain, coherent. To the equally lay audience in the courtroom that day, it is easy to imagine the whole ordeal as straight-up boring, opaque and repetitive. But to people like my father, so vested in these results, the expert testimony— the elevated, technical language surrounding the processes of scientific certainty—was *impressive*. And it was damning. At least that's how he remembers it.

Allen Robillard, the FBI's microscopic analysis expert who had initially conducted comparative examinations on the ropes in evidence, had flown into Evangeline Parish from Washington, DC, to provide his testimony as an expert witness. "These ropes," he announced, holding up the ropes that had been tied around the body, "could have originated from the same source as these ropes"—the Balfa ropes, now raised in his left hand. They matched, he said, "microscopically, physically, and compositionally."

The FBI's instrumental analysis expert David Nichols echoed the assessment when it came to the automobile rims. The one tied to the body was different in every way from the other three, except for one: the top layer of black paint was "microscopically, microchemically, and instrumentally the same"—pointing back to the set of four mismatched flea market tires spray-painted black.

As for the mobile home rims, though they did appear identical, the one attached to the body had paint that was chemically different from the rest. Despite Pucheu's inclusion of them in his puzzle, the mobile home rims were, decidedly, not a match.

Nichols was, though, also able to tie the orange paint sample taken from the Balfa home to paint flecks found on three of the ropes in evidence: the ropes used to tie the rims to Aubrey's body, the rope used to tie up Emily, and rope found in Harry Balfa's workshop. On all three ropes, the paint appeared to have been applied while it was wet. In each instance, it was the same color and was consistent microchemically and instrumentally. Later in the trial, Harry Balfa would challenge this match, claiming the paint on his property had come from Sunland Construction. He had only purchased it about six months before the investigators came to his house, over a year after Aubrey's abduction.

In cross-examination, Cullen asked the experts to elaborate on the actual significance of their assessments. What did "from the same source" mean? Does the degree of scientific accuracy compare to that of fingerprints, or ballistics?

Robillard shook his head, "I cannot say positively that these ropes came from the same source." He explained that he couldn't certainly say that they had previously been attached to each other, came from the same spool, or even came from the same manufacturer. "But I can say that they *could* have come from the same piece of rope; they *could* have come from the same spool; they *could* have come from the same manufacturer; or they *could* have come from different spools or lengths of rope at two different sources, made by the same manufacturer."

Cullen asked him if he knew what manufacturer that could be. He did not. He did not know how many manufacturers were making this kind of rope, or anything about the rope in particular. So, Cullen concluded, "there is really not much you can say about the source other than it could have come from the same source. Is that right?"

Robillard didn't seem to wholly understand the problem Cullen was articulating. Vexed, he reiterated, "That is a significant finding, because in order for this rope to come from another source, that other source would have to have the very same characteristics."

But, Cullen pressed, what source were we talking about anyway? The manufacturer, the Balfa residence? "Well, it could have come from the Balfa residence. On the other hand, it could have come from another piece of rope that was not in the Balfa residence." So, essentially, Cullen seemed to ask—it could have come from anywhere? Robillard concluded: "I can't say absolutely that the rope came from the Balfa residence."

Likewise, Agent David Nichols was unable to offer insight as to who manufactured the paint on the rims, how old it was, or whether the paint came from the same manufacturer. He could only say that the paint was the same on all four rims, and that the orange paint on each of the ropes was consistent when tested microchemically and instrumentally—that they all "could have come from the same source."

What Cullen was getting at is a critique still raised today in the field of comparison forensics. What does this conclusion actually *mean*? How rare is it for two samples of everyday materials such as rope or paint— discovered in different parts of a small town—to be derived from the "same source"? Especially when that source itself—The manufacturer? A spool? A bucket? A batch?—is unidentified. Are the chances one in ten? One in a thousand? One in a million? On this issue, the jury was pro- vided only this response from Robillard during a traverse examination by Pucheu, who asked him to explain again *why* his conclusions were significant to this case.

"Well," he responded, "the significance is simply this. All these ropes that were from the Balfa residence had the same physical microscopic characteristics as the ropes found on the body—the synthetic ropes found on the body—and as we have seen right before us, there are one, two, three other ropes that are different. So the significance is that some of these ropes match. To me, it is significant."

The Nezpique

ENEATH ALL THE DISCUSSION OF RIMS AND ROPE, THE
State and defense were each building their own undercurrent arguments concerning the Nezpique itself: What might the bayou
reveal about PawPaw Aubrey's death? About his killer?

This line of questioning was initiated by Julie Cullen, who asked Dr.
BJ Manuel about the bayou's flooding habits. A slow-moving, swampy
tributary off the Mermentau River, the Nezpique is historically notorious for flooding out into the prairie during the rainy season, spurring
several damming projects to control it, including John LaHaye's creation
of Miller's Lake, and countless efforts initiated by Aubrey himself.

Manuel explained to the jury that the Nezpique typically flooded
twice every winter and once in the spring, rushing out over the bridge and
the road as high as three to five inches. Such a flood had taken place in
the first few days of 1983 and was only just receding the week of Aubrey's
kidnapping. Dr. Manuel testified that on January 4, 1983, the road was
dry. Over the next two weeks, as the search parties wandered the parish,
the bayou continued to drain. On January 16, there was only about five
or six feet of water in it.

Dr. Manuel explained that when the water gets that low, a second
bank is revealed. There is the high bank, level with the bridge—and then
the lower bank, a small, wet beach beside the dwindling bayou. When
this much land has been undrowned, the thinned stream reveals its true
center, its deepest point—which does not line up with the center of the
bridge. This is where Aubrey's body bobbed, at the Nezpique's center.

Pucheu used this information to suggest that whoever dumped the
body had to be intimately familiar with the bayou. The person had to
know where the true center of the bayou was, even when it was concealed
by higher waters on January 6. They couldn't simply toss it from the middle
of the bridge, or it would have been swept to the bank as the water receded.
Whoever did this likely knew well how the Nezpique ebbed and flowed.

When questioning Harry Balfa, Pucheu wrestled loose the fact that one of Harry's brothers once had a camp near the bridge where Aubrey's body had been found, that John Brady and his brothers had all visited the area frequently, hunting the squirrels and the deer that passed through the Nezpique. "They knew the bayou," Harry said.

But Cullen was working a different angle. After all, if there *had* been a plan for the body to remain enshrined at the bayou's deepest point, its center, that plan had obviously failed. The body revealed itself, despite their efforts.

She suggested that the body hadn't been tossed over the bridge at all. These rims—clanging around the courtroom—were heavy. Add that to two hundred pounds of dead weight, and lift it over the side of a bridge? For it to fall exactly into its intended place? Unlikely, she asserted. It was far more probable that whoever had done this had dragged the body down the bank and into the water themselves, directly placing it at the bayou's deepest point. And John Brady, per the testimony of his now ex-wife Deborah Kinney, did not know how to swim. He could have used a boat, sure. But never had any member of the Balfa family or anyone else reported that the family boat was used on the morning of January 6.

And then there were the glasses, unbroken, right beside the waterline. The water had been receding for over a week. Kurt Vezinat testified that between January 15 and 16 alone, the water level had dropped about a foot and a half. So, if the body had been tossed into the Nezpique ten days before, when the water was several feet higher—how did those glasses come to be right there on January 16, undamaged, unmuddied, dry?

Time of Death

SHORTLY AFTER EMILY TOOK THE STAND—BEFORE SHE EVEN got to the story of the kidnapper entering their home—Billy Pucheu started asking her about Aubrey's bowel movements. She had been prepared for it, answering the questions straightforwardly and with as much dignity as she could muster. But to speak of such private matters before the whole town, before the media, must have just about killed her.

She told Pucheu her husband suffered no problems or irregularities when it came to his bladder or his stomach—though occasionally he did have "acid stomach." Yes, his bowel movements were regular. Yes, he usually went in the morning. She did not believe he ate or drank anything the morning of his abduction, nor did he get a chance to go to the bathroom.

Later, Bruce Guillory, a local rice farmer, would tell the court of Aubrey's last meal: chicken and sausage gumbo. On the evening of January 5, 1983, Guillory had hosted a group of local men at his home for dinner and a card game. Aubrey had not had any alcohol—"He never drank." But he had smoked a cigar, maybe two. They ate around 8:15 to 8:30 p.m. and then played cards until around 10:30—passing around a can of peanut brittle as they went.

On the third day of testimony, Pucheu called Wayne LaHaye back to the stand—this time as his father's primary doctor. He testified that Aubrey suffered no digestive problems and was on two daily medications to treat mild hypertension. A side effect of these, both diuretics, was that they can cause someone's bladder to fill more frequently.

All this was to come together with the much-anticipated testimony of Dr. George McCormick. At the time, McCormick was working as the elected coroner for both Bossier and Caddo Parishes in north Louisiana, as well as operating a private consultation practice, which conducted forensic autopsies for forty of the state's sixty-four parishes. In 1985, he was president of the State Coroners Association and had conducted over nine hundred autopsies.

McCormick's autopsy report, which I find in the DA's file, describes Aubrey LaHaye's death in a section titled "Narrative of Findings." A story of macabre: "This subject's death was due to cardiorespiratory arrest due to multiple traumatic injuries, of which the most severe were injuries received from multiple blows to the posterior scalp."

The document is so clinical. Full of words designed to be descriptive, but somehow cleanse the mutilated body of the true violence enacted upon it: *contusion, abrasion, laceration, hemorrhage.* A list of injuries a page long, all of which add up to the final blow: "Shock (due to combined effect of above head injuries), with acute congestive heart failure," which is what led, directly, to "cardiorespiratory arrest and death." PawPaw Aubrey was violently beaten to death. But from a strictly scientific standpoint, he died because his heart stopped.

McCormick described the state of the body when he received it as at a point of "moderate postmortem decomposition"—and riddled with the Vezinats' bullet holes. Tiny, bloodless trails carved through lax, lifeless muscle, organ, bone. Where the rope had been tied around Aubrey's neck remained a deep indentation, also bloodless—suggesting the rims had been attached only after he was dead. His hands were wrinkled and swollen—a telltale sign of a body that has begun its decomposition process underwater.

In the second section of the autopsy, McCormick goes into greater detail of his time with the corpse. He describes its arrival, in a black disaster bag. Unzipped, the body of an old man lay inside, wrapped in a single white sheet. He was 69 inches tall, estimated to weigh between 190 and 205 pounds. "He was covered with a large amount of dirt, grass, aquatic debris, and mud."

With intensive detail, McCormick spoils all fancies of grandeur I attempt to retain for my great-grandfather with testaments to his raw humanity, emphasized by his loss of it. "His hair was salt-and-pepper gray along the edges, with bilateral receding hairlines and central thinning." He was missing some of his teeth, had stubble growing on his face, and his sideburns were trimmed above his ears. "Both eyes were decomposed, but appeared to be dark in color . . . blood was present in the nose and mouth."

To examine Aubrey's head wounds, McCormick had to shave his

head. The first laceration was two centimeters wide, and four millimeters deep. Inside of it, he found a greasy blackened substance, which he wiped off to preserve as evidence. The second laceration was larger, seven centimeters wide, and four and a half millimeters deep. On the back of his head, a mass of mud and branches was tangled in his hair—along with the tiny piece of brown glass, "similar to glass used in beer bottles." On the back of Aubrey's neck was a large, red "abrasion" measuring seven centimeters in width, and on his lower back there was a deep bruise that measured eleven by eight centimeters.

McCormick goes on to document the "internal examination"—the process of taking Aubrey apart. People aren't meant to know so much about each other's insides. What sequence of events has led me here, to know the color of my great-grandfather's lungs, the smell of his gastric contents, the weight of his heart? It feels sacrilegious, the way we justify carving people up to answer our questions, dissecting each organ, each cavity—taking notes. Hoping to find revelations in the mangled flesh. Early decomposition fluid in the lungs. A bullet clanging to the ground with the removal of a skullcap. Fragments of peanuts in the small intestine. I google "cerebral edema" and the words *swelling of the brain* are bolded in the first results. My stomach turns at the words *skin slippage*.

With the autopsy, there is a small manila envelope. When I open it, I catch a glimpse of what's inside, then close it fast. I take a deep breath before pulling the stack of photos out, blurring my eyes to prolong the looking.

Already, I can see a smear of red. When I focus in, though, and allow myself to absorb the unfiltered horror of what happened to my great-grandfather, it's not the blood that repulses me. It's the mud. Clinging to his ears. Caught in the hairs of his face, the skin behind it flaring angrily—from rot or bruises I cannot tell. Up close, the wound on the back of his neck rages—glowing from folds of skin white as snow. The rope is still tied to him, clenching around his belly in an awful accumulation of flesh. Old-man belly, swollen and naked, caked in mud. The knots look so clean, so precise against the mayhem of the dead man they hold. The mortal wound is captured like a portrait, revealed in blinding light, marked. A ghastly, curved slice through the skull, deep enough that the doctors can stick their fingers in it. A canyon in a white, balding head.

But the worst photo of all is the close-up of his face. Bloated, eyes squeezed shut. He almost looks like a sleeping baby. The mud cakes his mouth like a beard, the mouth partially opened, as if he has just taken a breath. His hair wet, messy. His skin so many shades of pink, red, yellow, and blue.

Pucheu entered many of these images into evidence in court, but unlike in the television dramas, they didn't show them on a big screen—instead passing the four-by-sixes to each member of the jury. The only LaHaye who has seen what PawPaw Aubrey's body looked like, besides myself, is my dad. He's seen these photos, too.

Around six months after McCormick's testimony, my father was in his second semester at LSU School of Medicine in Shreveport. Each student was tasked with finding an externship opportunity, a chance to follow an area doctor around a few days a week. It occurred to Dad that the pathologist from PawPaw's trial had been from Bossier City, just down the road.

McCormick gladly took him on. Two afternoons a week, Dad would go to his lab to assist with autopsies of "floaters"—unidentified bodies found floating in the Red River.

By the time McCormick asked Dad if he wanted to view his grandfather's autopsy, Dad felt he could stomach it. He had read and observed the human body at its most grotesque, had handled many, sewed them back up. He only told McCormick he didn't want to see his pawpaw's insides.

I ask Dad what he remembers about them, what parts of those photographs have burned into his mind these forty years. "It was just this big . . . white . . . kind of hairless, pale body. Fat. On that table." He tells me, "It shocked me how little it impressed upon me that this was my grandfather." He doesn't remember the wounds—"I may have asked not to see them," he says. "I remember seeing pictures of the bullet holes, though. How they didn't bleed."

What he remembers best, though—this young medical student fated to someday become a urologist—is that, according to McCormick's examination, Aubrey had the first signs of prostate cancer. He hadn't even known it.

On the third day of arguments, Dr. McCormick took the stand. After establishing his credentials as an expert witness in the field of forensic pathology, he began walking the jury through the autopsy report. He explained the distinction between a "laceration" and a "cut"—the first suggesting the use of blunt force, as opposed to a knife. The depth of the lacerations on Aubrey's scalp, he said, went all the way through to the bone.

When Pucheu asked him to deliver his opinion on how Aubrey had died, he summarized his findings as follows: "We found that Mr. LaHaye had been struck on the back of the head with a blunt object. We were not able to tell what the blunt object was. It was not a sharp object such as a knife, which would have cut the skin . . . after these blows, he suffered hemorrhage around his brain and mild hemorrhage into his brain. Because of these blows to the head with a brain injury, he died." McCormick went on to assert that most likely, Aubrey had been hit on the head twice, and maybe even three times.

Anticipating Cullen's certain interrogation on the matter, Pucheu asked McCormick why there was no date or time of death listed on the autopsy. He replied that he was unable to give an accurate date of death without access to certain information. In response, Pucheu delivered the promised hypothetical:

"Now, doctor, *assuming* Mr. LaHaye was abducted from his home on January 6, 1983, at approximately 5:30 a.m., *assuming further* that on the morning of January 6, he took no medication, had nothing to drink, ate nothing, did not go to the bathroom to relieve his bladder, or did not have a bowel movement; *assuming further* that his bowel habits were regular, and they were in the morning; *assuming* that the night before he had nothing to drink other than perhaps one Coke; *assuming further* that he had eaten about 8:15 or 8:30 that night, had eaten chicken and sausage gumbo and thereafter had eaten some peanut brittle anywhere from 8:45 to 9 something or 10 p.m. when the poker game broke up—with that hypothetical question, can you, sir, give us an estimate of the time of death of Mr. Aubrey LaHaye?"

McCormick replied, without hesitation, "With those assumptions, in a hypothet, the best answer I can give you is that he died shortly after leaving his house at 5:30 that morning."

When Cullen got her chance, she demanded to know why McCormick had never tried to estimate a time of death before now, at trial. He responded that he hadn't been given the information he needed to make the judgment until today.

"So, when Mr. LaHaye was killed almost three years ago, the first time the prosecutor in this case has ever given you enough information for you to determine a time of death is today?"

"Yes."

Upon further questioning, McCormick admitted he and Pucheu had been discussing the time of death since the day the body was discovered—but never in certain terms. He said that in a conversation held a few weeks prior, he told Pucheu that the condition of the body was consistent with him being in the water since the day he'd disappeared, but that he needed more information to be certain. The information McCormick was "missing" up until just before he testified was (1) what sort of medications Aubrey had been on (2) what his bowel and bladder habits were like, and (3) whether he had emptied his bladder and bowels that morning.

Of course, all this information would have been readily available to Pucheu, and by extension McCormick, long before the trial. All they had to do was ask Wayne and Emily the questions.

In fact, a document I discover in the DA file confirms that McCormick did in fact make an estimate long before the trial—before John Brady Balfa was even tapped as the main suspect. Though it is not dated, the FBI's "Psychological Profile" on the then-unidentified subject who killed Aubrey LaHaye appears to have been created sometime after the body was discovered, but before John Brady's indictment. And in it is a summary of McCormick's findings during the autopsy, including the statement: "Victim was killed between 5:45 a.m. and 9 a.m. on January 6, 1983, and immediately thrown in the water, where he was later found."

Billy Pucheu had access to the estimate the entire time. He had just figured out a way to keep that information from Julie Cullen until the trial. And McCormick had gone along with it. The whole thing was a thinly veiled stunt to prevent her from adequately preparing John Brady's case.

Openly frustrated, Cullen asked McCormick to elaborate on how he had come to his estimation. He explained that during the autopsy, he had found peanuts in the beginning of the large intestine, in addition to colonic content through the rest of the large intestine. Aubrey also had a full bladder. This, he said, indicated he had not used the restroom in between consuming the peanut brittle at 10 p.m. on January 5 and his death. "If he had, the peanuts would have been farther down the intestinal tract," he explained.

Cullen asked him to imagine another hypothetical: What if Aubrey had gotten the chance to use the restroom between leaving his home and his death?

Based on the location of the peanuts in the digestive tract, McCormick said that this was impossible. "I would tell you that in all medical probability that is not true."

The medicine mattered, because if he had taken a diuretic that morning, it would have been more difficult to determine if the full bladder was his first or second of the day. But because he had not gotten a chance to take his pills, it was most likely his first.

All of this, he qualified, was only an estimate—but a significant one. "There is no totally accurate test of time of death," he said. "It is the thing you, in the legal profession, always ask us to do and it is the thing we can very seldom do." The second most difficult request he received from lawyers, he said, was to determine whether a victim found in water had drowned, or not. Despite common belief, this is extremely difficult to know for sure. The fact that the lungs did not have any debris in them, though, indicated Aubrey had likely ceased breathing before his body entered the Nezpique.

As for Aubrey's wounds, McCormick estimated that—based on the lack of white blood cells present—they had occurred between fifteen and thirty minutes before his death. It had happened fast, all at once, likely before the ransom call was even made.

Dr. McCormick's testimony was then bolstered by that of his colleague, the forensic anthropologist William Rodriguez. With deep-set eyes and a mustache that rivaled John Brady's, the thirty-one-year-old scientist was already a sensation in the burgeoning field—one of three full-time forensic anthropologists in the country and named a top expert on human decomposition by the American Academy of Forensic Scientists. He had studied under William Bass, who was at the time considered *the* national expert on the topic. Together, he and Bass had opened the University of Tennessee's now-renowned Body Farm—a research facility dedicated to the study of human decomposition, where bodies are meticulously analyzed as they decompose under various environmental conditions.

Today, forty years since this trial, Rodriguez is regaled as a global forensics superstar, having led investigations on war crimes in Iraq, Somalia, and Kosovo, as well as numerous terrorist attacks. He served for twenty

My great-grandfather
Aubrey LaHaye in
the early 1960s, in
his signature pose—
relaxed in the recliner
in his sitting room,
chewing on a cigar.

Aubrey with his eldest
granddaughter, Smokey.

Aubrey and Emily LaHaye,
known to me as PawPaw
and MawMaw, at their 50th
anniversary party in June 1981.

Aubrey and Emily LaHaye, their children and spouses, and their grandchildren, photographed in Aubrey and Emily's backyard in the early 1970s. *Back row:* Susan, Wayne, Aubrey, Emily, Tot, Sonny, Janie, Glenn, Richard. *Middle row:* My father Marcel, Danny, Jay, Nick, Dusty, Anne, Billy, Smokey, Jody. *On swing:* Suzette, Kaye, Sandy.

MawMaw Emily and me
at Christmas, 1998.

Aubrey and Emily LaHaye, pictured with their three children—Flora Jane ("Tot"), Glenn, and my grandfather Wayne—at their 50th anniversary party in June 1981.

The front page of the *Ville Platte Gazette* on January 13, 1983, featuring a photograph from the January 11 press conference led by Aubrey's son-in-law Sonny DeVillier. Standing behind him are, from left to right: FBI agent Ed Grimsley and Aubrey and Emily's three children, Tot, Wayne, and Glenn. **Courtesy of the *Ville Platte Gazette*.**

One week after the kidnapping, the *Mamou Acadian Press* photographed investigators from the FBI, the Louisiana State Police, and the Evangeline Parish Sheriff's Department working on the Aubrey LaHaye kidnapping case at Emily and Aubrey's dining room table. **Courtesy of the *Ville Platte Gazette*.**

The eight composite drawings from the Aubrey LaHaye kidnapping investigation preserved in the Evangeline Parish District Attorney's file—all created by FBI and Louisiana State Police investigators using Emily LaHaye's descriptions of the man who kidnapped Aubrey on January 6, 1983. Only composites A–D were introduced as evidence in the case of the *State of Louisiana v. John Brady Balfa* in 1985. In the DA file, I found a copy of composite A with a mustache drawn on it in ink pen (bottom row, center left). The mustache, or lack thereof, in these composites and Emily's descriptions became a major issue in the case.

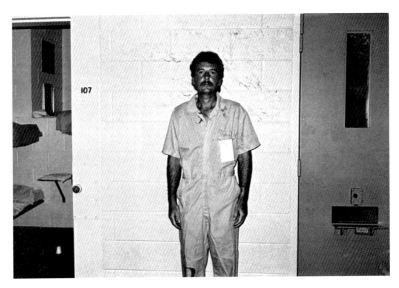

A photograph of John Brady Balfa in the Gregg County Jail in Longview, Texas, on January 12, 1983. The photo was taken with the intention of creating a lineup to show to Emily LaHaye when Balfa was an initial suspect in the kidnapping case. Per the testimony of FBI Agent Owen Odom, the photo was never shown to her. The defense used it to demonstrate that Balfa had a substantial mustache only six days after the kidnapping, despite Emily's description of a "clean-shaven" suspect.

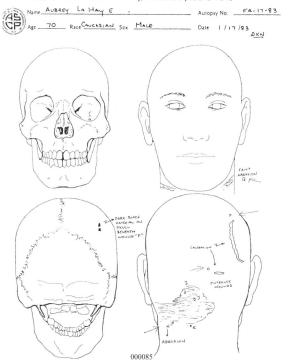

Head, surface and skeletal anatomy, anterior and posterior views.

Name AUBREY La HAYE E   Autopsy No. FA-17-83

Age 70   Race CAUCASIAN Sex MALE   Date 1/17/83
                                                    DKN

FAINT
ABRASION
R

DARK BLACK
MATERIAL ON
SKULL
BENEATH
WOUND "P"

LACERATION

ENTRANCE
WOUNDS

ABRASION

000085

From Aubrey LaHaye's autopsy file, as documented by Dr. George McCormick: diagrams of Aubrey's head wounds when he was found in the Bayou Nezpique, including the blows to the head that likely killed him.

An article published in the January 27, 1983, edition of the *Ville Platte Gazette*, asking the public to notify investigators if they had any information related to the pictured tire rim, which was attached to the body of Aubrey LaHaye when he was found in the Bayou Nezpique on January 16, 1983. **Courtesy of the *Ville Platte Gazette*.**

INFORMATION SOUGHT -- Investigators in the case of the kidnapping death of Aubrey G. LaHaye released this photo today of the tire rims which were used to weigh down the body of LaHaye to the bottom of Bayou Nezpique. One of the rims is "distinctive," according to investigators, and anyone knowing anything whatsoever about this particular tire rim in this photo is asked to call the Evangeline Parish Sheriff's office or the Evangeline Parish District Attorney's office, the Evangeline Parish Sheriff's office or the FBI with that information. Any information will be kept confidential. See accompanying story.

Investigators Ask Information On 'Distinctive' Tire Rim

The Federal Bureau of Investigation today released copies of photographs of the two tire rims which were used to weigh down the body of Aubrey G. LaHaye in Bayou Nezpique.

Ruby Guillory, investigator for the Evangeline Parish District Attorney's office, said one of the rims is "distinctive" in its features. Police are asking, in releasing the photograph of the tire rim, that anyone with any type of information whatsoever concerning the tire rim

in question please contact the District Attorney's office, the Evangeline Parish Sheriff's office or the Federal Bureau of Investigation.

In the meantime another press conference has been called for 10 a.m. today concerning the LaHaye case investigation.

A spokesman for the FBI in New Orleans had said earlier this week no substantial progress can be reported at this date in the kidnapping death of LaHaye, a well-known Evangeline Parish

businessman, but that investigation continues into the case.

LaHaye was kidnapped from his home near Reddell in the early morning hours of Jan. 6 and was found dead in Bayou Nezpique Sunday, Jan. 16.

Funeral services for LaHaye were conducted Tuesday, Jan. 18, in St. Ann's Catholic Church in Mamou.

(For a special tribute to the life of Aubrey G. LaHaye, see page 4, this Section.)

June 4, 1984   850100

Charles A. Watts
Harrison County Jail
1300 29th Ave.
Gulfport, Ms. 39501

To Evangline Parish Sheriff's Dept.
Evangline Parish
Ville Platt, Louisiana

Dear Sir:

Because of my need to remedy a problem I presently have in Livingston Parish, this letter is to provide you with some information concerning a murder in your area. And if you feel that you want additional date on this subject then we can discuss the deal I want.

There is a fellow named Danny Singleton whose incarcerated here at the Harrison County Jail, with me, and he has told me about a banker from Mamou, La. that was kidnapped from his home to be held for ransom. It was a fake ransom demand and the banker had been killed for someone. Danny told me he was beat & throwen into a bayou. His son-in-law, (which Danny was suppose to know), has a deal made, and Danny had gotten a couple of fellows from Mobile, Ala., and they had met with some other fellow concerning the deal. After the business was completed, Danny had took them back to Mobile, Ala.

If you are interested in additional information about this subject, then I'm willing to provide enough to let you know that I do know something about it and once a deal can be made about my problem in Livingston, Louisiana, then we can determine how much you need from me.

Charles Watts

A letter found in the Evangeline Parish District Attorney's file, written to the Evangeline Parish Sheriff's Department by Charles Watts on June 4, 1984. Watts, a prisoner at the Harrison County Jail in Gulfport, Mississippi, recounted a story he'd heard from a fellow inmate, Danny Singleton, regarding "a banker from Mamou, Louisiana, that was kidnapped from his home to be held for ransom." He wrote that, according to Singleton, "the son-in- law . . . has a deal made."

The front page of the March 11, 1985, edition of the *Ville Platte Gazette*, picturing John Brady Balfa being transferred to the St. Landry Parish Jail on March 8, after his arraignment in Evangeline Parish for the robbery, kidnapping, and murder of Aubrey LaHaye, to which he pled not guilty. **Courtesy of the *Ville Platte Gazette*.**

Jordan,

Christmas wishes from the heart.

Merry Christmas to you and your family.

John Brady

The Christmas card I received from John Brady Balfa in December 2017. Despite multiple letters and outreach efforts on my part, this is the only correspondence I've ever received directly from him.

(above) St. Ann's Cemetery, where Aubrey, Emily, Glenn, Janie, Smokey, and Robert are all buried. In the background are the Mamou Rice Dryers, funded and built by Aubrey LaHaye, his brother Elvin, and his business partner Leslie Ardoin in 1949. Local reporters at the time described them as the "Cadillac" of all rice dryers in Southwest Louisiana. They remain an instantly recognizable feature of the Mamou skyline.

LaHaye Road (middle photo), where Aubrey and Emily first built their homestead and established LaHaye Brothers Farm in 1938. They lived in this house for almost fifty years before Aubrey's murder. Today, it is owned by Aubrey and Emily's grandson, my godfather ("Parrain") Danny, and the two-mile stretch is home to dozens of other LaHaye descendants. **Photos by Olivia Luz Perillo.**

Aubrey and Emily's last living child, Wayne LaHaye, and his wife, Susan—or, as I know them, Papa and Mommee. They stand in their pasture on LaHaye Road, the last remnant of the LaHaye Brothers' cattle empire. **Photo by Olivia Luz Perillo.**

My dad, Marcel LaHaye, who was eighteen years old when his grandfather was kidnapped and murdered. The event altered the trajectory of his life, and ultimately of mine. It is he who set me on this journey and guided me all the way through. Photo by my mother, Chantel LaHaye, on their new property, which runs right up to the Bayou Nezpique.

The Bayou Nezpique, where my great-grandfather Aubrey LaHaye's body was discovered on January 16, 1983. **Photo by Olivia Luz Perillo.**

years as the chief forensic anthropologist and chief deputy medical examiner for special investigations for the Department of Defense Armed Forces Medical Examiner's Office. And he testified as a forensics expert in some of the most intensely publicized cases of the twenty-first century, including that of Casey Anthony and of Adnan Syed, whose case was made a sensation in the first season of the podcast *Serial*.

Rodriguez had started working in Caddo Parish as the deputy coroner under McCormick just a few months before the trial. In testifying to his expertise, he told Cullen he had made about three hundred time-since-death approximations and had never yet been proven wrong.

Cullen was unimpressed by the experimental, revolutionary nature of Rodriguez's field, and objected to his testifying based on "veracity or exactness of science." Judge Coreil overruled the objection.

In his testimony, Rodriguez explained that he had used climatological data, the autopsy report, and the images taken in the morgue to determine a time-since-death estimation on Aubrey's body. Because water tends to be anywhere from three to ten degrees cooler than the air at any given time, and bodies underwater decompose at roughly half the rate of bodies on land—he calculated that the time-since-death was between ten and twelve days before January 17. Since Aubrey had been alive until at least 5:30 a.m. on January 6, he had to have died that day or the next. And based on McCormick's testimony, he likely died shortly after Emily saw him walk out the door. *Exactly* during the small window John Brady could still have been in Evangeline Parish.

The Alibi

To keep Pucheu from introducing John Brady's colorful criminal history to the jury, Julie Cullen could not put him on the stand. So the closest thing the jurors got to "John Brady's side of the story" came in the form of the four statements he had made to law enforcement between January 1983 and September 1984.

With slight variations between each statement—the main matter of concern was timing. Over the course of the four interviews, the time John Brady claimed he left his dad's house changed from 5 a.m., to 5:30 a.m., to 6 a.m.—inconsistencies that typically check with the basic imprecision of human memory.

But the difference between 5 a.m. and 6 a.m. was huge here. The Balfa home, according to testimony by Detective Rudy Guillory—who had driven many of the significant routes in this case as part of his investigation—was 8.8 miles from the Aubrey LaHaye home. To be knocking on Emily's doorstep at 5:15, John Brady would have had to leave his house by around 5 a.m. This is true even allowing for some error on Emily's part—as phone calls reporting the kidnapping to Glenn, Guillory, and Thomas Lupkey were reported to have gone through by 5:45 a.m. 5 a.m. was the absolute latest John Brady could have left his father's house to possibly have time to get to LaHaye Road, perform the abduction, and leave. If there was solid evidence that he had left at 5:15 or later, then he couldn't have reasonably been the abductor.

The best the defense had was Harry Balfa's testimony. John Brady's father pleadingly told the jury that when he woke up to use the restroom on the morning of January 6, 1983, he had found it occupied by John Brady. When he looked at the clock, he saw it was 5:08 a.m. Hearing him, his son called, "Daddy, you need the bathroom? I'm through." He then opened the door and stepped aside into the hallway.

When Harry came back out, John Brady asked him if he wanted any coffee. Harry wasn't feeling well and said he was going back to bed. He remembered the way the kettle was sitting on the stove, the water already boiling.

According to Harry's telling, before John Brady left, he came down the hall and poked his head into his father's bedroom to let him know he was off. Harry told him, "Be careful on the road. And if you need, let Daddy know. Call."

Pucheu asked Harry if he'd be surprised to know John Brady told the FBI he had left the house at about 5 a.m. Harry said he would.

Assuming John Brady *did* leave the house at 5 a.m. or slightly before—giving him time to get to the LaHayes' doorstep—there remains the question of whether it is possible for him to committed the kidnapping and murder before leaving for Texas.

To take John Brady's own word for it is to place him at the Best Western at "noon," "shortly before noon," "shortly after," or at "12:30." He told Owen Odom the drive took him about five or six hours, meaning he would have had to start driving west by 6 a.m. at the earliest, 7:30 at the latest.

This still allows for just under two hours for John Brady to have left the LaHaye house, killed Aubrey, taken him to the Nezpique (or taken him to the Nezpique, then killed him), tied him to the rims, dumped him in the water, and made the ransom call. It's a tight window, but—especially if the whole thing was well planned ahead of time—it isn't impossible.

Of course, John Brady's own word, alone, meant little. His father's testimony was helpful, but it directly contradicted John Brady's own statements to authorities, in which he repeatedly claimed no one saw him leave the house that morning. Of course, Pucheu was sure to point this out. For the alibi to be totally exculpatory, Cullen needed more than the defendant's father's sleepy recollections. And she needed those two hours to be accounted for. She called her next witnesses, Deborah Kinney and her mother, Geraldine.

Immediately, their testimony as to the time frame of John Brady's activities on January 6 conflicted with John Brady's. Both placed him in Atlanta, Texas, at 10:30 a.m.

According to Geraldine, this is when John Brady called her from the Best Western to let her know he had arrived. She was working as the manager of the Kentucky Fried Chicken across the street from the hotel and was going to open the doors when the phone rang.

She said that later, John Brady and Debbie came by the restaurant to visit—before the lunch rush, around 11 a.m. Then, the couple left, drove around, and came back around 1:30 p.m. to visit some more. That evening, a little before 6 p.m., John Brady came to the house to pick up Debbie for their double date.

The next day, she testified, John Brady came back to their house for lunch. Geraldine's husband was reading the newspaper and noticed that someone had been kidnapped in Mamou, Louisiana. "How close is that to your home?" Geraldine had asked him. John Brady had taken the paper, read the article. "I knew him," he said.

Geraldine told the court that on their drive to Evangeline Parish from Atlanta, Texas, for this trial, they had taken the time to clock their mileage and time. She said the drive from the McDonald's—which sits right beside the Best Western in Atlanta—to Harry Balfa's house took five hours exactly, was 238 miles driven at 55 miles per hour in Thanksgiving Day traffic.

Pucheu picked up his pen, made a note.

He made another later during Cullen's questioning, when the defense attorney asked Geraldine about John Brady's marriage to Debbie, and Geraldine was unable to recall the date of the wedding.

When Pucheu got his chance to cross-examine her, the first question he asked was "Where did you sleep last night?"

"At Mr. Balfa's house." A clear violation of witness sequestration.

Pucheu asked Geraldine if she and her daughter had discussed the case with the Balfas. Geraldine responded that they had. He nodded, then moved on to the wedding date.

"Tell me—tell the jury why you remember *so much* about January 6 and 7 of '83, and so little about your daughter's wedding?"

"We were glad to have John down there when he came," she said.

"That's not answering my question."

"That's why I remember it. We had so looked forward to it."

Pucheu gestured toward John Brady, whose eyes were downcast, refusing to engage with the drama unfolding before him. "You weren't glad when he married your daughter?"

"Oh, we were glad."

"You were not glad to have John in the family?"

"We are thrilled to have John in the family."

"But you don't remember the day he married your daughter?"

"No, I don't."

On the stand, Geraldine was becoming increasingly agitated, and Pucheu was leaning into it—finally smacking his underlying suggestions right on the table in a direct insinuation of perjury. "Are you telling the truth about everything you've testified to in reference to this case? Did anyone—myself, anybody in John's family, John, Debbie, anybody involved in this case—suggest to you at any time that you should lie or should fabricate anything in order to assist John in this matter?"

"I don't have to lie. John was with us. John called. We don't have to lie about it."

After Geraldine's testimony, the judge ordered a recess for lunch. Out of the presence of the jury, Pucheu objected to allowing Deborah Kinney's testimony—based on her mother's own admission of their breaking sequestration.

That Cullen either allowed the Kinneys to stay at the Balfas, or was somehow unaware of it, mystifies me. These two women, along with Harry, were the bones of her strategy to establish John Brady's alibi. Each of these testimonies was already subject to doubt; they all came from people who held some allegiance to him. In addition, their accounts directly conflicted with John Brady's statements, which Cullen had full access to prior to the trial. Why allow the chance for any additional suspicion to cloud their trustworthiness?

In response to Pucheu's objection, Cullen argued that the purpose of sequestration was to prevent witnesses from acquiring knowledge from courtroom testimony—and at that point neither Harry nor Tim had yet testified. They had never been in the courtroom; they could not share information from witness testimony with the Kinneys.

To my surprise, Judge Coreil, who had almost uniformly ruled against Cullen's motions at every chance until now, ruled in her favor.

When they called the jury in, Debbie took the stand. She corroborated Geraldine's testimony, saying her mother called around 10:30 a.m. on January 6, 1983, to let her know John Brady had arrived and was waiting for her at the Best Western. She was able to pinpoint this time because she had been watching *The Price Is Right*, which ran from 10 a.m. to 11 a.m., when she got the call.

Debbie went straight to him, she said, arriving a little before 11. Her account mirrored her mother's, telling of how she and John Brady had gone to KFC to visit before lunchtime. Afterward, the couple went to buy some cigarettes, drove around town a bit, and went back to her mother's house to watch a movie. She took John Brady back to his hotel room around 4 p.m., where they sat and talked for a while. She left him, and he met her back at her mother's around 6 p.m. for their double date.

This, it should be noted, is a significant departure from John Brady's initial January 11, 1983, statement to FBI agent Lloyd Harrel, in which he said he drove about thirty minutes to Lodi, Texas, to visit with the Sunland Construction crew there. According to that account, Debbie dropped him off at the hotel around 3 p.m., and he stayed on the worksite until 6 p.m.

Debbie said that after their date, which ended around 11 p.m., she and John Brady spent some time in his motel room. She left around 3 or 4 in the morning.

Before tendering, Cullen asked Debbie why she and John Brady ended their marriage. "John always wanted kids," she said. "He always wanted a bunch of kids, and me, I wanted to work. And he didn't want me to work, and he pressured me to have a baby, and I wasn't ready."

Pucheu smiled.

In cross, the first question he asked her was, "You say you're not ready for a baby?"

"Yes, sir. Right."

"And yet you slept with John the night of January—"

Cullen stood up. "Your Honor! I'm going to object to this line of questioning."

"Ah, it's a perfectly good question," Pucheu said, hands out, grinning.

Cullen was furious. "Your Honor, I strongly object to the question. Whether Mr. Pucheu thinks it's a good question or not, I object to the question."

Judge Coreil overruled her, allowing Pucheu to continue his taunting— "I presume, young lady, y'all were not playing tiddlywinks?"

Debbie scrambled to clarify that they had not "slept together"— allowing Pucheu to initiate a debate over what exactly that term consists of. At one point, Debbie desperately looked around at the room, saying "I don't know, I'm confused."

He was trying to mar her character, but he was also suggesting something nastier: *Oh, you divorced this murderer because he wanted a baby? Yeah, right.*

It's a tactic one assumes might have been effective in a small, conservative, Catholic town in the 1980s. But reading it in 2018 as I was, it aroused an instant revulsion toward the district attorney—intensified by how the judge allowed it to continue, as Cullen objected and objected.

Changing course, Pucheu asked Debbie if it would surprise her to learn John Brady said he arrived in Atlanta at noon and met her between 12:30 and 12:45.

". . . but it was earlier," she said.

Throughout the course of the trial, three different time spans were given as to the length of time it takes to get from Evangeline Parish to Atlanta, Texas, or vice versa. John Brady consistently said the trip took five to six hours. The Kinneys claimed it took them five. Guillory, who made the trip twice, said it took him four hours and fifteen to twenty minutes.

If the Kinneys' testimonies were true, and John Brady was in Atlanta as early as 10:30 a.m.—his window to get Aubrey from alive in his bedroom to dead in the Nezpique narrows to an hour, per the shortest driving time. Impossible? Perhaps not. But the probability tapers. This also means John Brady could not possibly have been the person who made the 7:10 ransom call, which was determined by the FBI to be a local call. He would have had to be on the road by, at latest, 6:15 a.m.

All this depended, of course, on whether Harry, Geraldine, and Debbie were telling the truth. On whether John Brady was telling the truth. And they couldn't all be. Who would the jury believe?

At least one aspect of John Brady's alibi was corroborated—though not before the jury—by the hotel records. While questioning Detective Guillory about his trip to Atlanta to clock the time, Cullen asked him if he had spoken to anyone at the Best Western. He admitted that he had and had retrieved some records there.

"Who is in possession of those records?" Cullen asked him.

"The district attorney."

Cullen then requested a brief recess. When everyone returned to the courtroom fifteen minutes later, she held up the record Guillory had mentioned, which she'd just retrieved from Pucheu. The document was a Xerox copy of the Best Western's check-in records and indicated John Brady Balfa had in fact checked into the motel, Room 116, on January 6.

"Mr. Guillory, to your knowledge, has anyone in the District Attorney's Office ever advised me that you all were in possession of this document?"

At this, Pucheu stood up to object—"Your Honor, we better remove the jury. I think this is highly prejudicial to the State."

After the jury was dismissed, Pucheu turned to Judge Coreil. "What is she doing? She is trying to make the State look like we are concealing some evidence."

Cullen reminded the judge that in her discovery motions made in March, she had requested access to *any and all information that could possibly be exculpatory.* "They have known all along that my client checked into that hotel on January 6. They have known that I have been trying to get in touch, or get copies of, these records." Cullen said she had even gone to Atlanta herself to speak to the people at the Best Western, who told her they had already given the records away to "some law enforcement person" months before. "I have been trying since January of 1985 to get a copy of this and I find out now it has been sitting in the district attorney's file since September of last year."

Pucheu argued that Cullen already was in possession of John Brady's own statements and had witnesses to prove he had been in Texas on January 6. This document, a Xerox copy, was not certified and couldn't be used as evidence anyway.

The document couldn't be introduced by itself, she rebutted, but she could have subpoenaed someone from the Best Western to verify it. "What the district attorney feels is exculpatory or corroborative of my client's testimony is not for him to decide," she went on. "I was entitled to this, and I did not get it. That is my objection . . . this is just one more occurrence of what has happened in this case from the time this man was indicted."

Judge Coreil ruled that ultimately, the evidence in question, as a Xerox copy, was hearsay and couldn't be used as evidence. The trial would proceed.

What interests me about this interaction is the omission of the *other* records in existence, obtained by the FBI in January of 1983, which indicated John Brady had checked into the hotel specifically *by noon* on January 6. The sentence reads loud and clear: "Hotel records indicate he checked into motel between 9 a.m. and noon, January 6, 1983."

The Motive

B Y THE TUESDAY AFTER THANKSGIVING, THE EIGHTH DAY OF trial, Billy Pucheu had laid out the bulk of his case. He'd connected the dots—rims on the body to rims in the Balfa yard, rope on the body to rope in the yard. And Emily had pointed right at him, right there in the courtroom. "He was the man," she said.

But he still had to answer the resounding question: *Why?*

It was all about money, Pucheu posed. Isn't it always?

His last witnesses were a series of five local individuals who had, in some way, been involved in John Brady's financial struggles—which reached their peak in 1982, leading right up to Aubrey LaHaye's murder.

Pucheu called Eddie Soileau, owner of Sunland Construction, to the stand. John Brady's boss. Soileau testified that in January of 1982, he lent John Brady $5,000, which had been paid in full via money taken out of John Brady's paycheck over the course of the next two years. Soileau then testified that John Brady had approached him, just six weeks after receiving the loan, asking for $12,000 more. "He indicated he was in bad financial trouble," Soileau said. "I told him I couldn't do that."

Over the course of 1982, John Brady attempted to acquire loans through his hometown bank, Guaranty, which he had been visiting with his father since he was a young boy. They'd deposit small bits of cash into his checking account, smiling at the round man in the suit who greeted them by the door, a cigar hanging out of his mouth.

John Brady's first petition to Aubrey was for a signature loan of $3,000, for which the banker recommended he get a cosigner. Harry testified that he had planned to sign for it but had gotten sick. Lying in the hospital bed after having most of his stomach removed, he told John Brady, "Son, I'm sorry. I can't sign that . . . I don't know if I can keep working after this." Without a cosigner, Aubrey wouldn't approve the loan.

He returned a few months later, applying for another $3,000 signature loan. Aubrey was in the process of approving it but changed his mind at the last minute when someone alerted him to John Brady's bad checks.

The third time, John Brady was asking for a $6,000 loan, which he told Aubrey was to purchase a vehicle. Since an auto loan would be secured, Aubrey agreed to approve it and told Joyce Reed to get the details together. Then, John Brady clarified. The loan wasn't to finance the vehicle, it was for the down payment—another signature loan. Aubrey had to turn him down again.

During Reed's testimony, Julie Cullen asked her if any of these interactions had been recorded on paper. "I've never known Mr. Aubrey to take a written application on anybody," she answered. "He knew most families. He went by families, the appearance, you know, the way a person presented their application verbally."

John Brady did somehow manage to get his vehicle loan. According to testimony from a banker at American Security Bank in Ville Platte, in August 1982, John Brady signed for an $8,569.08 loan, payable in thirty-six monthly installments of $238.03 beginning in September. The pickup was the same one he'd be driving a few weeks later in Longview, with the Edwards '83 sticker on the back and no license plate, when the cops caught up with him after he raped the woman at the 7-Eleven. It was the same truck he'd drive from Evangeline Parish to Atlanta, Texas, on January 6, 1983. Remarkably, the owner of the dealership cosigned the loan himself.

By November 1982, it was delinquent. In December, the bank was demanding the entire balance back in full. In January 1983, John Brady also had to start paying back $7,500 of student loans, which Guaranty Bank held, at a rate of $113 a month.

On top of all this, according to a Guaranty Bank bookkeeper, Ramona Ortwein, between the dates of November 17, 1982, and January 6, 1983, John Brady had signed off on $7,200 of dishonored checks at Guaranty, which included payment to his lawyers and bondsmen for the Longview rape case.

In total, on the day Aubrey was kidnapped, John Brady—out on bail and accused of rape—was on the hook for almost $16,000 (equal to more than $50,000 today).

For whatever reason, John Brady's gambling addiction was never mentioned to the jury. But knowing of it as I do, it lingers beneath each and every dollar—multiplying them in undocumented dealings, raising the stakes.

What sort of state was he in, in January 1983?

Did the weight of his situation steal his sleep? Did it ignite that wild impulsiveness within him, the one that had gotten him into so much trouble in the past? Maybe he still held some sort of misaligned hope, that characteristic arrogance. He just needed one good bet.

Was John Brady Balfa the kind of person who might be driven, by the threat of financial ruin, to commit murder?

I ask this question now, almost forty years later—knowing so much, knowing so little. But the jury had far less to work with: only a man very bad at paying his bills, who had a reason to dislike my great-grandfather just before he was killed.

And you already know how this trial ends.

Closing Arguments

AY IT PLEASE THE COURT: LADIES AND GENTLEMEN OF the jury: It's been a long nine days. . . . Here we are in the State of Louisiana, fortunate enough to have what we consider the most perfect system of government yet known to man" —a system whose leader, Governor Edwin Edwards, was in court himself that very same day, accused of mail fraud, obstruction of justice, and bribery.

"[This is] a system where when somebody like the defendant is charged with crimes—murder, armed robbery, aggravated kidnapping—he gets to be tried by members of his own community. That sure is the epitome of justice."

This was the introduction for Richard Vidrine's closing statements on December 4, 1985. Billy Pucheu had given him the honor.

In 2017, almost forty years since the trial, Vidrine recites the beginning to me in that little meeting room at the courthouse, the DA file splayed before us, his arms gesturing to an invisible jury. He reads from a legal pad filled with his notes—the very same he had referenced on the trial's last day. He's transported back to his glory days, when his peachy hair was a more robust red and his college football body a less distant thing. But his voice still rolls out from his chest, deep and firm, the rhythms of lawyerspeak still instinct.

Julie Cullen's closing arguments—which I read neatly typed in the official transcript some years later—found their romanticism elsewhere. This trial had left her with little love for the machinations of the American justice system, after all. Instead, she drew on the quiet, and the not-so-quiet, dramas she'd witnessed unfold during her time in this peculiar little parish. She set the scene, asking the jurors to imagine themselves omniscient observers, on January 6, 1983:

"Ladies and gentlemen, you need to think back to a cold, dark, wintery morning. It's been raining a lot lately, but apparently, the rain has stopped. It's not quite dawn and you're in a relatively sleepy, quiet rural area, Mamou. A lot of people are getting up early. People work hard in this area of the country.

"It's about five o'clock in the morning. Mrs. Aubrey LaHaye's getting up to set her pot. It's five o'clock in the morning. John Brady Balfa's getting up to drive to Texas to see his girlfriend. It's probably five o'clock in the morning. And Mr. Harry Balfa Sr.'s getting up to go to the bathroom. It's 5:08 in the morning."

The attorneys each took their time, walking the jury through the events of January 6, 1983—Vidrine calling the abductor "John Balfa," Cullen calling him "someone." They relaid their arguments, reemphasized the high points. Vidrine kept telling the jury he was "sure they would agree" that the State had proved its case beyond a shadow of a doubt. Cullen kept pleading with them to consider all the details, very, very carefully—to let the seriousness of sending a man to prison for his entire life weigh upon their conscience. "I don't want to use the term, 'play God,' but . . ."

In 2017, Vidrine tells me how, in preparation for this finale, he'd gone into the courtroom before the jury came in. He'd laid out each of the automobile rims in the four corners of the space. He asked the jury to think of the evidence as a jigsaw puzzle. "The pieces of the puzzle fit," he said. He pointed, one by one, to the three corners of the room where he'd placed the Balfa rims. "We went to the Balfa residence, and we found three trailer rims. And, *boy*, they looked for that fourth one. They were surprised, Charles and Harry Sr. They were surprised they couldn't find that fourth one. But where was the fourth one?"

He pointed with both hands to the last corner: "It was tied to Mr. LaHaye's body."

"I was real proud of that whole orchestration," Vidrine tells me, grinning.

It isn't until years later, when I review this speech in the form of the court transcript, that I catch the error. *Trailer rims*, Vidrine had said. But the Balfa rims the analysts had connected to Aubrey's body, the ones that "could have been a match," were the automobile rims. The trailer rims had not matched at all. Vidrine's closing statements reveal that the State didn't understand its own evidence. But no one, not even Julie Cullen, noticed the blunder—an indication of how incomprehensible the forensic testimony had truly been, to everyone. Including, of course, the jury.

Despite missing her chance to point out the State's false representation of their own evidence, Cullen tried to emphasize the significance, or lack thereof, of those two words: *could have*.

"What did all those experts say? *Could have* come from the same source. Ladies and gentlemen, what the State wants you to do in this case is convict John Balfa and send him to prison for the rest of his life on testimony and evidence that says it *could have* come from the same source. . . . We're talking proof beyond a reasonable doubt, not maybe, not possibly."

Even if the rims and rope and paint *were* a true, exact match, she allowed, what evidence has the State shown to prove John Brady is the person who took the rope and rims from the Balfa property? She reminded them that the yard and junk pile were not monitored or fenced; anyone could have come and taken them. Cullen even went so far as to point out that John Brady's brothers and father—who had as much access to the property as he did—were never investigated as the person who could have tied the materials to the body.

Throughout both closing arguments, the mustache loomed large. As Vidrine reminded the jury of testimony from various witnesses, he'd stop to ask them: "Did that man have a mustache? Can you even remember?"

When Cullen got her chance, she turned to the jury—"Al Robillard, did he have a mustache? *Did he not?*" Of course, all of you remember that he did, she insisted—rejecting Vidrine's attempt at ridicule. But even if the jury didn't remember, she appealed—"Would you put Al Robillard's life on the line for the validity of the description you would make of him?"

At this point, Cullen turned her frustration upon Emily, raising her voice and relinquishing all grace to the surviving victim of the crime that had brought them here. She reminded the jury of how the widow had requested a second look at not just John Brady, but also another member of that lineup in Opelousas. "*Why*, Mrs. LaHaye? *Why*, if you're so sure, why were they brought back?"

She mimicked Emily's testimony: "'Well, the police officers suggested it. To satisfy the police officers.' . . . She's made *damn* sure that she's not going to let you know that she's doubtful . . . Oh, she's sure now! She wasn't sure in September, but she's even less sure of the person's looks and the person's identification and description when it all first happened, when it should have been most fresh in her mind."

Vidrine put it to the jury very simply— "Either you're going to have to believe Mrs. Emily LaHaye, or you're going to believe the defendant's family from Texas. Who do you believe?"—before pointing out all the problems with the Kinneys' testimonies. In fact, he said, even if they didn't believe Emily, the jury would have to choose whether to believe the Kinneys or John Brady Balfa himself, since their statements on his time of arrival in Atlanta conflicted with his so significantly. He posed: Are the Kinneys the most believable people in this courtroom? Of course, they weren't.

Speaking of Geraldine, he said outright: "It's obvious she was lying on the stand. You remember her testimony, her demeanor, on the stand? She was hostile. She was evasive . . . Do you remember that lady? She's the same person who can't remember her daughter's wedding date, but she *does* remember January 6, 1983. She was trying to protect the defendant."

To close, Cullen asked the jury to consider the exact logic Pucheu had laid out at the beginning of the trial, only now as evidence that John Brady *couldn't* reasonably be the murderer. John Brady had had a savings account at Guaranty since he was a teenager, and he had conducted business there every semester for his school loans. His father had done business there. He and Aubrey were familiar to each other.

"You have to decide if this person . . . instead of going to see his girlfriend like he told everyone and like everyone was expecting, instead he goes to the home of a man he knows, without a mask, walks in and says, 'You know me. My name is Vidrine. I live around the corner.'"

John Brady's financial situation, she argued, was not a believable motive—"If people killed for $15,000, bankruptcy courts wouldn't exist. Loan companies wouldn't exist. People are in debt all the time." John Brady was someone who functioned in society, she said. He had gone to college, had kept a job. In January 1983, he was engaged to be married. "He was looking forward to a new future," she said. "He would not go to someone he knew—that he knew would recognize him—to rob him on his way to Texas."

The jury entered deliberations at 3:45 p.m. And then, everyone waited. A woman sold pralines in the courthouse hallway. The LaHayes sat with the DA's staff in Billy Pucheu's office; the Balfas and the Kinneys across the hall in a room with Julie Cullen. The reporters whispered in groups, reviewing their notes. Most everyone expected the verdict to be delivered the following day. But after just over an hour, at 4:50 p.m., everyone was called back into the courtroom.

"Ladies and gentlemen," boomed Judge Coreil, "have you chosen a foreman and reached a verdict?"

The foreman, the nurse who had traveled to Mexico with my grand-parents, stood, "Yes, we have, Your Honor."

The deputy clerk of court retrieved the written verdict from her, then read the document aloud. "Count number one, that John Brady Balfa at the Parish of Evangeline, State of Louisiana, on or about the sixth day of January 1983, committed second-degree murder of Aubrey G. LaHaye. Verdict: Guilty. Is that y'all's verdict?"

"Yes," said the foreman.

"Count number two, that John Brady Balfa at the Parish of Evangeline, State of Louisiana, on or about the sixth day of January 1983, committed aggravated kidnapping of Aubrey G. LaHaye. Verdict: Guilty. Is that y'all's verdict?"

"Yes."

"Count number three, that John Brady Balfa at the Parish of Evangeline, State of Louisiana, on or about the sixth day of January 1983, while armed with a dangerous weapon, robbed Aubrey G. LaHaye. Verdict: Guilty. Is that y'all's verdict?"

"Yes."

Collectively, the LaHayes retain almost no memories of this moment. When I ask them about it, they recall a general sense of relief, certainly. Relief that it was all over. But no one remembers the verdict as a moment of "Thank God." It's as though it were the inevitable conclusion, as though this were always how things would end. Now, they could all go home, and never speak of this again.

As for the Balfas, who occupied almost the entire left side of the courtroom—a local journalist described the way they sniffled and sobbed, listening to the jury affirm their worst fears. Debbie sat straight as a rod, tears silently pouring down her face. Harry's entire body slumped forward, one of John Brady's brothers patting his back beside him.

John Brady Balfa, they wrote, betrayed no emotion as the word *Guilty* rang out, again and again—his fate sealed. He would live out the rest of his life at Louisiana State Penitentiary at Angola, the "Alcatraz of the South."

PART IV

The Mystery

At Least They're Near the Light

'VE ALWAYS HATED MAUSOLEUMS. COLD, CONDENSED CITIES, shining walls of death dressed in faded silk flowers.

PawPaw Aubrey helped fund his own, was on the building committee for it. In the newspapers of the time, the project was celebrated as state of the art, a modern addition to St. Ann's burial options, built of imported marble embellished with bronze.

I haven't visited MawMaw Emily since the day we slid her casket into its slot in 2006. That day, against the scraping of slate on wood, I remember asking my dad if they would move her to the ground later. Since then, we've both, half joking, proclaimed to anyone who will listen that we want to be buried in the *Platin* cemetery near our house, where every grave lies level with the dirt, surrounded on all sides by open rice fields and Miller's Lake sunsets.

It's not that St. Ann's graveyard isn't beautiful in its little way—a square carved out of the prairie, flowered tombstones against a backdrop of the rice dryers PawPaw Aubrey built all those years ago. It's that the humidity here is thick, the wildflowers the same as those in my parents' front yard. It's that I know these last names, every one of them: Guillory, Morein, DeVillier, Fuselier, Fontenot, Vidrine, Soileau, Deshotels, Molitor, LaHaye.

I feel uncomfortable here, mortality laid so directly atop my home. Approaching thirty, I've yet to know true mourning. I'm remarkably unfamiliar with the act of grieving, with the experience of loss. I've watched from a distance as death reaches into the lives around mine, pulling a four-wheeler backward onto the tiny body of my sixth-grade classmate; wrapping a senior football player's car around a tree; nudging the three-year-old I once babysat off his father's lap and tumbling out the tractor door; stifling my coworker's father in the summer heat after Hurricane Ida; projecting two old men out of their fishing boat into the Atchafalaya, and then my brother's two teenage friends into another body of water a year later. At their funerals, I sit in the back, clutching my heart in between my chest bones, reaching in vain to grasp and carry my residual share of their families' suffering. I stop short of immersing myself in it, every time. I backtrack in terror, reminded that someday my world will break open too.

Inside the mausoleum, though, I try to at least place myself in front of it, of death. The room opens at the top of a T, with a hallway extending to a stone altar against stained glass, sunlight pooling fractured beams and pastel drippings onto the tiled floor. Littered all down the hallways are stray flower petals, faded by time and sunlight. Dead mosquitoes sit in piles, having found no lifeblood here. They join the resting on the stone-cold floor. The few still living encircle me. Buzzing around my ankles and up my skirt.

I find MawMaw Emily and PawPaw Aubrey's graves in the corner, on the bottom shelf right up against the glass. *At least they're close to the ground*, I think, the dirt only a few feet below these tiles. PawPaw's epitaph reads, "An honest man is the noblest work of God." MawMaw's: "Go. Bear much fruit that will remain." *At least they're near the light.*

Try as I might, I find myself unable to conjure any sentimentality about it all. No part of me, within or without, feels a stirring of Maw-Maw's presence. Wherever she is now, I feel to my core that it isn't here.

And as for Aubrey . . .

He would be so proud of you, someone who barely knows me, who didn't know him, told me recently, learning of my quest. It's the sort of thing you say, I guess.

But I'm skeptical.

I imagine the stern man looking out at me from MawMaw Emily's bedroom wall. The man whose pockets jingled when he walked, who drove to Sugartown to buy the family watermelons in the summer, whose cleanest suit smelled of cigar. I can imagine myself a child, my face buried in his chest, his big hands rubbing my back.

But as an adult, as a woman—there is a void there that I do not know what to do with. A silence resounding from the silences in my grand-mother's memory, my great-aunts' and my aunts'—whose recollections of PawPaw are held in the ways he treated their children, and how he worked with their husbands. Aubrey was a man's man. A perfect gen-tleman, a wall of propriety separating all he was interested in, all he was passionate about, from the world of women. Their inner lives were of little interest to him, with the exception, perhaps, of his wife. I wish I could ask her about it, about the selves they exchanged behind the walls of their home.

"Are you proud of me, Pawpaw?" I ask later, away from his grave, the question released into *my* world, landing among the books and the dog hair and the citrus-scented candles. "Is this what you would have wanted?" His great-granddaughter, running around Evangeline Parish asking questions of his business dealings, his bank? Speaking the un-spoken horrors back into existence, dreaming of bodies in bayous? In certain corners of my mind, I see him telling me to sit down, be quiet, let it all lie.

But in others, a gentle whisper, a grasp, and a shake on the shoulder: "You're getting closer."

There's More We
Don't Know

'VE ALWAYS BEEN SURE BALFA DID IT," MY DAD TELLS ME. "HE
did it. Or he was involved. But I mean, I think most people agree
there's no way he did this just because of a loan. So, why? *Why* would
he do this?"

The verdict was guilty. The case was solved. PawPaw Aubrey's brutal
death avenged. Justice served. The world set right. Life could go on.

But the year was 1985. The LaHayes had more tragedies to endure.

In 1990, when Uncle Glenn was found bleeding in that ditch, John
Brady Balfa had been locked away for four years. But when Aunt Michele told Mommee Susan what had happened, the first thing Mommee
said was: "This has got to be related to PawPaw's stuff. Someone killed
Glenn, too."

The closure that had been promised with Balfa's conviction never
quite arrived. The story Richard Vidrine and Billy Pucheu left us with is
all too unsatisfying. The loose ends lingered:

Why didn't John Brady, knowing Aubrey might recognize him, wear a
mask? Why did he leave a witness alive?

Why did he use the name "Vidrine"?

How did John Brady, alone, manage to convince Aubrey to stand still—
using the threat of a pocketknife—while he tied his wife to a bed?

Why a knife? Why not a gun?

Could John Brady, a skinny twentysomething alcoholic, have possibly han-
dled Aubrey's body and those rims all by himself?

What was the point of the ransom call, if he was just going to kill him? If
he had already killed him? How did he expect to get any money from this?

Where did he kill him?

What did he kill him with?

Could it have been an accident?

Was it part of something bigger?

THE 1990S BROUGHT A BLESSED PAUSE ON TRAGEDY FOR MY family, who turned inward and upward—building new identities directed toward the new generation, mine. These were new beginnings. The questions that remained around PawPaw Aubrey's murder weren't to be spoken of, except in whispers. And any suspicions that the story told in the courtroom in 1985 wasn't the *whole* story were relegated to midnight insomnias, gently shoved into the recesses of the memory. Life must go on.

By all accounts, MawMaw Emily never wavered in her confidence that Balfa was the man who came into her home that day, the man who killed her husband. She benefited from a deep trust in the justice system, in Billy Pucheu, and in herself, which allowed her the conclusion she needed to embark on her golden years with any promise of happiness, of peace. Eventually, she agreed to sell her house to her grandson Danny and his wife, Michele, and "MawMaw and PawPaw's house" became "Nana and Parrain's house," PawPaw Aubrey's office transformed into a nursery. MawMaw Emily moved into a custom mother-in-law suite added onto Mommee Susan and Papa Wayne's house and hung PawPaw's portrait on the wall. Each time her great-grandchildren would visit her, it would look out at us—a familiar stranger no one spoke of.

But peace was had on LaHaye Road. It's held firm there now for almost forty years. Embarking on this journey, I've asked myself so many times: *Can I resurrect the past without casting darkness onto the present?*

Again and again, I make my way down LaHaye Road, asking my family members, ever so carefully: *Do you ever have questions about the verdict, about whether they got it right?*

"I think we all feel pretty sure . . ." says Aunt Suzette. "No, I *know* we all feel like we don't know the whole story. But for some reason they proved it was him . . ."

"I mean, even at the time, it didn't seem realistic that there was just this man who killed him without a true reason," Uncle Jay tells me. "And since then so many people, old people, have said, 'Well, there's other people involved, and one day it's gonna come out,' and all that stuff. We've heard that story so many times."

"It's like he wasn't a big enough fish . . . to do all this by himself," says Uncle Nick.

Aunt Anne always thought there were two or three abductors. "The way they tied MawMaw up and held PawPaw, to me that would take three people. To me they couldn't do that and keep watch, make sure nobody was coming . . . I have no doubt he did it. I think there are other people that did it, too. I think there is a lot of stuff we don't know about."

"I used to . . . back in my dark mind, I used to think PawPaw Aubrey and my daddy were all kinda tied to something and somebody," says Uncle Billy. "I don't know. Do I still kinda feel that way?" He pauses. "Yeah . . . I kinda do."

"Someone out there knows more about this," says Aunt Michele.

"If something comes to light in twenty years, I think it'd be okay," says Aunt Kristy. ". . . but for this generation, my generation, I think they're better off not knowing. If something happened that's more than what they've told us."

"Everybody wondered," says my papa Wayne. "I wonder still."

The Alcatraz
of the South

EVERY SINGLE MORNING, AT 5 A.M. SHARP, A WHISTLE WAKES John Brady Balfa from his slumber. From my king-size bed and wealth of privacy, I think of him lifting his body to a sitting position, yawning, and sitting on the edge of his bunk to be counted, along with five thousand of Louisiana's most forsaken men, in the nation's largest maximum-security prison.

He's now lived more of his life inside the gates than out of them. To complete his sentence in whole, he'll have to be here until he dies. Then he will have to be reborn and do it all over. Twice.

The Louisiana State Penitentiary, also known as Angola, occupies eighteen thousand acres cradled inside the curve of the Mississippi River that rushes from Mississippi into Louisiana. It is often noted that this property of rolling hills and verdant pastures—stretching as far as the prisoner's eye can see—is larger than Manhattan.

And as in so many other swaths of beautiful, fertile land in this part of the world, there is blood in the soil. Angola earned its mythic moniker of "the bloodiest prison in America" in the 1960s, but it arises from a long legacy of horrors, interrupted sporadically by bouts of attempted reform. The history of violence goes back even further, though, to the beginning of the nineteenth century when the prison was not a prison, but a cotton plantation. Then, it was owned by Isaac Franklin, who is credited with bringing two-thirds of all enslaved Africans in the South to its plantations.

Angola's history as a state prison begins in 1900, when the State purchased the property and ended the brutal leasing system of convicts—which allowed planters and companies to "rent" out convicts to perform hard, unpaid labor. In the name of reform, lawmakers posed agriculture as the only sort of hard labor the convicts would be subject to, calling it a "convict farm." Quite prettily, less than fifty years after the Civil War's end, the antebellum farm was resurrected on that curve in the Mississippi—packaged as a more progressive form of punishment, pastoral and full of meaning. While it was an improvement from the convicts' treatment under the leasing system (the death rate of Louisiana prisoners dropped 62 percent in 1901) the new order essentially reestablished plantation slavery in Louisiana, granting it another name. During that first year, the food produced by the convicts' labor was enough to feed all 1,076 of them, with enough surplus to earn the state over $13,000 (equal to over $400,000 today).

Over a century later, at the Louisiana State Penitentiary at Angola, teams of predominately Black men (who make up almost 75 percent of the prison population) bend over cotton crops while armed white guards on horseback, called "freemen," look on. Angola may no longer be the bloodiest of prisons, but this portrait, shamelessly, prevails. Prisoners are paid, but at rates between two and twenty cents an hour. No longer solely benefiting the state, the cheap labor is also capitalized upon by private corporations, largely in the agricultural industry. The inmates plant, harvest, and process commodity crops like cotton, wheat, corn, milo, and soybeans; they oversee around 2,000 head of cattle and annually produce over 4 million pounds of vegetables. They also participate in various manufacturing operations, making soap, garments, mattresses, mops, furniture, and more. In the 2021/2022 fiscal year, the entire prison labor system in Louisiana reported over $30 million in sales—most of which were the result of enterprises at Angola.

I do not know how much time John Brady Balfa has spent in those fields, if any at all. I do know that he is white and educated, though. Now in his sixties—an age that studies indicate, for prisoners, is the equivalent of almost eighty in the outside world—he lives in one of the trusty dormitories, indicating he enjoys medium-to-minimum security privileges and access to some of the least demanding job assignments. If John Brady has ever been a part of that infamous tableau, it would have been shortly after his arrival in 1986, when most incoming inmates endure their rite of passage into the Alcatraz of the South: ninety days of hard labor in the cotton fields.

As Louisiana's State Penitentiary, Angola earned its notorious reputation as a place of violence early in its legacy. In the 1930s and 1940s, reports of abuse in the form of leather whippings and sweatbox torture made their way into the news. In 1951, thirty-seven inmates slashed their own Achilles tendons in protest of the abuse they faced from their overseers, poor working and housing conditions, and food quality. The ensuing investigation brought forth a nurse who described the dormitories as "filthy and stink[ing] like the hold of a slave ship" and testified to the frequency of sexual and physical abuse inmates were subject to, calling Angola a "sewer of degradation." The committee reported their findings to Governor Earl Long, recommending an end to all corporal punishment, the appointment of a new warden, updated accommodations, and rehabilitation programs. Long laughed, then shuffled about, half-heartedly trying to find a new warden. In 1952, Long's gubernatorial opponent Robert F. Kennon made penal reform a major part of his campaign. The people of Louisiana voted in his favor.

That year, Kennon allocated $4 million for a new Main Prison complex. He appointed a "progressive" warden, who prohibited private deals for the use of prison labor outside of the farm as well as all forms of corporal punishment. Black-and-white stripes were switched out for the signature denim blues so well known today. A vocational education program was underway. "We can take it for granted that Angola will never be allowed to revert to its former state of bestiality," wrote journalist and investigative committee member Edward Stagg in a now-famous article for *Colliers* titled "America's Worst Prison."

But alongside all this reform, another brutal evolution was underway. In 1956, state executions—which had previously taken place in the parish where a crime was committed—were moved to the Angola grounds. A small building on-site became the execution chamber, where an electric chair, called "Gruesome Gertie," would end eighty-seven inmates' lives before 1991, when lethal injection became the method of execution. Since then only eight men have been executed by the State of Louisiana, and only one person since 2002, in large part because of a difficulty in sourcing approved lethal injection drugs. (This is likely to change, though, and soon; in March 2024, Louisiana's governor, Jeff Landry, signed into law a bill that allows the state to keep confidential all records of its execution methods—opening the door for easier access to obtain lethal injections. Landry has also now made it legal to utilize the controversial nitrogen gas method of execution, and he's bringing back the electric chair.)

The reforms of the 1950s were forgotten by the 1960s. America's Worst Prison became America's Bloodiest Prison as a wave of inmate-to-inmate conflict arose, lasting through the 1970s, spurred in part by tensions around the civil rights movement. Nine wardens walked in and out between 1964 and 1968, and in 1971, the American Bar Association described conditions at Angola as "medieval, squalid, and horrifying." Forty inmates were murdered between the years of 1972 and 1975 alone, and over 350 were treated with serious knife wounds. In 1972, an officer was discovered dead after having been stabbed thirty-eight times. Two Black inmates were convicted of the crime, and each served over forty years in solitary confinement, the longest period of imprisoned isolation in American history.

In 1976, the Louisiana legislature approved over $90 million to expand Angola and to build other prisons in the state to relieve the burdens of overcrowding. The money helped, and general infrastructural conditions improved. Violence was curbed, for a time. But the gospel of "tough on crime" was starting to spread. The prison population in Louisiana was about to mushroom, and the state was not prepared for it.

John Brady Balfa may not have entered Angola during its most violent era, but it was certainly one of its most hopeless. In 1986, he joined the 14,580 others imprisoned that year by the State of Louisiana, which then held the fifth-highest incarceration rate in the nation. For most of the twentieth century, the State of Louisiana had kept its prison population down by implementing an unofficial "10–6" rule, which allowed for the release of prisoners with a life sentence after ten years and six months of good behavior. Shortly before John Brady arrived, that rule had been abolished. In 1972, 193 people were serving "natural life" sentences in Angola. By 1994, that number had risen to 2,400. The tide of public opinion was shifting away from concern over prison conditions and toward locking up criminals.

In 1988, Governor Buddy Roemer denied the pardon board's clemency recommendation for the freedom of Wilbert Rideau, a now-revered prison journalist whose memoir is one of the most revelatory firsthand accounts of life in Angola. Rideau had, by that time, served twenty-seven years for killing a woman during a burglary attempt at age nineteen. His prison record was sparkling clean, and he was perhaps the most famous prisoner of his time, writing for national publications and receiving some of the country's most prestigious journalism awards. He frequently served as a bridge between administration and other inmates, helping to maintain peace and foster improvements from within the prison. Every warden and most of the officers who had worked at Angola during Rideau's imprisonment, as well as the director of the ACLU, supported his release. But Roemer denied it anyway.

This denial of freedom for a long-term inmate described as "the most rehabilitated prisoner in the United States" had a visceral effect on the 4,800 other men with life sentences at Angola, John Brady among them. The next several months ushered forth a deluge of murders, suicides, and escape attempts—performed almost exclusively by lifers with clean records, who had just lost all hope of ever getting out of prison. "Hopelessness is contagious," wrote Rideau in his memoir.

The sudden wave of violence brought US district judge Frank Polozola to declare a state of emergency at the prison. Yet another host of rehabilitation efforts followed, but the systemic culture of abuse and poor conditions continued to rear its head. In 1991, the Department of Justice issued a report condemning the prison's poor medical care, citing a lack of doctors and nurses in the infirmary, the practice of locking up mentally ill patients for up to twenty-four hours a day, and the fact that un-air-conditioned cells often reached temperatures of ninety degrees. In May 2013, the Center for Constitutional Rights and the International Federation for Human Rights condemned Angola's death row conditions—in oppressive heat, isolation, and without mental health care—as torture. In 2021, a district judge ruled in favor of a class action lawsuit filed by a dozen inmates with more complaints about the prison's medical care—describing conditions in the medical ward as inadequate and often neglectful enough to meet standards of cruel and unusual punishment. In a 2024 exposé by ProPublica, an inmate's visiting mother described the infirmary as a place reeking of feces, with dirty medical equipment, and patients screaming relentlessly.

Problems within Angola's medical system have been exacerbated in recent decades as Louisiana's incarceration rates continue to rise. When a 1990 federal court order demanded the state reduce overcrowding in its larger prisons like Angola, the solution came in the form of financially incentivizing local sheriffs to build facilities to house convicts in their parishes. Overcrowding was alleviated, but now there were more jails to fill, and the business model was based on head counts. More people were being imprisoned for longer sentences, and motivation to reduce existing sentences decreased.

Since 2005 Louisiana has incarcerated more people per capita than any other state in the United States, with a brief unseating by Oklahoma in 2018. In 2020, 680 out of every 100,000 people in Louisiana were incarcerated—a number higher than most nations'—granting the state the title "the world's prison capital."

Efforts at reform have moved at a snail's pace, pushing against remnants of the public's "lock 'em up" attitude and various entities who share a financial interest in maintaining a high prisoner population to supply cheap labor and line sheriffs' pockets.

A 2017 bipartisan effort led by Governor John Bel Edwards's administration promised change in the form of the "most comprehensive criminal justice reform in the state's history" combating mass incarceration. But those efforts were quickly rolled back by the Jeff Landry administration in 2024, which, among other things, totally eliminated parole in Louisiana and passed a law requiring inmates to serve 85 percent of their sentences before reducing their incarceration through good behavior—a move criminal justice experts estimate will nearly double the number of incarcerated people in Louisiana by 2030. Prior to becoming governor, Landry frequently insisted that inmates are only entitled to "adequate" medical care. As part of his new legislation, existing programs that allowed the sickest of inmates to be released were eliminated. They aren't letting anyone out.

As a result, the populations at long-term facilities like Angola are becoming increasingly geriatric. John Brady Balfa is one of over 80 percent of Louisiana lifers over the age of forty, and one of nearly 1,200 over sixty. As he continues to age, and his health worsens, he will face the horrific reality of living out the rest of his days at the mercy of the prison's medical system, which will only become more overburdened as his fellow inmates age with him. Many of these prisoners face significant, often expensive, health problems that make them statistically very little threat outside of prison. But the State is determined they live out their sentence, that they die in Angola.

Elma Meyer

T WAS CHRISTMAS 1985–JOHN BRADY BALFA'S LAST IN EVAN-
geline Parish.

His family would have made sure he didn't spend the holiday alone, as much as they could. They'd have brought blankets, books, magazines, cookies. I imagine little Naomi, age nine, glittering in the visitors' room in her Christmas dress. Trying to make her brother smile.

Julie Cullen was working on a lead, though. Something that could perhaps get John Brady another trial. Everyone prayed for a Christmas miracle.

She had gotten the call a few days after the verdict was delivered— "You've got to appeal." The woman, Elma Meyer, was the sister of an old client. "He didn't do it. I *know* he didn't do it." What Meyer told Cullen next brought the defense attorney back to the Evangeline Parish court- house to file a motion for mistrial, based on newly discovered evidence.

The sentencing was scheduled for January 17, 1986. Judge Coreil also intended to hear Cullen's arguments for a new trial on that date, but some- where along the way wires got crossed. Cullen arrived January 17 unpre- pared to present her case. But the court had already subpoenaed Elma Meyer, along with two witnesses for the State—who *did* come prepared.

Cullen requested more time so that she might further investigate the issue, a request the judge denied. After almost an entire year of proceed- ings, he was ready to get this case off the docket. "Let us proceed, Miss Cullen." A drama of absurdity ensued.

Meyer took the stand. A local bartender with a drinking problem, she spoke nervously and distractedly, and kept descending into wild tangents.

Meyer's story was that she had been a patient in the Mamou hospital in January of 1983, right around when Aubrey was kidnapped. She said she was being treated for diabetes by Dr. A. John Tassin, and at one point her blood sugar had gotten so low she temporarily lost her eyesight. "I couldn't see, but I could hear," she repeated, over and over. "That's the thing, I can hear real, real good."

Meyer testified that she overheard some "boys" talking in the room next door. "I heard they was talking to this other young boy that was in the hospital about Mr. LaHaye."

"What actual words did you hear being said?" asked Cullen.

According to Meyer, one of them had said something like, "Did you get everything fixed?" The other responded that he had. "And you're sure we're not going to be in no trouble?"

"No," he'd said. "Because John Balfa promised he was going to take the whole blame."

They went on to describe how they'd killed Aubrey LaHaye, saying they'd hit him on the head with a 2-iron, twice. "That's all I heard," said Meyer. "And then they kept on laughing and laughing."

Meyer testified that she had yelled at them, through the walls "What y'all was talking about, Mr. LaHaye and John Balfa? John Balfa didn't kill. It's y'all that killed him!"

Because she couldn't see, she couldn't be sure, but she believed that afterward, the men came into her room. One said, "Well, listen to Miss Priss, we have to cut her britches off." Someone, from farther away, addressed this voice, "Come on, big boy, let's go. We're in enough trouble. Let's get out of here before she gets us in some more."

A nurse that came in afterward asked Meyer why the room smelled like cigarettes.

Meyer said that she would have come forward with the story earlier, but she had assumed John Brady wouldn't be convicted. When she saw the news report in December that he had, she knew she needed to say something.

She testified that she had not ever learned who the voices belonged to, but she suspected one to be "Mr. Granger's"—Feryl Granger's. Because he had "came out of the pen in the same days Mr. LaHaye got killed."

Granger, of course, had been discussed as a person of interest from the beginning. Still to this day, his name arises all around conversations of the LaHaye case. Many people who attended John Brady's trial tell me they remember him being there for at least some of the days, sitting alone in the back of the courtroom.

But Granger could not have been the actual person who abducted Aubrey. Aubrey knew him and probably wouldn't have let him into his house. Emily likely knew him, too. But even if she didn't, everyone who has ever seen him remembers his eyes, chillingly blue. "Evil eyes," my dad says. Even more exculpatory is the fact that Granger was in prison in Texas in January 1983. He wasn't released (his first-degree murder conviction reversed and remanded) until a month later, in February 1983. Meyer was mistaken.

When Billy Pucheu asked Meyer if she knew Aubrey LaHaye, she offered a confusing, dialogue-heavy account of a night spent at the Evangeline Downs Racetrack & Casino, where she met four men in suits: one she didn't know, two with known Mafia connections, and Aubrey.

One of the Mafia men was Clifton Thibodeaux, who owned a nightclub in St. Landry Parish known as a headquarters for Acadiana vices of all sorts—most famously prostitution and illegal gambling.

Pucheu, mockingly, asked if the fourth man was the notorious New Orleans mob boss, Carlos Marcello.

It wasn't Carlos, she responded, in all seriousness. She knew Carlos.

The four men, she said, were in a back room, counting money. She knew because Thibodeaux spent the evening trying to buy her a drink.

"Are you saying that Mr. LaHaye was with the Mafia?" Pucheu asked her.

"Well, anybody that is gonna follow Clifton Thibodeaux has gotta be mixed with the Mafia . . . I heard too that Mr. LaHaye was a Mafia. Now, I can't prove that. But a lot of people said he was."

Pucheu pressed on, "Are you saying that it is the Mafia that had him killed maybe?"

"I don't know," she said. "But it's sure not Balfa."

Pucheu asked if Meyer was at any point afraid of testifying, afraid there might be consequences. Meyer said she had never been threatened by anyone, but that some eerie things had happened since 1983. Feryl Granger had been calling her house, saying he wanted to fuck her. On another occasion, a vehicle full of men came and sat in their truck, right in her driveway.

Back at the hospital, shortly after those men left her room, she said a "fat man in blue jeans, with a mustache, black wavy hair, and some cow boots" had been caught wandering the halls at the hospital. When Pucheu asked what made her afraid of him, Meyer said, "Because I didn't know who he was. I didn't know why he come and lean against the hall and watch straight in my room."

After the judge dismissed Meyer, Pucheu presented two witnesses: Dr. A. John Tassin, and Dr. Frank Savoy[1] Jr.—Meyer's doctors.

Tassin testified that Elma Meyer had not become his patient until October 27, 1983—ten months after Aubrey's murder. She had, however, been under Savoy's care for a few months beginning on January 30, 1983— over three weeks after Aubrey's kidnapping. During this time, she was suffering from the effects of her untreated diabetes and was in a state he described as "more or less combative and not too aware of her surroundings for at least four weeks." She was also suffering from liver failure, causing elevated ammonia levels, which he said could induce a continuous hallucinatory state that would yield very few concrete memories. She was experiencing normal vision, according to his notes.

In her concluding arguments, Julie Cullen admitted that the evidence presented by Elma Meyer wasn't convincing enough on its own to warrant a new trial. She said she was still looking for the names of the individuals checked into the hospital room adjacent to Meyer's to corroborate her story. She asked for more time, and another hearing. She also argued that John Brady Balfa deserved a new trial because "the verdict is contrary to law" on the grounds that he did not receive a fair and impartial trial. "The evidence was not to such an extent that the burden of proof, which is required, was in fact met."

In response, Pucheu told Judge Coreil, "I have never had a trial where the court has leaned over so often to be certain the defendant got a fair trial." He cited the mock jury and pointed out the fact that just as many people, in both the mock jury selection and the real one, had been prejudiced toward John Brady as against him.

And as for Elma Meyer, he said, "A jury hearing that testimony could only reach one conclusion. That it was a desperate, ill-founded, rather entertaining—but proving zero—effort by a defendant. A desperate defendant."

Judge Coreil denied Cullen's motion, and promptly delivered his judgment: For the armed robbery, kidnapping, and murder of Aubrey LaHaye, John Brady Balfa would be sent to Angola, where he would serve two life sentences and ninety-nine years of hard labor, without parole.

---

1 Pronounced "Sah-vwah."

He Said He'd
Take the Fall

WHEN I FIRST READ ELMA MEYER'S TESTIMONY, I'M EN-
thralled by it. And so frustrated by it. I'm kept awake at night
connecting threads that draw me forward, only to break off
ragged. When I dream, I dream of Granger's blue eyes staring at a be-
draggled, bedridden woman as she shouts at him. He holds a cigarette,
and then he holds a 2-iron. The cigarette smoke changes course, snaking
into another mouth, PawPaw Aubrey's, with his sunglasses and his cowboy hat. A cigar, not a cigarette. A handful of cash. All of it—the cigar,
the 2-iron, the rims, the cowboy hat—in the Nezpique. PawPaw Aubrey
standing on the banks, beside Clifton Thibodeaux, beside Granger, a
dent in his head. John Brady Balfa raising his handcuffed hands, in surrender or desperation, I cannot tell.

So much of the rumorous vapor still shrouding the Aubrey LaHaye murder emerges in Meyer's testimony, but without anywhere to go. Meyer's
story, uncorroborated, was clearly not enough to justify a new trial.

And still, it's an elaborate story, dressed in detail with names, dialogue,
and the smell of cigarettes. Meyer did not seem to be a cunning woman,
nor did she seem capable of crafting such a tale on her own. Why would
she make it all up? There is no evidence that she had any significant relation to John Brady or to the Balfas. What did she have to gain?

And if it was a hallucination, it was a pretty damn specific and timely
one. What are the chances her confused mind conjured such a conversation, joining Aubrey with his convicted-killer-to-be, so early on? What
are the chances of her remembering it?

I can't help but feel that some part of this, some small piece, *happened*.
That there's a whisper of truth to it. Even the conflicting dates don't
bother me. Meyer said she was in the hospital right after Aubrey was
kidnapped on January 6. She wasn't until January 30. It doesn't seem

outlandish that such conversations from plotters might have continued in the weeks beyond the actual murder.

Still, that truth—whatever it may be—remains elusive, all these years later. Any records of who might have been in that adjacent room are long gone. And even *if* Meyer's story is true—John Brady is still not proven innocent of the crime. He said he'd take the fall.

March 2, 1986

Late on Sunday evening at the Evangeline Parish courthouse, Deputy Leon Fontenot[1] was opening the door to his office when his radio went off. An escape attempt. *Lord,* he thought, turning around to rush back to the jail. *Haven't had one of those in a while.*

It was Balfa, they said. The one who killed Mr. Aubrey LaHaye. Sheriff Floyd Soileau[2] met Leon in the hallway heading toward the cell in question. "The dispatcher said he saw his arm sticking out outside his window," the sheriff said, shaking his head. "Like he was waving at someone."

When they got there, they found John Brady sitting on his bed, reading the newspaper. "Good evening, Officers," he said with a smile. Leon unlocked the door, and Sheriff Soileau stepped inside. "Get up, Balfa, give me your hands." Deflated, he stood up and offered his wrists, saying nothing while the sheriff cuffed him. Leon walked around them to look at the window, where three of the bars had been sawed right off. "What did you use to do this?" Leon asked, picking up his pillow, lifting the blankets. John Brady didn't say a word.

The next day, they still hadn't found any tools in or around the cell John Brady had been sleeping in. The sheriff put a rush order on John Brady's transfer to Angola. They had to get him out of Evangeline Parish.

John Brady never took any fall. Not voluntarily. He denied being a part of Aubrey LaHaye's murder from the beginning. He pled not guilty, and over the past forty years has never stopped trying to get out of prison.

Julie Cullen submitted the first appeal right after trial, arguing assignments of error to the judge's denial of several motions, including the

---

1 Leon Fontenot is of no relevant relation to my husband Julien Fontenot's family.

2 Floyd Soileau (who was a deputy during the initial Aubrey LaHaye investigation) was elected Evangeline Parish Sheriff in 1984 after Ramson Vidrine completed his term.

change of venue and her motions for discovery. She also argued the court should have never let Dr. McCormick testify to the time of death, since she had not been provided the information before trial. In the application, she submits that these denials and others constituted a "system of denial of rights" from the Evangeline Parish DA's Office and court.

A year later, the Louisiana Court of Appeals disagreed with her, affirming John Brady's conviction. The Louisiana Supreme Court followed suit in September 1987.

At this point, Cullen told John Brady she would push onward, moving up to the federal courts. For two years, he—trapped within the infinite boredom of prison life—waited for an update. When he reached out to Cullen in 1989 to ask about the new appeal's progress, she informed him she could no longer represent him. She had accepted a post as the assistant to the attorney general of Louisiana.

At this point, John Brady, with the assistance of a fellow inmate attorney, wasted no time filing his own application for postconviction relief, the thrust of which was a lengthy complaint of "ineffective assistance of counsel before, during, and after trial."

John Brady argued Julie Cullen had failed him, her incompetence opening the door for his allegedly unlawful conviction. He said she had failed to adequately prepare for the trial itself, pointing out that she never made any effort to interview Emily LaHaye ahead of time, or any of the other state witnesses. He charged that instead of complaining about all the State was not giving her, she should have been making a greater effort to conduct her own investigation. If McCormick wouldn't cooperate and give her a time of death without certain information and the State's blessing, Cullen should have tracked down the information herself and subpoenaed him before the court in a pretrial hearing. Instead, she went to trial without the time of death.

At the end of the complaint, John Brady does grant Cullen the grace in acknowledging her heavy caseload in 1985, consisting mostly of capital cases. This enormous pressure and obligation was at its height right around the time of John Brady's trial, which she was fighting pro bono. He cited a case Cullen tried in April of that same year, in which Cullen presented arguments trying to reduce her client's sentence from death to life in prison. While appealing to the jury, she broke down, weeping and apologizing. "I'm sorry," she said. "I thought I was tougher than this. I've never had to do any of this before. I'm a wreck."

John Brady's complaint earned him a postconviction relief hearing on March 6, 1992, with new court-appointed representation. Richard Vidrine, still serving as the assistant DA, represented the State, with Preston Aucoin (who had been a close friend of Aubrey's) presiding as judge.

After two years of waiting to hear from Cullen, then months of preparing the application, then two more years spent awaiting a hearing, and roughly two hours of testimony, John Brady listened as Aucoin casually announced he would deny the application for postconviction relief. John Brady would have to reboard the bus to Angola, doomed to serve out the rest of his sentence.

Two years later, another Evangeline Parish convict arrived at Angola, at some point becoming John Brady's bunkmate. In 1992, Terry Campbell had been convicted of second-degree murder and sentenced to life in prison after, in a drunken fury, killing his wife's lover.

The moment Campbell arrived at Angola, he set about appealing his conviction based on an allegation of racial discrimination in Evangeline Parish grand juries. John Brady would have been keeping up with the sequence of these events closely. Campbell's appeal was based on a systemic exclusion of Black people from the position of Evangeline Parish's grand jury foreperson. Over the course of sixteen and a half years, from March 31, 1976, to February 12, 1992, every single one of the thirty-five forepeople selected by judges for Evangeline Parish's grand juries were white. (Also of note, though never mentioned: only two of these were women.) This time frame, of course, encompassed John Brady Balfa's trial as well as Campbell's. And Campbell, like John Brady, was a white man.

So, in 1998, when the United States Supreme Court reversed and remanded Campbell's conviction, John Brady was ready. By the end of the year, he had prepared a new postconviction relief application, arguing the exact issue raised by Campbell.

Due to the implications such an appeal might have on cases in Evangeline Parish, the hearing was promptly scheduled to take place in two months. John Brady requested a continuance so that his new lawyer, Arcenious Armond Jr., would have adequate time to review the case. In a handwritten note I find in the DA file, John Brady explains to his court-appointed lawyer, Chuck West, that one of his brothers paid for Armond's services. They really thought this might work. This might get him out. Left field as it was, it had worked for Terry—why not him?

The hearing was rescheduled for April 1, 1999. Armond would be presenting the same argument for both John Brady and another client: that the Supreme Court's ruling on the Campbell case could apply retroactively. If affirmed, this would open the doors for every single criminal trial that took place in Evangeline Parish between the dates of March 31, 1976, to February 12, 1992, to be retried.

Aucoin, who was once again the judge, had also presided over the original Campbell trial—and had been the one to deny the initial motion alleging discrimination in grand jury proceedings. "I guess if there is one district judge in Louisiana that knows about the Campbell decision, it's me," he told Armond.

Ultimately, though, Aucoin sided with the State, whose argument emphasized that Terry Campbell had raised the objection at hand *during* his trial, not afterward. For this argument to be applied to their cases, these defendants (i.e., their lawyers) would have had to have done the same. It was too late now.

And just like that, Evangeline Parish's Angola residents—anxiously awaiting the results—had their hopes of getting out like ole Terry dashed to bits.

Over the next two years, Armond pushed the issue through each level of courts until he was finally dismissed by the US District Court "with prejudice" in March 2001. They were done.

So, John Brady maintains his innocence.

If he has ever agreed to "take the fall," he isn't holding up his end of the bargain. John Brady has been trying, as hard as he can, to get out.

This begs the question: If he did do it, but he wasn't alone—why not name names? If John Brady did not in fact kill Aubrey on his own, then any information he does possess about the murder could be leveraged to get a lighter sentence. To get out sooner. To get out at all.

The fact that he has not leaves, in my mind, three possibilities:

First, John Brady did it, maybe not exactly as the court portrayed it, but close. He did it, and he did it alone. And he is, quite simply, lying.

Second, John Brady did not do it, had nothing to do with it, knows nothing about it. Everything he is saying is true. And he is justifiably desperate to clear his name.

Third, John Brady was part of something bigger, whether it be a conspiracy or an impulsive group decision, that resulted in the kidnapping and murder of Aubrey LaHaye. These people let him take the fall. But they have threatened him, or the people he loves, if he reveals any other knowledge about the affair. I say people and not a singular person, because the only way he would be in danger by selling someone out is if there was a third person who could come after him. If he gets out by his own merits, he will be safe—so all he can do is try. These people, at least some of them, must still be alive.

This theory is the one his sister Naomi feels is closest to the truth. "Do I think my brother killed Mr. Aubrey? Absolutely not," she says. "Do I think he knows a lot more than he's saying? Absolutely, yes. And he won't say it. And it gives me the chills. I think he's protecting us to an extent."

Right after John Brady was arrested, she tells me, "they" burned down a home right by Harry Balfa's house; and the family took it as a warning. "They sent him a message," says Naomi. "Burned it right to the ground. And this happened within days after he was arrested. Like a few days."

Later, I'm unable to confirm with certainty if and when this fire took place, but it's clear when speaking to Naomi that it has become a principal plot point in the Balfa family's telling of what happened to John Brady. "Somebody was sending him a message to keep his mouth shut."

The Meyer Characters

W HAT MOST CAPTURES MY IMAGINATION WHEN IT COMES
to Elma Meyer's testimony, I think, is the idea of PawPaw Aubrey sitting around a card table with Clifton Thibodeaux.

Aubrey was one of the most powerful men in town, was connected
to the most powerful men in town. He managed most of the money in
town. He *had* most of the money in town. And he didn't keep records.
Could any of this darkness have originated with him?

Mafia involvement, or at least Mafia associations, isn't a leap.

And while others I speak to echo this suspicion, even members of the
LaHaye family, I can find no evidence. None. It is virtually impossible to
connect Aubrey to any of the vices. He didn't drink. He didn't dance. If
he gambled, he gambled well, and discreetly. If he did anything untoward
at all, he did it without his family, or the community at large, knowing. If
Aubrey was involved in Thibodeaux's corner of the underground, he was
successfully living a double life—a true Jekyll and Hyde—and he pulled
it off until the day he died. No one ever saw him in "cathouses," places of
intoxication, of ill repute. Or if they did, their lips have been well sealed.

Except for Elma Meyer's.

Meyer is certainly not the most reliable source. She could have
been mistaken, or a liar. But I entertain the prospect, if only for a moment. PawPaw Aubrey in his banking suit, smoking a cigar with Clifton
Thibodeaux—pimp, drug dealer, bookie, murderer.

Thibodeaux owned the Turf Lounge—a notorious nightclub sitting
right on the St. Landry-Evangeline line—and was known to operate two
nearby brothels, called The Spot and The Gates. The main clientele for
these venues was a rotation of roughnecks home from stints working for
offshore oil companies. Men whose amphibious lives shifted between
the hypermasculine world of the Gulf rigs and brief excursions into
family domesticity. With wives who either counted the days until they
came home or counted the days until they went back, and more money

in their pockets than they had reasonable time off to spend. Places like the Turf curated a rare utopic space where the two dimensions collided. The crowd was made up of their brotherhood, men like them. But there was no backbreaking work here. *Enjoy your break. Take advantage of the world's pleasures. Empty your pockets here. Le joie de vivre.*

Throughout the 1970s and 1980s, Thibodeaux was known as the head of St. Landry Parish's local Cajun Mafia and linked to the larger Dixie Mafia—a decentralized system of criminal operations taking place across the Old Confederacy, whose members were frequenters of the Turf and its affiliates. (The Dixie Mafia, it is worth noting, operated independently from the larger and better-known Sicilian Mafia, or Casa Nostra, and its operatives in the South—though the two "organizations" occasionally did business.)

In a newspaper profile on Thibodeaux written a year after his death, former state police officer Lieutenant Harry Courville described the club owner as someone whose "tentacles went far." One of the attorneys working for the St. Landry DA's Office during those years said Thibodeaux got away with just about everything. "The people who operated in the criminal element were afraid of him," he said, "and rightfully so."

In one of the few examples of repercussions Thibodeaux faced for his criminal activities, he was charged with conspiracy to commit aggravated burglary with two coconspirators, Darrell Morris and Jack Joy. Four months before the May 1970 trial, Joy was able to get out on bond. When he did, he told his bondsman, "I think I am signing my own death warrant." A few days later, his body was found in an oil field, burned to a crisp with a bullet in his head. His murder has never been solved. At trial, Morris refused to testify against Thibodeaux. The jury had no choice but to deem him not guilty.

The only charge Thibodeaux ever served real time for was the distribution of narcotics, for which he accepted a plea deal that sent him to prison in Bastrop, Texas, for four years. Those four years spanned 1981 to 1985—meaning Thibodeaux himself was in prison the day Aubrey LaHaye was killed. Of course, he was in prison the day Jack Joy died, too.

Feryl Granger was also a known member of the Dixie Mafia, working in the drug distribution schemes and as the occasional hit man. In all likelihood, he and Thibodeaux crossed paths on occasion. In fact, a 1988 newspaper article places Granger at the Turf, where he was arrested for simple battery. While Thibodeaux's criminal activity was calculated and careful, Granger wrought chaos wherever he passed. In 1990, he stabbed a man right on Sixth Street, in the middle of Mamou, where everyone could see. My dad describes Granger as a snake. If you offended him, he'd probably smile at you and walk away, then come back later when you weren't suspecting it and stab you from behind.

Granger's claim to fame was an incident that took place in Sugarland, Texas. On January 3, 1978, Steve and Marjorie Anderson were discovered in their home, their eyes and mouths duct-taped shut, each shot several times in the head. Their daughter Mary Lou, a local prostitute, would later confess to law enforcement that a roommate had connected her with Granger, who she understood to be a hit man. Mary Lou hired Granger to kill her parents so she could collect $5,000 on an insurance policy she had taken out on them. She told officials she later changed her mind (she purportedly possessed photographs of herself in bed with a Louisiana mayor, which she planned to use as blackmail to get her money), but Granger wouldn't relent. He forced her, at gunpoint, to come with him to her parents' neighborhood while her roommate held her teenage son captive. Granger left her in the car, tied up, while he went inside the house. He came back with blood all over his gloves and a "horrifying"—as she would testify—look on his face. Convicted unanimously by a jury of first-degree murder, Mary Lou was set to be the first woman executed in Texas since 1863. The Department of Corrections had to build a death row just for her—though her sentence would later be reduced to fifty years in exchange for her witness testimony in Granger's trial.

Like Mary Lou, Granger was convicted and sentenced to death by lethal injection. At his sentencing, noting that the defense presented no arguments from friends or family on Granger's behalf, the prosecutor bellowed: "Feryl Granger's lived thirty years on this earth and not one human being came in and said one good thing about him, because they can't."

Granger was in prison for about two years before a judge remanded his case back to the trial court due to lack of sufficient evidence. After paying a bond of $45,000, he reentered the streets until May of 1981, when his second trial delivered a life sentence. This time, Mary Lou refused to testify, and the prosecution was forced to read the transcript of her previous testimony. This paved the way for a new appeal, which would result in Granger being set free in February 1983. Over the next thirty years, he'd continue on as he always had, rotating in and out of jails around Acadiana until 2010, when he was riding his motorcycle over the Mississippi River bridge in Baton Rouge and crashed into the wall. He died on the spot at sixty-two years old.

By that point, he'd had a daughter, and she had a daughter, too—with MawMaw Emily's nephew. Camille was born the same year I was. I don't know if Feryl played a part in her life, but her mother didn't. Her father tried. She was raised by her Deshotels grandparents, on LaHaye Road. Every summer, we'd meet at Mommee Susan and Papa Wayne's pool, flipping off the diving board and racing each other across the deep end. She was stunning, even as a little girl, and always a little dangerous, a little more adult than I was. She had the lightest blue eyes you've ever seen. Cool, steely, unforgettable blue. Just like they say her grandfather's were.

Besides the notorious personalities of Granger and Thibodeaux, the shadow of organized crime enters Meyer's testimony in a more unexpected persona too: that of her doctor, Frank Savoy Jr.

The heir apparent to the founder of Mamou's hospital—which was built in 1950, the same year Aubrey LaHaye had opened Guaranty Bank—Frank Savoy Jr. was not only one of the state's best doctors; he was also a brilliant businessman. After his father's death in 1960, Savoy made it his life's mission to bring high-quality health care to Mamou and the surrounding areas, expanding the hospital every few years, ensuring it offered the most state-of-the-art treatments, and bringing in doctors from every specialty to the prairie. My papa Wayne was among them, followed by my father, and then my uncle. For decades, the hospital was the largest employer in the area.

Alongside Aubrey, Savoy was without a doubt one of the most powerful men in Evangeline Parish. "But Aubrey wasn't like Frank," Ted Smith, who worked for years at Guaranty Bank, tells me. "Everybody knew Dr. Frank was tied up with the Mafia, treated those people, did business with them. Aubrey wasn't like that."

This wasn't the same drug-dealing, murder-for-hire Mafia that Granger and Thibodeaux associated themselves with, though. This was bigger. According to the enduring rumor, Savoy was the personal doctor for the Sicilian New Orleans godfather Carlos Marcello, who headed Louisiana's intricate illegal gambling network and was dubbed by the United States Senate's 1951 Kefauver Committee on Organized Crime as "one of the worst criminals in the country." To this day, Marcello is believed by many to be the mastermind behind President John F. Kennedy's assassination; he's even said to have admitted it.

Mamou, a key stop along the "Acadiana Trail" funneling the mob's illegal wares from New Orleans to Houston, is said to have been a favorite haunt of Marcello's. Legend paints a picture of a sleek black limousine driving up to the entryway at Savoy Medical Center, an entourage of guards escorting a mysterious figure inside. According to Eugene Manuel, son of the legendary Mamou nightclub tycoon T-Ed Manuel, Savoy met Marcello during his residency in New Orleans.

T-Ed himself is often today called the "Cajun Godfather," remembered for wearing fancy suits in a town of farmers, pockets full of cash, and for his buddy-buddy relationship with Governor Edwin Edwards. He was the owner of the Holiday Lounge, where Edwards's cardboard likeness greeted each and every guest. T-Ed's fortune was made in the coin-operated machine business—jukeboxes, pinball machines, cigarette dispensers. And the slots, which were illegal until the 1990s. As Daniel Baham, a former employee of T-Ed's, puts it: anything coin-operated in Louisiana, especially if it was illegal, was controlled by Marcello's family. "You couldn't buy jukeboxes in those days unless you were connected," he says. Eugene confirms this, saying, "You had to get approved by them people over there."

Eugene remembers, as a child, waking up to breakfast with Marcello sitting at his kitchen table. "I watched them talk on the phone so many times," he says of his father's relationship with Carlos.

And one of the most frequent patrons at T-Ed's bars? Dr. Frank Savoy Jr. "My daddy was best friends with Dr. Frank," says Eugene. "They were like brothers." Savoy would come to the club, which was two miles from the hospital, after a long shift, and drink with T-Ed until daylight.

To corroborate Eugene's claim that Savoy was Marcello's personal physician, the Eunice journalist Todd C. Elliott once tracked down the doctor's widow, Bobby Savoy (now deceased). She told him that, as she remembered it, the Mafia man Savoy had treated was *not* Marcello but someone else from New Orleans: Sam Roselli.

"It wasn't Marcello," my dad echoes her when I ask him about his time at Savoy Medical Center. "It was Sam Roselli who would come to see Frank." Not long after my dad started his urology practice in Evangeline Parish in 1995, he crossed the old man surrounded by what appeared to be bodyguards in the hallway at the hospital. "Somebody told me, 'That's

Sam Roselli,' and that he was one of these big Sicilian-based New Orleans Mafia guys."

When I try to track down information about Sam Roselli, though, I
come up empty. I learn about the Chicago mobster Sam Giancana, who
controlled most of Louisiana's illegal gambling, liquor distribution, and
various political affairs through the 1940s and 1950s. Giancana's name
joins Marcello's on the list of suspects associated with the JFK assassination, along with his number-two man, John Roselli—whose activity
was connected to Al Capone and mostly focused on Hollywood and the
Las Vegas Strip, and who on at least one occasion used the alias "Sam
Roselli." Giancana and Roselli were both killed by hit men, Giancana
shot in his home while frying sausage in 1975 and Roselli strangled and
dismembered, his body discovered in a drum floating in Dumfoundling
Bay in 1976. Both were dead long before my dad could have possibly
seen them in the Savoy Medical Center hallway. But, in the absence of
evidence that a well-known mobster by the name of "Sam Roselli" exists,
I can only speculate that the name was used by other gangsters—perhaps
as a sort of symbolic alias. Or that the man who visited Mamou was
perhaps one of John Roselli's descendants, the result of one of his many
romantic affairs.

Whoever Savoy's Mafia connections might have been with, my dad
tells me as long as he knew the old doc, he was involved in "all kinds of
weird business." Papa Wayne, working at the hospital with Savoy and the
other Mamou doctors, some of the richest men in town, was frequently
invited to invest in properties and oil fields that had a shadow about
them. He always politely declined.

During the twentieth century, the Acadiana underworld romped and
raved and schemed and squelched beneath the utopia of LaHaye Road
and the average upper-middle-class family's life in rural Evangeline Parish. The loose ends of PawPaw Aubrey's mysterious death, though, dangle and swing, drawing the eye to where the fabric separating these two
dimensions grows thin. Absent of informants, there is no definitive proof
the characters from Elma Meyer's testimony—Thibodeaux, Granger,
Savoy, Marcello, the elusive Roselli—had any knowledge or involvement
regarding Aubrey's kidnapping. Thibodeaux, Granger, and Marcello
were all in prison at the time of the abduction. Roselli may not have even
existed. Savoy's association with the mob, by all accounts, was limited

to business deals and medical care—to some degree removed from the more violent activities of organized crime. To suggest he might have had an interest in harming Aubrey LaHaye feels far-fetched. But to entertain the notion is to grant a motive for his presence in the courtroom the day of Elma Meyer's testimony, a reason to quash her account. It also explains why someone in his hospital might have felt safe talking about the business there.

Jimmy Sylvester

JANUARY 7, 2006

NAOMI WRAPPED HER HANDS AROUND THE STYROFOAM coffee cup, more for warmth than with any intention of drinking it. She was sitting with her mother, Mildred, and her brother Tim in the corner of her cousin Inis Balfa's Chevron station in Ville Platte. Over the grimy little café table between them, a trail of smoke curved from her mother's mouth. When Inis stepped out from behind the register to check on them, she asked, "You do . . . , like, you trust this man?"

Inis wasn't a close relative. Naomi barely knew him. But he had called Mildred a few weeks before with a story.

A man named Dominick Dupré[1] had tracked him down, asking if he was related to "that Balfa that's in prison." He said he knew something, that he wanted to have a meeting with the family. "I know he didn't do it," he told Inis.

Dupré was a known drug dealer in the area and had spent much of the previous decade on the run after escaping from the St. Landry Parish Jail on charges of marijuana cultivation. Now, though, he was an old man. The Balfas watched him through the window, climbing out of his truck, shuffling to the door. Inis walked over to greet him. "Hey hey, that's my buddy right there." He locked the door behind him, flipped the Closed sign.

"I'm here," Dupré said. "But I won't do it again. I can't barely walk no more."

Inis pulled a chair for him. Tim caught Naomi's eyes over the table. The man looked like he'd keel over any minute. "He was kind of confused. You could tell he was kind of senile," she'd say later.

"*Parlons en français?*" Dupré asked them.

"*Ouais.*" Mildred nodded.

Naomi was the only person at the table who couldn't speak French conversationally. She'd be able to pick up most of what was going on, but she had brought a tape recorder with her, which she'd later have Sheriff

---

1 Of no relevant relation to the Dupré family from which Susan and Janie LaHaye came.

Eddie Soileau translate and transcribe as a record of the conversation, a record she would share with me.

"When was the last time you saw John? His name is John, right?"

"Yes," said Mildred. "About two months ago."

Dupré nodded. He looked at John Brady's mother, sister, and brother, and he said, "I know it's not him. I know that."

Tim furrowed his brow. Mildred leaned forward. "Okay . . ."

"I told Inis who it was," he said. "I told the sheriff and the DA who it was. They did nothing."

Mildred asked him how long ago this had happened. Dupré shook his head, "There's a long time, a long time ago. This didn't happen yesterday." He went on, "If you want to see him die over there, that is on you. It makes no difference. But I think the little fella can come back over here."

Then he started muttering something indecipherable about a car. A Buick Skylark with purple wheels. "He got those wheels with Jimmy Sylvester," he kept saying. "It's Jimmy Sylvester who gave him the wheels. He kept one to put on the old man's neck when he drown him. It was Jimmy who drowned him."

Everyone was quiet, minds spinning.

Jimmy Sylvester was the son of Ville Platte millionaire Oscar Sylvester Jr., who joined Aubrey LaHaye and Frank Savoy Jr. as one of those powerful, entrepreneurial old-timers of twentieth-century Evangeline Parish.

Oscar's older son, Jerry, had been boxing buddies with my papa Wayne when they were teenagers; Papa had even been in his wedding. That was before he moved to Baton Rouge, though, and got involved with the Louisiana Teamsters Union while it was still controlled by Mafia man Jimmy Hoffa. Shortly before going to trial on charges of criminal conspiracy and aggravated battery, Jerry was killed in an airplane crash in 1969. Most Evangeline Parish folks, to this day, assume it was a hit.

Jimmy, Oscar's younger son, stayed closer to home. In Evangeline Parish, he became a sort of mogul in the salvage business, opening several used car lots, scrap metal shops, and body shops. The businesses were small, but the money must have been big; he was known to make significant contributions to political campaigns, and when someone robbed his home in 1981, he reported two pieces of jewelry had been stolen at a value of over $15,000.

But according to Sheriff Eddie Soileau, who was working as a deputy with the department in January 1983, Jimmy was in serious financial trouble at the time of Aubrey's death. At one point the bank had even locked up his salvage yard. Newspaper articles show that by December 1983, Jimmy's building was occupied by a new salvage business, owned by someone else.

In the West End Chevron in 2007, Dupré told the Balfas he had tried to tell Billy Pucheu from the get-go that Aubrey LaHaye's death was Jimmy's doing. "*He* should be over in Angola because I told him who did this. Their answer was, 'Jimmy is the son of Oscar Sylvester. He is rich, and we can't do him anything'. . . . It's a crooked deal they have there."

At this, Tim spoke up for the first time: "I know it's crooked."

"Yes." Dupré knocked his wrist a couple of times on the table. "It's crooked."

It was another local criminal, Emerson Morgan, who had purportedly told Dupré that Jimmy was behind Aubrey's murder. Morgan told a story of how Jimmy approached him and said something along the lines of "Son, we can make ourselves $500,000 real fast."

But Dupré suspected Jimmy even before that. When Sheriff's Deputy Floyd Soileau came knocking on his door in the early days of the investigation, the composite in hand, Dupré held it up and said, "Well, that's easy. That's Jimmy."

"'But we can't do him anything. That's Oscar's son.' That's what he told me."

The next day, Dupré went straight to Sheriff Ramson Vidrine himself. "I told him, 'Doc, it's Oscar's son who did that.'" But nothing ever came of it.

"Anyway," Dupré went on, "Jimmy said he wanted to go kidnap a rich man in Mamou. He didn't name LaHaye, but he was the only rich man in Mamou."

Dupré started to stand up, his mission completed. "Well, I guess that's it." Inis grabbed his elbow to help him. "I have nothing else. He's not the only one they did that with."

Mildred nodded, saying only "*Ouais*" as she stood up to shake his hand.

"You don't have to go tell them tomorrow, no," Dupré told her. "But go, see, don't wait too long. I only got a few months to live. I want to take care of this boy before I die."

"*Merci*," Mildred whispered, sitting back down, pulling out another cigarette from her coat pocket, eyes red.

"Don't thank me too much. When I was a criminal, I was a criminal.

But now I made my peace with God. Thank God for this, 'cause he took me to you with this."

As he was walking away, Mildred called to him, "Merci. Merci au coeur."

"I didn't always feel this way," Naomi tells me. "I had a little bit of doubt, like maybe John *could* have done something like this." She was aware of his criminal record, after all. His gambling problem. His rape conviction. "Maybe he could have."

Emily's identification of John Brady, so confident, loomed in the back of her mind. "It bothered me that your great-grandma said, 'That's him. I know his face. That's him.' Like how can she sit there and be *so* sure of herself?"

At some point, working in the Sheriff's Department, Naomi decided she wanted to dig deeper. "I think God kinda pushed me . . . I had questions. I wanted answers. I wanted to know what went on. And Rudy wouldn't let me have all the transcripts. And there's a reason he didn't let me have all the transcripts. *So* many mistakes were made. From the beginning, it wasn't a fair trial."

It was right in the middle of Naomi's personal investigation, wading through whatever files she could, that Dominick Dupré approached Inis. After that meeting in the Chevron station, Naomi never doubted her brother's innocence again. Back at work the next week, she asked Sheriff Eddie Soileau if he could help her track down a photograph of Jimmy Sylvester.

When Soileau brought the photo to her, she remembers, "it gave me the chills."

Seeing the photograph, everything clicked right into place for Naomi. To her, Jimmy looked *exactly* like John Brady. "I knew right then and there how that woman could mistake the two. There's no doubt she honestly thought John was him. She thought it was him."

Sheriff Soileau confirms this and says that from the beginning, back in January of 1983, Jimmy's name had come to mind whenever he looked at the composites. "I said it from the beginning," he tells me. But no one ever took him seriously. "So, when Naomi came up with this, and Dupré said it was Jimmy, it all came together for me. I don't know if he knew your great-grandfather, or if he had a plan. Maybe it's not even him. But I always thought it was, and this kind of confirmed it. Jimmy would wear a little tam hat all the time. Had a little round face."

I turn to the newspaper archives and scrounge up a handful of photographs of Jimmy Sylvester. The best one is a portrait taken in 1974. I place this image beside two images I have of John Brady Balfa from the DA's file. One is the infamous photo used as evidence at trial, taken in January of 1983. John Brady stands before a cinder-block wall, wearing a jumpsuit. The lighting is poor. He has the thick caterpillar mustache. The second photo is better quality, a close-up of his face taken in 1981 for his Louisiana Operator's License. The mustache is more of a shadow, and he's smiling.

I can see what Naomi sees. Both men are dark-complected, with slightly protruding ears and deep-set eyes. Both have thick eyebrows, a round face, and—in these photos at least—a wan little smile. The biggest difference between them is in weight. Where John Brady is angular and bony, Jimmy is full and even a little round. In most of the photos I find, he's clean-shaven. Jimmy is about ten years older than John Brady, and he would have been thirty-six years old in 1983. This is not a far departure from Emily's original description of someone in their "early thirties." While I don't find the resemblance overwhelming, as Naomi did, I do find it plausible to imagine Emily getting these two men confused. And Jimmy matches her actual description just as much, if not more (clean-shaven!) than John Brady does.

It has now been almost twenty years since Dupré's revelation, though. And, of course, John Brady remains in prison. Jimmy Sylvester died in 2002, at the age of fifty-five, of a "long illness" according to his obituary. When the Balfas asked John Brady about Jimmy Sylvester, he said he had never heard the name before in his life. All they had was the rambling, uncorroborated account of a dying criminal, who had heard from another criminal, also dead, that Jimmy did it. "We didn't have the money to get an investigator, or to get every attorney we could find to try and . . . and the man was dead," says Naomi. "How are you gonna prove any of this?"

Even if it were possible to prove Jimmy Sylvester had, in fact, killed Aubrey LaHaye—there remains an avalanche of questions to be answered, starting with: *Why?* According to Sheriff Soileau, it was about money. Jimmy was going through a hard time and decided to try to get some quick cash.

Naomi has her own theory.

"If I can be honest with you, Jordan . . . well, I think it was someone in the LaHaye family that hired Jimmy. So they could collect an insurance claim on Aubrey."

When Naomi tells me this, she says it so carefully, so earnestly. She studies me. She might not trust me totally, I think. But she trusts me this much. She trusts that if this is true, that I will hear her. And when she says it out loud this time, I'm surprised at how little it moves me, how I naturally find myself nodding, absorbing, taking notes.

I've allowed myself to go there, of course. I've had to. Stripping away the Technicolor filters that have rosied my coming of age, my perceptions of who I am, who we are. I've stepped outside of the snow globe and tried to peer inside, imagining a world in which one of our own could have killed my great-grandfather. I've even pushed myself into unthinkable realms, dimensions in which my own gentle grandfather might know more than he is saying, might be more than he reveals. "Papa . . ." my dad told me once about his father, "Papa clings to peace, more than he clings to truth."

But in the end, my family stood to benefit nothing from the loss of PawPaw Aubrey. They all relied on him so much—for guidance, for money, for stability. The devastation and chaos of the 1980s on LaHaye Road revealed how much he was holding it all together. Who, of us, could have wanted him gone? Who, of us, could have done this?

I try to tell Naomi that the greatest degree of guilt I can realistically grant my grandparents, my aunts, my uncles, my father is knowing there may be more to this, knowing—perhaps even with some degree of certainty—that the wrong man probably took the fall. And looking the other way. Even this feels far-fetched to me, after speaking so intimately with each of them, listening to the way this has affected their lives, hearing their own reverberating questions. I truly believe that they, like I, have no way of knowing for sure what really happened to PawPaw Aubrey. And, for them, the wondering had to end somewhere.

But I hear my own bias echoing against the walls. I tell her that no LaHaye got rich after PawPaw Aubrey's death, that none of these people had the motivation or the character to do something like this. I tell her that they loved him.

She is looking at the floor, the trust between us waning. I decide to give her the one name I do have, the LaHaye who isn't really a LaHaye.

"There is someone . . . Do you know who Sonny DeVillier is?"

She shakes her head, whispers his name, "Sonny DeVillier . . ."

Uncle Sonny

YOU KNOW," DAD TOLD ME, EARLY ON IN OUR CONVERSAtions about PawPaw Aubrey, "ever since I started my practice here, I've had patients tell me—so many of them, they tell me that anyone who's anyone in Eunice thinks Sonny DeVillier had something to do with killing his father-in-law."

It's a line of investigation I've toed with caution, a dreadful accusation against a man still living, whose daughter, my aunt Anne, I love. But it emerges everywhere, the name Sonny DeVillier spilling forth from people's mouths, unprovoked, across all corners of my research.

But with the name comes nothing solid: not a motive, not a shadow of proof. Only, again and again, "People say he had something to do with it."

"Who are these people?"

People in town, they say. *People all over town. Old people. Bad people.*

Few of them have names, and the ones that do claim they know nothing. Or they are dead.

Beyond the potential reward of Aubrey's life insurance—which feels like a stretch to me—the closest thing to a viable motive I get comes from Ted Smith, a former board member at Guaranty Bank. He tells me the rumors emerged right away, as soon as the body was found. "The conspiracy theories . . . that it was Sonny, or it was a setup . . . when they found the body it changed from 'it's probably a local' to 'it was a setup the whole time' and then they reached back into the family . . . it became just unbelievably harsh character assassination. And once it would start, there was nothing to stop it."

"But why would people think Sonny did it?" I ask him.

"I always thought it was about the Community Rice Mill loan," he says. The loan had at one point passed from Guaranty to Acadiana Bank, causing Sonny all sorts of grief before the FDIC demanded Guaranty take it back. "Mr. Aubrey put Sonny's bank in jeopardy."

WHEN I TELL MY DAD I'M PLANNING TO VISIT UNCLE SONNY IN the nursing home, he sets his coffee down. "Are you?"

"I'm just going to ask him about what he remembers," I say. What he remembers about PawPaw Aubrey, what he remembers about 1983. Aunt Anne is going with me. "He's got to be on his deathbed," Dad says.

"Aunt Anne says he's not doing great," I tell him. He'd been diagnosed with Parkinson's. She said she thinks he's had it for decades, the nerve cells wilting away, the dopamine disintegrating, little by little, for thirty years.

"Parkinson's . . . wow." Dad pauses, considering. "You know, people on their deathbed . . . that's when they start to talk."

"I always felt sorry for your mother," Uncle Sonny tells me when I visit in September 2017. I can't remember the last time I saw him; it must have been at least a decade. But he's instantly familiar. Flashes of those piercing blue eyes and that sly, elflike smile broach the surface of my memory. This is despite the sunken state of him now—entirely bald, except for white tufts on either side of his head. He's folded over, set deep in a leather recliner, his hands convulsing. I sit gingerly on the edge of his unmade bed while his daughter Anne fusses around the room, straightening things up. A nurse comes in and out over the course of our visit, making jokes with Uncle Sonny about turning the stark, depressing bedroom into a law office. "He's so sweet," she tells me on her way out. When she's gone, he laughs. "I don't even know her name."

He tells me I look just like my mom, and that he remembers when she first moved to Evangeline, how she so often sat quietly in the corner at the rowdy LaHaye gatherings. An introverted Texan girl who grew up with a small family in a trailer house, so far from home. "I knew what it was like to be an outsider in that family," he says.

Years later, Aunt Anne tells me that toward the end of his life, Uncle Sonny asked to join her for the LaHaye Christmases and Thanksgivings again. "I wouldn't bring him," she says. The last few times he attended, he had stunned everyone with his sheer meanness. Had called some of my older cousins, teenagers at the time, "too stupid to get into LSU" and my mommee Susan a bitch. It has been years since those outbursts, but that is how he is remembered on LaHaye Road. "He was a dick," says

Aunt Anne. "Not all the time, he wasn't. But he pissed people off. People didn't like him. And I can't blame them."

Despite the family's belief that Uncle Sonny did not like the LaHayes, I find tiny clues to the contrary in his things. There's a scrapbook filled with newspaper clippings of his and his daughters' achievements—there are school portraits of Jody and Richard and Billy, of Smokey, of Danny and Suzette and my dad. There are newspaper clippings from several of PawPaw Aubrey's exploits, and a saved program from my papa Wayne's graduation from medical school in the 1960s. In the years after Aunt Tot's death, Sonny writes in his journals about his loneliness, saying he wants to remain in close contact with his wife's family, "even if I don't recall every LaHaye's name."

PawPaw Aubrey's name is not mentioned once in Uncle Sonny's journals. But MawMaw Emily's is, and with a certain tenderness. "She is a warrior," he wrote in the months before her death.

My conversation with Uncle Sonny is a struggle, more in regard to his declining speaking abilities than his mental state, though certain things barb him, cycling back again and again. Like the fact that my dad didn't raise us on LaHaye Road. "That drove Emily wild," he says, laughing. "Marcel built his house away from the family."

When I ask Uncle Sonny what he remembers about PawPaw Aubrey's death, he delivers an often difficult-to-follow monologue. From the beginning, he tells the story of the kidnapping as though there were two, maybe three, abductors—"Two yo-yos from Eunice." This is how Aunt Anne always tells the story, too; indicating this is not simply a case of an old man being confused. This is how the tale was always told in the DeVillier home.

He goes on a mostly indecipherable rant about PawPaw Aubrey and his land, and his taxes, and his involvement with KATC News and CLECO Energy, the rice dryers. The end of each sentence disintegrates into a mumble. "Daddy," Aunt Anne begs him, "try to talk better. Even I can hardly understand you."

"I can't help it, baby," he says. "I'm trying my best."

He tells me about how he was the one who had to identify Aubrey's body, how he watched from above, at the top of the bridge, as they pulled it out of the Nezpique. "And the body was perfect."

He tells me about the rims, then adds: "That's how they got caught, too. And you know who the people were that did that?"

"You're talking about Balfa?" I ask.

"Yep. Mr. Aubrey knew who he was. He knew he was a crook."

When I ask Uncle Sonny if he attended the trial, he tells me he didn't. I can see that he's fading. He asks Aunt Anne to get him something to drink. When she opens the mini fridge, she tells him: "Your options are Boost, wine, and coconut water." He wants the Boost.

For an agonizing few minutes, the room is silent as he struggles to wrap his lips around the top of the straw, his tongue wagging, the creamy white liquid rising up into his mouth, dribbling down his chin a little, falling onto the sheet on his lap, which appears to be covering the fact that he isn't wearing pants. Could this pitiful, lonely, dying man be capable of fabricating this entire story right now? How much can someone possibly hide in such a vulnerable state?

One of the last things Uncle Sonny tells me, before I pack up my things and go, is that PawPaw Aubrey was a good man. "He was very kind," he says. "A good man."

I nod, disappointed. I'd hoped Sonny DeVillier, of all people, might tell me something else.

No Formidable Plan

THE MYTHOS OF THE CONTRACT KILLER THEORY, ATTACHED to mafiosi and conspiracy as it is, was rejected by the FBI from the beginning—when Sheriff Ramson Vidrine was shouting it to the heavens.

In the FBI's "Psychological Profile," which used data on similar criminal cases to characterize Aubrey LaHaye's kidnapper, the investigators begin by asking key questions about the details of the abduction:

> *First, why did the subject tell victims his car was in a ditch, but parked it in the victim's driveway?*
> *Second, why did subject use a small knife as a weapon, and not a gun?*
> *Then, why did subject take only a wallet and no other valuables?*
> *Fourth, why did the subject tie the victim's wife very loosely?*
> *Last, why didn't the subject recontact victim's family for the ransom?*

These details, the report concludes, suggest the abductor entered the LaHaye house without a "formidable" plan. Someone who had thought this through or was an experienced criminal would have anticipated that Aubrey's wife would be present and armed himself with something more intimidating than a knife. The subject either was not afraid of being identified, or the thought did not occur to him; he was unmasked, and not only did he leave one of the victims alive, he left her poorly constrained—able to quickly and easily contact law enforcement. "After the first phone call to the victim's family, subject realized he was not going to be able to obtain the ransom money without being apprehended. It is at this point the victim became a liability to the subject." Aubrey died, the report says, because his kidnapper was a poor planner.

Continuing on, the profiler suggests the subject's age is between twenty-five and twenty-seven years, and that he is of "medium intelligence"— which has been altered by drugs or mental illness. He has a high school education, and maybe some college or trade school. The subject would have either a minor or nonexistent criminal record and likely resides within a one-hour drive from the LaHaye home. He is either unemployed or works sporadically as a laborer. "Subject will feel increased stress as a result of this crime."

The report offers a compelling case against the more outlandish speculations of organized crime, and though imperfect, the profile does come pretty close to describing John Brady Balfa. A young man struggling with addiction (of alcohol, and likely not drugs), who had attended some college and up until recently (the previous September, when he had been charged with rape) had only a minor criminal background. He lived close by. He was in between jobs with Sunland at the time, working as a laborer.

Accepting the premise that Aubrey's murder was the result of a poorly planned ransom attempt, the profile might as easily point to Jimmy Sylvester. Though I am able to raise far fewer details of Jimmy's life, I do know that he was close to the right age, he had either a minor or nonexistent criminal background, he lived nearby, and he worked in salvage and mechanics. He, like John Brady, reasonably matched Emily's physical description. And he had *plenty* of access to tire rims.

Dominick Dupré's accusations as he told them to Mildred, Tim, and Naomi not only are implicative of Jimmy but also are damning to members of Evangeline Parish law enforcement and the DA's Office. Dupré claimed he told a sheriff's deputy, the sheriff, the DA's investigator, and the DA himself that Jimmy Sylvester killed Aubrey LaHaye—only to be told by each of them that nothing could be done, because Jimmy was Oscar's son. None of these men—Floyd Soileau, Ramson Vidrine, Rudy Guillory, or Billy Pucheu—are alive to deny or corroborate that these conversations occurred. Is it possible that the entire system of Evangeline Parish law enforcement would so thoroughly protect the perpetrator of one of the parish's most sensational murders, simply because his father was rich and powerful?

The biggest problem I have with this is a basic one: What are the chances that four different members of law enforcement confided in Dupré, a well-known criminal, that this was a cover-up?

But I suspend my disbelief, for now. After all, on the list of potential categories of corruption in Evangeline Parish, nepotism is the least surprising. In his totemic history *Opelousas Country*, Robert Gahn claims it was intrinsic, suggesting that the parish's high crime rates at the start of the twentieth century might be attributed to the fact that most of the population was related by blood. It bred a literally incestuous system of favors and protection. In Evangeline Parish, even if you aren't related to the people in power, chances are you know someone who is.

From the beginning, I've been unable to shake my discomfort with Billy Pucheu's aggressive suppression of information from Julie Cullen, especially concerning the time of death. Why go to such lengths if you trust your case is solid?

"Rudy *knew* John was the one who did it," Eva Guillory, his widow, tells me. "This was the big case of his career. He spoke about it for the rest of his life. He often would go over the details of what happened, and how much the whole thing affected him personally." She tells me she doesn't believe the case would have been solved by any other investigator, by someone who was less personally invested. "He was so committed to doing the right thing, dedicated in ways you don't see in a lot of people . . . he pursued this case because it was personal to him. He was not going to let it go. He wanted to do this for people he loved and cared about."

Even if Guillory and Pucheu did wholeheartedly believe in their case, is it possible that their close relationships to the LaHaye family clouded their judgment? Is it possible that this proximity motivated them, even subconsciously, to get someone, *anyone*, behind bars for this?

And then there is that darker possibility, the one suggested by Dupré. What if Pucheu and Guillory—or even just Pucheu, or even just Guillory—*needed* John Brady to be the fall guy? What if they were protecting someone else? With some reluctance, I think of Uncle Sonny. Of the rumors. *What if they were protecting us?*

Jimmy is the son of Oscar Sylvester Jr. He is rich, and we can't do him anything.

Like Aubrey LaHaye, Oscar Sylvester Jr. was of the "great generation" of Evangeline Parish elders. While Aubrey was building Mamou's first bank atop John LaHaye's lending philosophies and a fortune on his farming instincts, and Dr. Frank Savoy Jr. was fulfilling Frank Sr.'s dream of bringing a hospital to the prairie, Oscar was mastering the art of customer service.

At the start of the twentieth century, Oscar's father, Oscar Sylvester Sr., owned a neighborhood store in Plaisance, a community east of Mamou and Ville Platte, right over the border in St. Landry Parish. As a twentysomething working for his father, Oscar faced multiple run-ins with the law concerning bootlegging and moonshining.

But by 1937, Oscar's criminal days seemed behind him. He was farming along the east side of Evangeline Parish, and much like Aubrey, attempting to acquire as much land as he could get his hands on. He made most of his money as a local contractor, winning major road and gas line projects from the city and police jury. By 1946, at the age of thirty-two, Oscar became one of the first men in Evangeline Parish to own a private plane. As his contracting business grew into a house moving business, and his rice and farming operations expanded, Oscar became one of the biggest landowners in the area, and an important investor in local industry. Standing right there beside Aubrey at the meetings for bringing a textile mill to Evangeline and at the opening of Guaranty Bank in Mamou—there was Oscar in his suit, eyes squinted and savvy, hair combed to the side, hands in his deep, deep pockets.

While Oscar's and Aubrey's circles overlapped, there is little evidence to suggest they were close. They occupied similar places in the parish's power structure, but Oscar did so in a manner that was just a little darker, just a little messier, just a bit more vogue. Oscar had more style than Aubrey. There was the plane, and an airstrip behind his house for it. And the house—it's still there today, home now to the parish's now-retired resident orthopedist. Palatial, with a pecan orchard lining the long, long driveway, obscuring all but the rising peak of something mysterious and grand. We passed it every day on our way to school as kids, as we shifted from the scattered farmlands of Vidrine and into "town" (Ville Platte). On this property, in 1969, Oscar hosted a literal circus—elephants and all—in the backyard. His outdoor kitchen was outfitted in the finest antiques and noted for its grand dining table, which seated sixty. In his front yard, goldfish swam in a ten-thousand-pound historic bathtub once housed in the United States Capitol Building, where, legend has it, Speaker of the House Joseph G. Cannon used to relax while he dictated notes to his male secretaries.

Oscar was more political than Aubrey. He was frequently selected as part of local delegations to make cases for the parish, particularly in matters of infrastructure, in Baton Rouge or Washington. In 1956, he was even named an alternate delegate for the Democratic Party's National Convention. Locally, he never ran for office, but he shoved his weight around as one of the parish's biggest taxpayers.

242 | HOME OF THE HAPPY

In civil court, where he faced quite a bit of litigation, Oscar lost as often as he won. Suits for alimony from his ex-wives and worker's comp claims, mostly. He was sued at one point by the US secretary of labor, who accused him of failing to pay his employees the minimum wage. When a local couple won a suit after Sylvester's house moving company dropped their home and damaged it, Oscar "sold" the company to Jimmy, who was in college—a tactic the courts, after an appeal, saw right through. At one point, Oscar even sued Jimmy for his truck. There are at least two instances of simple battery, both of which resulted in plea deals.

He wasn't entirely above the law, though it is plausible he faced more lenient consequences than most. Some have told me they believe Oscar was involved in the mob, and even suggested he had a role in his son Jerry's death in that plane.

What could Oscar Sylvester Jr. have had on the 1983 deputy, sheriff, district attorney, and his investigator that would so radically protect his son, a failing businessman at the time, from a murder charge? What threat could he represent that would lead them to conspire together to send the wrong person to jail for the rest of his life?

PART V

The Question of Relief

The Gospel of John

Y EARS AGO, IN ONE OF THE HALF-DOZEN CATHOLIC PERIOD-
icals my mommee Susan reads, she found an article with John
Brady Balfa's name in it. "He's given his life to the Lord!" This
brought her great joy. She cut the article out, folded it, and saved it somewhere in her massive house of infinite folded articles and poems and
photographs—shoved into books and on shelves and in folders. I'm sure
we'll find it someday. But every time I see her, and we discuss the Aubrey
LaHaye story, she tells me, "Gosh, I just wish I could find that article."

Google—a far less poetic repository than my grandmother's house of
papers—brings me to three articles published in 2016. They announce
John Brady Balfa as one of six inmates from Angola who completed a
prison program in pastoral studies through the Loyola University New
Orleans Institute for Ministry. The course was meant to grant him deeper
knowledge of the Catholic faith so to better share it with fellow inmates.

This program was one of an influx of religious initiatives that have
come to characterize rehabilitation at Angola during the reign of Warden
Burl Cain from 1995 to 2016, which coincided with over half of John
Brady's time at Angola.

A charismatic Southern Baptist from Pitkin, Louisiana, Cain cuts
an almost caricatured figure of a good old boy come to save the day—
big belly, drawl, and all. He arrived at Angola with his legacy as a radical force in the penal system clearly in view, delivered prophetically and
matter-of-factly in Bible quotes. He was gonna change this hellhole, and
he was gonna do it through Jesus Christ. Cain's religious crusade func-
tioned around a concept he coined as "moral rehabilitation"—the idea
that by instilling morality through religion, he might transform Angola's
rapists, murderers, and thieves into people who can better contribute
to society and live meaningful lives. For much of his tenure, Cain was
lauded across the country for the way he was transforming Angola into

a peaceful, God-focused place. In his memoir, Wilbert Rideau described Cain as someone who "enjoyed being dictator" and "regarded himself as a benevolent one," who would habitually refer to himself as "the father" and the prisoners as "his children."

Cain's wardenship would come to be marred by various degrees of scandal, eliciting more than one investigation into corrupt business dealings and criticisms of his role as a quasi-dictator of Louisiana's notorious prison labor industrial complex. Still, his commitment to rehabilitation, during a time when sentiment toward prisoners was out of fashion, has left an impact in the form of expanded vocational and quality-of-life programming prisoners at Angola continue to benefit from. The biggest mark Cain left on Angola was the 1995 establishment of a seminary program.

The "Bible College," as it is often called, is offered through the New Orleans Baptist Theological Seminary and gives inmates the opportunity to acquire an associate or bachelor's degree in theology, qualifying them to serve as ministers in the prison—and for some of them, someday, outside of it, too. The opportunity arrived only a year after Congress signed into law the Violent Crime Control and Law Enforcement Act, which made incarcerated individuals ineligible to receive Pell Grants, enormously restricting access to higher education for prisoners across America. In the early 1990s, there were almost eight hundred college-in-prison programs across the country; by 1997, there were eight. (The law was overturned in December 2020, and in July 2023 Pell Grants were once again made available to incarcerated individuals in United States prisons. Due to administrative challenges, as of 2024 there is still only one eligible prison college program in the country.)

For thirty years, the Bible College—which is funded by outside donations—has been the sole opportunity for inmates to earn a college degree at Angola. The curriculum for the ministerial degree includes general education classes such as English, algebra, and history, as well as more specialized courses like Greek and Hebrew, and various instruction on Christian history, theology, and preaching strategies. Though the degree is conducted with a focus on Baptist teachings, inmates are not prohibited from participating based on their chosen denomination or religion. Graduates of the program are considered inmate ministers by the administration, responsible for facilitating Bible studies, worship services, and prayer groups. They often receive jobs in the chaplain's office.

These jobs—along with prison lawyers—are the best paying in Angola, at twenty to forty cents an hour.

In this way, Cain was able to assert control over inmate religious organizations and leadership, while at the same time reaping the benefits—financial and otherwise—of allowing "trained" religious leaders to emerge from the inmate population itself. Religious leaders under Cain's wardenship were not simply leading a club of faithful. They were community leaders, political leaders, in Angola. The prison became a place where commitment to a faith grants you power.

Catholic inmates at Angola have had as much incentive as anyone to participate in the benefits the Bible College offers: education, access to better jobs, and lessons in religious leadership. As Christianity burned throughout the prison, the Catholic chaplaincy, with Cain's support, also worked to increase programming for its parishioners, in the form of retreats, training programs, and additional opportunities to worship. During Warden Cain's tenure, inmates worked around the clock to build five new chapels across the Angola property, including the Our Lady of Guadalupe Catholic Chapel at the Main Prison. For thirty-eight days, forty prisoners worked to build the chapel, laying bricks and building scaffolds. And for thirty-eight nights, another crew would replace them, working in freezing temperatures beneath the West Feliciana moon. It was completed just before the Feast Day of Our Lady of Guadalupe on December 12, 2013, and was blessed in a special ceremony conducted by the bishop of the Diocese of Baton Rouge, Robert William Muench. Official documentation testifying to the chapel's consecration was signed by the bishop, by the Catholic chaplain, and by two Catholic peer ministers—one of them John Brady Balfa. At the end of the ceremony, Bishop Muench announced he had a personal message from the Vatican: "Pope Francis gives you assurance of his prayers and imparts his apostolic blessings to the community and benefactors of the Our Lady of Guadalupe Chapel."

Just about everything I know about John Brady Balfa's time at Angola is tied to his religious journey, a map I draw by cobbling together mentions of him in various newspapers published over the past thirty years.

The earliest evidence I've found of John Brady's recommitment to Catholicism is a letter written in 1989 to the editors of various newspapers across Acadiana by a woman named Susan Balfa, who claimed to be John Brady's wife. I do not know how Susan met John Brady, or when they married, only that it was sometime during the first few years of his imprisonment. The ceremony had to have taken place in one of the on-site chapels, likely the circa-1940s St. Augustine Catholic Chapel, and was overseen by one of the prison chaplains or an outside minister selected by the couple. Couples were allowed to invite a best man and a bridesmaid, as well as their parents and any children Susan might have had. For Susan to enter the front gate, she had to present the official marriage license, with John Brady's address listed as 17544 Tunica Trace, Angola, LA.

Published under headlines "Balfa Wrongfully Convicted, Says Wife" and "Wife Says Balfa Is Not Guilty," the letter aims to clear John Brady's name to the public, letting them know he is innocent of Aubrey LaHaye's murder, and that she, his wife, is fighting for his freedom. "My faith does not lie in our judicial system," she says, "nor in the fact that John is indeed innocent . . . We serve a big GOD—a miracle working GOD, who will get all the praise and glory for John's release. I even praise Him for John's incarceration! . . . My husband was lost in sin without Christ as his Savior, and in the parish jail 'Brother Ray' met John and loved him enough to introduce him to Jesus."

Susan's words drip with earnestness, with hope, with confidence in John Brady's innocence and in a just world, where truth and goodness always win out. A world where God, in his omniscience and omnipotence, makes sure of it. It is this same confidence in cosmic justice, in God, that reassured MawMaw Emily—that continues to reassure my grandparents and many of my aunts and uncles—that John Brady is exactly who did this. That evil was justly discovered, and rooted out, and punished.

Surely, the Lord has heard all their prayers, seen John Brady's wife kneel every night beside her bed while miles and miles away Emily LaHaye kneeled beside hers. One begging for divine justice to save him, the other offering thanks for locking away the wrongdoer, forever.

It's been over thirty years since Susan sent these letters. I wonder if she has lost faith. If she has, where did she lose it? In John Brady? In God? I don't even know if she is still married to him, though I find no documentation of a divorce.

Eventually, though, I do find "Brother Ray." Ray Jones is an evangelist minister whose Radiance Ministries specializes in spreading "The Word" through song. On his website, he mentions how over the years he has frequented prisons in Louisiana. In news articles, I find a handful of references to him, by prisoners, as "Brother Ray." I send an email, asking Jones if he has any recollection of meeting a man named John Brady Balfa in Evangeline Parish around 1985, attaching a clipping of Susan's letter. He responds the next day:

> He was very broken. If he is the same man, he was desperate to share his story and declare his innocence, but he was broken over the direction of his life. All I did was share the love oe [sic] Christ with him and pray 'The Sinners Prayer' with him. I am pretty sure I gave him and [sic] paperback New Testament and told him to start by reading the Gospel of John. I may have communicated with him by way of a letter after that, but [it] was a long time ago. After our prayer, he seemed to have a newfound purpose and there was a definite change in his perspective.

According to John Brady's own spiritual testimony—delivered in newspaper interviews over the years—he didn't wholly recommit himself to the Lord until 1994, when he went to confession for the first time in twenty-two years. The priest serving as chaplain at the time listened for over an hour as John Brady spoke his sins aloud, clouding the confessional. Afterward, the priest embraced him. He told him God loves him, that God forgives him. That the air, within and without, has been made clean, has been made clear. He did not have to live his life a forsaken man.

Around this time, Warden Burl Cain was establishing the country's first fully operational prison hospice program in Angola, a prison where over 80 percent of its inhabitants are doomed to die there. Cain worked with the University Hospital Community Hospice in New Orleans (UHCH) to create a program to the standards of the National Hospice and Palliative Care Organization, without significant costs to the prison. The secret to this structure was, of course, to use inmate labor to support trained hospice staff; inmate volunteers received training as caregivers who would then support their peers until their last breath and ensure they are not alone when they go. The program has been hailed as an initiative of radical empathy and humanity and has since been replicated in prisons nationwide. To this day, the inmate volunteers are considered "anointed ones" among their peers, many of whom will die in such arms as theirs someday.

I do not know when John Brady started volunteering with the hospice program, nor how long he participated. It's possible that to this day some of our world's most reviled men see his face before they say goodbye to it. In 2001, though, the inmate hospice volunteers were asked to vote for the individual among them who had "put forth the best effort in end-of-life care." And John Brady Balfa was named the Inmate Volunteer of the Year, an honor described by a representative of the GRACE Project who bestowed the award as "tantamount to the best volunteer caregiver in the country, because Angola has the nation's best program."

By 2004, John Brady was named one of Angola's twelve Catholic Peer Ministers. These ministers were granted the responsibility of assisting the Catholic chaplains with counseling, burials, and distributing Holy Communion throughout Angola. One of John Brady's main tasks was to visit the prisoners in isolation cells, to talk with them, to ask them if they wanted to discuss the Word of God.

In 2005, he was reassigned to Camp D—a more violent dormitory in Angola—to lead ministry efforts there. Before his arrival, only two men in D participated in Catholic programming. Within a few months, John Brady was regularly leading a cohort of thirty faithful. "I answered the call with my heart, but the rest of my body didn't want to go," he is quoted saying about his new appointment. "We all work as a team in reaching out to our brothers, helping one another to live and grow in faith."

In 2007, John Brady had risen to the role of clerk in the chaplain's department, granting him the role as spokesperson for various initiatives within the prison's Catholic community. He was transferred from Camp D to the Main Prison, where he still to this day lives in the Ash dormitory, home of the trusties.

In one of the 2016 articles my grandmother initially led me to, John Brady explains his motivation to continue his education through programs like the Loyola Institute for Ministry. "Our focus is when we grow, we help other people grow," he says. "Our ministry is a ministry of presence. We're in prison, so we all have a commonality. We all come from the same place. Ministry is helping people find hope in a hopeless situation."

Something about the religiosity of Cain's Angola has always unsettled me. Part of it is the image he poses, a white "man of God" overseeing a farm labored over by a largely Black, barely compensated population held against their will. Part of it is, if I'm being honest, my own scrambled feelings about religion—and the cynicism such doubts breed. Rideau himself described Cain's use of religion as a mechanism of control, of power. As a way to pacify men into submission.

But at the same time, I cannot deny the very real hope that religion can offer men like John Brady. Men who have been told they are irredeemable have found, through faith, redemption and meaning in a life spent behind concertina wire, at the whim of a government that hates them. Certainly, there is value in hope; and where else are they to find it?

Other people's skepticism finds ground in John Brady himself, and his motives for becoming a Godly man in prison. A former Angola chaplain, Joseph E. Wilson, once described his experience of inmate ministers as largely motivated by power, "Some of them intend to try to promote the Lord's work," he said. "But on the other hand, you have a number of them who are in it because of the power and prestige they get out of it."

I see it. I can see it especially when you apply this view to John Brady as people remember him just before he was convicted—someone who spent his short time as a free adult dreaming of political acclaim, manipulating those around him to achieve attention and respect, lashing out when things didn't go his way, refusing to accept responsibility for his actions. Someone who craves power, always just outside his reach. Ministry would have been the fastest way to achieve something resembling power at Angola, especially under Burl Cain's rule.

But I hate this.

I, like my far-more-faithful grandmother, would like to believe John Brady has changed. I would like to believe he's earnest in his desire to be *good*, that he's found some way to make his life meaningful. It's easier that way. It makes us all feel a little better—as we sleep in our own comfortable beds enjoying the freedom of privacy and chosen company, of access to media and transportation and life without chains. Imagining that locking people away might lead them to be exactly what they were made for.

But even more than this, such transformation would mean redemption is possible. And with that, perhaps, forgiveness.

The problem comes when I try to account for John Brady's claims of innocence. If we are to believe his faith sincere, then what do we make of his enduring insistence that he did *not* kill Aubrey LaHaye? He is either lying, or he isn't. And if he's lying—the life he's turned over to Christ is one built upon falsehood.

If he's not . . .

Jane

DON'T ANSWER THE UNKNOWN HAMMOND NUMBER THE FIRST time my phone rings. When I see that they've left a voicemail, I bring the phone to my ear, and almost miss my next stop sign.

"Hey, Jordan, my name is Jane Hogan. I'm a postconviction lawyer out of Hammond, Louisiana. I'm calling because I've recently gotten involved in the case of John Balfa."

I call her right back. By the time I pull into my driveway, we've arranged to meet the following weekend. "You probably know a lot more about this case than I do," she says. "But I don't see how John could have done this. I'd love to pick your brain, to see what you think about it all."

For months, I'd considered taking my questions about the trial to a lawyer. I needed to know whether the red flags I saw—the acrobatics employed to keep the time-of-death information from Julie Cullen, the ambiguities of the forensic testimony—were significant, or exaggerated by my own search for a story. The courts, through every appeal, had held up John Brady's conviction. These were legal experts. Who am I? But this lawyer, she sees the problems too.

Jane Hogan, I learn, is about a decade older than I am. A few years' prior, she'd launched a literary journal with other Baton Rouge creatives, a project meant to explore the phenomenon of southern femininity while pushing against the "Southern Belle" stereotypes of hoop-skirted gentility. "I don't wear makeup," Jane said in one of the interviews that circulated around the journal's release. "I cut my own hair on my porch, and I drink whiskey till 7 a.m."

Jane hasn't been a lawyer for all that long, but I quickly discover she's established a reputation as a fierce advocate for criminal justice reform, a defender of the forgotten, the hopeless, the reviled. In an interview she gave to LSU's student newspaper, *The Reveille*, she reveals a little about her motivations as a defense attorney and a glimpse into how she sees the world. "I don't believe people are inherently bad," she tells the reporter.

"Look at why [the crime] happened. Look at the circumstances. Look at what we could have done, [what] could his family have done, what can we do now? I don't think we should give up on people. I think we should try to heal them." In the years to come, her advocacy for second chances would on occasion come to resemble leniency. One of her later clients was a Catholic priest convicted of raping a teenage altar boy. Thanks to Jane's highly publicized appeals, he completed his sentence under house arrest so that he would not be exposed to the coronavirus outbreak at the parish jail.

Jane started her work in postconviction representation—advocating for the rights of people already deemed criminal—shortly before we met, when she entered private practice at her parents' firm in Hammond. Part of this work is in conjunction with the Louisiana Parole Project, a non-profit dedicated to advocacy for incarcerated individuals up for parole, supporting them as they reintegrate into society. In this capacity, she would make a name for herself fighting for Angola's "10–6 lifers," men who, prior to the 1970s, accepted plea deals for life sentences with the expectation that they would be eligible for parole after ten years plus six months of good behavior, only to have the parole eligibility requirement increased to twenty years, then forty, then abolished altogether. In 2021, Jane would win freedom for two of these "forgotten men"—some of Louisiana's longest-serving inmates, both in their seventies—by negotiating new plea deals.

John Brady Balfa, who pled not guilty and entered Angola with an unambiguous "life without parole" sentence, isn't one of these men championed by the Parole Project.

No, Jane's interest in him is different.

"Ooooh, what a curious girl you are," Jane coos, her hands wrapped around the bottoms of my chocolate lab's ears. "I've got three," she goes on, before settling into my dining room chair. "All ladies." And a baby on the way. "Crazy, totally. It's bananas, not planned." Her face is pretty in a gentle way that reminds me of Brie Larson, and her voice has a quiet, musical quality to it.

Between us, laid out on the table, are most of the analog records I've got: the newspaper clippings, John Brady's Christmas card, the long sheets of paper from the clerk of court's file, the composites.

Jane tells me she's been working to slow down her practice. "No new cases," she'd tell her paralegal. "No more cases." But about two months ago, when the summary of John Brady's case came across her desk, she'd found herself enthralled. "I am just so fascinated by it."

John Brady's family hired her, she says—Naomi and one of his nieces, Bridget. He had recently gotten a response to a long-pending FOIA request, gaining him access to the same FBI files I'd been sifting through. Thirty-four years since his sentence, this was the first John Brady had seen of these records; even redacted, much of the information in them was new to him. His family wondered if there might be enough to make a case for his innocence, and if not that, then for a mistrial based on the fact that this information had been illegally kept from him all these years.

The "new information" that had captured the Balfas' attention included the discovery of the two knives recovered near Aubrey's home, the FBI's acknowledgment of at least thirty alternative suspects (all names redacted), Emily's positive identification of Taylor Strother in a lineup, the fingerprint lifted from the tire rim, and the blond hair—all elements of the investigation John Brady, and his previous lawyers, had never been made aware of. "These are things you would think that if they were dead ringers for John Brady, or if they would have helped them to put him away, they would have brought that out," says Jane. So why did they never come up in his trial? Likely, because they didn't support the state's case.

"Tell me if I'm wrong," she says, folding her hands on the table, "but I think the three of us have similar goals"—the three of us being her, John Brady, and me. "We all want to unveil the truth." Though, of course, her goal extends beyond that. She is candid about this: "I want to get John out of prison, and even if I found out he did do it, I'll still try to get him out of prison."

But she *doesn't* think he did this. It's part of what drew her in so immediately.

She asks if I've come up with any alternative suspects during my research. I tell her about Calvin Ware. I mention Jimmy and Oscar Sylvester; Naomi's already told her the story of Dominick Dupré. I tell her about Feryl Granger and the Mamou Mafia, about T-Ed and Carlos Marcello and the windy lists of names at the depths of the Aubrey LaHaye conspiracies. I even tell her about Sonny. I tell her that none of it seems to go anywhere, to land in any comprehensible order. There's nothing real, nothing solid.

I've seen the DA file, I tell her, but only under the watchful eye of the former assistant district attorney Richard Vidrine. "That is a public record," she tells me, shaking her head. "You have a constitutional right to view everything that's in this file. What he was doing was illegal." At the time, I'd felt Vidrine's approach to showing me some things, and holding others back, was sketchy, annoying. *It was illegal?* Jane asks me, "If everything was done right, why would he be protective of the file all these years later?" *Right.*

Jane has run into her own obstacles trying to access the DA's file. She submitted a records request to the Evangeline Parish Clerk of Courts Office shortly after agreeing to represent John Brady, only to have it returned because it was sent to the "wrong address." "Which . . . it wasn't. I double-checked," she says. When she visited the courthouse in person, requesting access to the files, she was told the woman who "handles these things" wasn't there. "I'm worried the current district attorney in Evangeline Parish is going to dig in his heels on this case, you know, where it was a high-profile case, and they have a conviction and they have a guy who is serving life," she tells me. "So why revisit it? Why, even if he didn't do it . . . to not have a replacement, someone to blame instead of him . . . it's hard."

I already know I'll be trying to get in front of that file again, and I tell her if I manage to get to it before she does, I'll share whatever I find.

"That's what I was kind of hoping for," she says. "I think this could be something we can maybe partner on, like share information. Within certain limitations of course."

I take a deep breath. "Right. There is one thing."

I'm fine with exchanging ideas, sharing records—excited about it even. This has always been about seeking truth, and the prospect of a collaborator is thrilling. But I do not, in fact, know with certainty that John Brady is not guilty. I imagine the look on Papa Wayne's face should he see me standing beside Jane Hogan and John Brady Balfa, their assistant, their helper. I won't jump entirely onto their side of the fence, yet.

"I'd like to avoid getting into a position where I'd need to testify on John's behalf," I tell her. "Not unless we can prove his innocence, and only then if the truth rests somehow with me. My family—"

"Oh, I know," Jane cuts me off. "I absolutely understand. This trauma, it's complicated."

She pauses, starts to ask a question, stops, aimlessly picks up one of the composites from the top of the stack of papers on the table. Then she goes for it, "Are there are any members of your family who are, like, 'I don't think John Balfa's the right person'? Like they don't know who did it, but they believe in his innocence?"

It's a question I wasn't expecting, a stance I haven't even firmly taken. "There's a lot of people . . ." I start, then hesitate. ". . . I don't think anyone is confident enough to say that. A *lot* of people have questions."

She nods, switches gears, assures me this arrangement will be a simple exchange of access. My connections to Evangeline Parish and her connections to John Brady and the Balfas. My extensive newspaper archive, court transcript, and historical context; her legal expertise and access to all ongoing efforts toward John Brady's legal case.

"I plan on filing an application by June," she tells me. Less than a year away. "These are so hard, though," she says. "It totally sucks to represent people you believe are innocent. It's so hard to prove these things. Especially when the cards have been intentionally hidden."

We start to go through my archive—organized with a chaotic logic only decipherable to me. She scans PawPaw Aubrey's lengthy résumé, picks up a photograph of him and MawMaw Emily. I tell her some of the stories I've collected about my great-grandfather: how he was a handshake banker, knew everyone in town. How no one ever saw him wearing shorts, not even at the camp. How he never cooked, except to barbecue, when he'd lay an old refrigerator sideways on the ground and grill a whole chicken in the trough. A true Cajun microwave.

As I speak, Jane smiles and asks questions, delicately flipping through the yellowed newspapers. When we get to my photographs of the Nezpique, she pronounces the bayou's name wrong, using the "z" and leaving off the "kay." She does know the Balfa Brothers, though, and when those news articles emerge, her head snaps up, "He *is* related to Dewey Balfa! I didn't feel like it was my place to ask, to fangirl. How wild!"

It's my turn to ask about John Brady, a chance to collect those rare scraps of his personhood not forty years ago, but now. "What is he like?"

"Yeah," she says. "Well, I can tell you . . . um, he's a really—and if he *is* the person who did this to your great-grandfather, I'm sure it's hard to hear—but he's very, *very* kind."

She tells me that in their first few meetings, John Brady was quick to admit he had done terrible things. When Jane offered to look into his rape conviction in Texas and his attempted murder conviction in St. Landry Parish, he told her "No, no, no, no, no. I did those things. I accept those charges. And I've done my time for that." But he didn't kill Aubrey

LaHaye, he told her. "And he's, like, 'I cannot say I did something I did not do.'"

Jane even goes so far as to say that if the DA came to John Brady tomorrow and offered him a plea deal for time served—"Just say you did it and walk free"—he'd refuse. "He won't do it."

One of the first things Jane does, while awaiting a response from another records request, is seek out a second opinion on Aubrey's time of death. "If the time of death that was testified to is not actually accurate, then it's really exculpatory for John," she emphasizes. Were Dr. McCormick's and Dr. Rodriguez's assessments correct? Did Aubrey LaHaye die immediately after he was kidnapped, or was it possible that it happened later, when John Brady was already in Texas?

Jane contracts the National Autopsy Assay Group, an independent forensic consultation service based out of San Diego, to review the Aubrey LaHaye case. She sends them everything she's got: the transcript with McCormick's and Rodriguez's testimony and the autopsy report.

When the results come back mid-2020, the report is 250 pages long, featuring assessments by forensic pathologist (and NAA Group CEO) Dr. Evan Matshes and forensic anthropologist Dr. Madeleine Hinkes, as well as pages and pages of relevant medicolegal studies and forensic pathology textbook pages to back them up.

Right out the door, Matshes takes issue with Dr. McCormick's expertise; he was not board certified (only "board eligible," according to his testimony) in forensic pathology and likely lacked formal training on the subject. Going into the autopsy itself, Matshes raises questions about whether or not Aubrey died because of his head injuries, which he writes are "potentially fatal, [but] not in and of themselves necessarily fatal." He notes that many of the findings on the body McCormick attributed to shock could also be attributed to drowning, particularly the hemorrhage in each of Aubrey's middle ears. McCormick's estimation that Aubrey's wounds were inflicted within fifteen to thirty minutes before his death Matshes deemed a "classic problem" in forensic pathology, without any scientific basis.

"Mr. LaHaye may have been thrown into the bayou while he was still alive (having already received the head injuries)," he writes. "More likely than not, drowning played a pathophysiologic part in causing his demise."

Reading this, I shake my head, wanting to reject it. It's absurd—who is to say what is the worse way to die? But something about the sudden finality of that death by blows seemed to shut PawPaw Aubrey's eyes, to dull the height of his fear. The lights suddenly blown out. He wouldn't have felt the cold water, wouldn't have struggled to breathe, tied to those rims like an animal, sinking into the Nezpique as though sinking into sleep, her churning waters ushering him into the next life.

But perhaps not. Perhaps he saw it all, felt it all.

When it comes to the time of death, Matshes's assessment is delivered in all caps: THE TESTIMONY OFFERED BY DR. MCCORMICK ABOUT TIME OF DEATH WAS IRRESPONSIBLE. Matshes argues against the use of the gastrointestinal contents as a measuring stick. "Patterns of human urination and defecation are so variable, highly personal, and unpredictable that they have never been recognized as factors that could or should be considered when determining time of death," he writes, even going so far as to call McCormick's rationale "pseudoscience."

According to Dr. Hinkes, Dr. William Rodriguez's estimate that Aubrey's death occurred ten to twelve days prior to the body's examination was indeed a legitimate line of evidence. But then she goes on to list all the factors Rodriguez did not seem to account for in his assessment: Did he consider Aubrey's clothing and how that might affect decomposition? What about the microclimate, whether the body was submerged, if the water was moving, plant life, degree of shade? "Dr. Rodriguez appropriately gave a time range," she writes. "But might not have considered all the factors listed above."

To Jane, the report has the potential to break things open, to raise enough questions to get John Brady back into the courtroom. For me, it only expands the gaping hole of possibilities surrounding PawPaw Aubrey's death. One less certainty, a dozen more questions. A degree more of sadness.

But in a cell in Angola, a tiny spark of hope.

Over the course of the first half of 2020, Jane Hogan keeps me updated on her progress. In April, I get the cell phone number of the current district attorney, Trent Brignac, from my little brother, whose college roommate is his son. It's the beginning of the COVID-19 pandemic. I'm furloughed with time to spare, and the courthouse is mostly shut down. Brignac tells me he'll have someone pull the file for me; it'll be waiting in an empty conference room. I drive the hour from Lafayette, where I am now living, to Ville Platte each day for a week, locking myself in that room with my notes and those boxes. And I dig.

I agree to share anything compelling I find with Jane, who still has not received a response to her public records request.

Besides mountains of records concerning the trial and investigation, I accumulate a collection of loose ends. There's a pocketknife, unfolded and rusted to the point of crumbling, in an envelope labeled "Rec. from Terry DeVillier on 11/18/85 at 10:30 a.m. Found by his wife about 8 weeks ago in ditch in front of his house." The date is the day the Aubrey LaHaye murder trial was set to begin, and over a year since John Brady's attack on his bookie. I imagine the knife got tossed in here in between strategy meetings, without time to test or follow up on before the trial—the assumption being, of course, that this could possibly be the knife used on both PawPaw Aubrey and Terry DeVillier. A loose end never tied. I hold the artifact gingerly, pieces of it coming off in my palm. Could something so small, so ugly, be the impetus of all this? Is this where it ended up?

Digging deeper, I find two photographs of footprints, framed in camel-colored sand by red pine needles and little rocks. Six ridges on the sole, narrowing like an egg toward the toes. Three bigger ridges at the heel, little wineglasses. Fingers hold a tape measure to them—a foot and half-inch each. Taken at the Nezpique, I can only presume.

Another envelope holds a folded-up paper towel, labeled: "White paper towel under left side of seat. 10/2/84 1980 Ford. Received S/A Owen Odom 10-3-84 2:55 p.m. Q49." This one I can trace back to the FBI file, which lists the evidence submitted for testing. The paper towel was taken from John Brady's truck in a search conducted in December 1984, in which a Louisiana state policeman vacuumed debris from various areas in the truck to be sent off to the FBI labs. I wonder what they were hoping to find in his truck over a year after Aubrey's murder. Then I see that the paper towel was submitted for fingerprint analysis, which came back inconclusive. It seems as though they were hoping to source a fingerprint from John Brady, likely to compare against the print found on the rim attached to Aubrey's body. The FBI's results report: "No fingerprint record was located here for John Brady Balfa."

But that can't be right? In 1984, John Brady was in custody for the Terry DeVillier case. Couldn't the FBI, or the DA's Office, have gotten prints directly from him? In the deposition given by John Brady's old landlord after his 1982 arson attempt, she claims investigators lifted seven latent prints from gas cans found on the property right after the fires, which were matched to John Brady's. I find this report *in* the DA file, indicating Guillory or Pucheu must have known about it. Couldn't they have connected with the police in Baton Rouge to get a copy of John Brady's prints for comparison? Why was it necessary to search his truck? Was any comparison ever conducted at all? And why, of all the evidence that was lost to the ether, did this ultimately useless paper towel manage to survive in the DA file?

In the box, I also find a single-page document titled: "Interstate Flight-Escape: WANTED BY THE FBI: Henry Cook Salisbury."

Salisbury, I discover, is evidence that the DA's Office did entertain, at least briefly, the possibility of the Dixie Mafia's involvement in Aubrey LaHaye's murder. Also known as "Little Henry," "The Hatchet," and various other aliases, Salisbury was once described by the sheriff of Biloxi as "the most dangerous man in the world." The sheriff knew, too. He was his coconspirator in various misdeeds, including Salisbury's grand finale—a plot to kill the Gulfport police chief, foiled by the FBI in 1983. In January of 1983.

When Aubrey was killed, Salisbury—like Feryl Granger, Carlos Marcello, and Clifton Thibodeaux—was incarcerated, and quite occupied. He had just been captured after seven years on the run, with a criminal reputation that struck fear into anyone remotely involved in the Gulf Coast's criminal underworld. His record goes back as far as the 1930s, with charges for running illegal gambling rings, manslaughter, and armed robberies—big ones, jailbreaks, wiretapping, drugs. When the FBI caught up to Salisbury in the summer of 1982, he was living in the Pink Panther Mobile Home Park outside of New Orleans.

He was arrested, facing multiple charges in several different cities— most of which he wouldn't have the chance to face before succumbing to liver cancer in March of 1984. Since then, stories have proliferated about his notorious reputation as a hit man. His fee wasn't even that high. He *liked* to kill.

Because of the timing of his arrest, Henry Salisbury couldn't have been Aubrey's killer himself. And it's difficult to imagine that amid the abrupt end of his life as a fugitive and the half-dozen charges being levied against him, he'd have had time or energy to coordinate a hit against a banker in middle-of-nowhere Mamou. But what do I know of criminal conspiracy? It's possible that he, a criminal ringleader based in Louisiana in the years before Aubrey's death, at least knew something about it. Someone at the DA's office thought so, at least for a moment.

I've got documents spread across half of the conference room table. The room is windowless and warm. I've forgotten to pack my lunch, but don't want to waste the time it will take to hunt down something to eat in early-pandemic Ville Platte. Each day I leave the courthouse feeling as though I've barely made a dent. I'm not even reading everything, am photographing most of it to peruse later. But so often I can't help myself; I step into the cavern, and half a day will pass before I emerge on the other side.

I almost miss the next Easter egg, squeezed in with the various pre-trial motions made by Julie Cullen and Billy Pucheu. Motion for Continuance, Motion to Suppress Evidence, Motion to Obtain a Private Investigator, Motion for a Change of Venue.

Motion & Order for Subpoena to Tim Balfa.

The document orders John Brady's brother Tim to appear for questioning in Pucheu's office on June 3, 1985, regarding "his wallet being found near the location where Aubrey LaHaye's body was found, and any information that he has concerning the death, armed robbery, and kidnapping of Aubrey LaHaye."

What?

When I tell my dad about this find, I see something rare on his face: surprise. "*Really?*" Tim would have been about eighteen years old in January 1983, and his presence anywhere near that section of the Nezpique during that time does not look good for John Brady. But while it's true this evidence might have helped the State's case, it would have also complicated it—made the story less cut-and-dry, raised questions.

"I saw Tim just the other day," Dad says. I've reached out to Tim more than once in hopes of meeting, and each time have been met only with silence. "How do you explain that?" Dad muses of the wallet. "Why was that not brought up in court?"

Tim must have shown up for questioning in June, because there is no evidence that he was ever charged with contempt of court. What did he tell Pucheu that would convince him to drop the matter altogether? What did he know? There is no further record of the interaction, or of Tim Balfa at all, in the file.

\\\\\\

THE MOST INTRIGUING DOCUMENT I FIND IN THE DA FILE, THOUGH, is a handwritten letter to the Evangeline Parish Sheriff's Department from an inmate, Charles Watts, at the Harrison County Jail in Gulfport, Mississippi. It's dated June 3, 1984.

> *Dear Sir,*
>
> *Because of my need to remedy a problem I presently have in Livingston Parish, this letter is to provide you with some information concerning a murder in your area and if you feel that you want additional dates on this subject, then we can discuss the deal I want.*
>
> *There is a fellow named Danny Singleton who's incarcerated here at the Harrison County Jail with me, and he has told me about a banker from Mamou, Louisiana, that was kidnapped from his home to be held for ransom. It was a fake ransom demand and the banker had been killed for someone.*
>
> *Danny told me he was beat and thrown into a bayou. His son-in-law (which Danny was supposed to know) has a deal made and Danny had gotten a couple of fellows from Mobile, Alabama, and they had met with some other fellow concerning the deal. After the business was completed, Danny had took them back to Mobile, Alabama.*
>
> *If you are interested in additional information about this subject, then I'm willing to provide enough to let you know that I do know something about it and once a deal can be made about my problem in Livingston, Louisiana, then we can determine how much you need from me.*
>
> Charles Watts

The banker's son-in-law. Sonny.

The Son-in-Law

THE LAST TIME I VISIT UNCLE SONNY IN THE NURSING HOME is in March of 2019, on his eighty-fourth birthday—about a year *before* I'll discover Charles Watts's letter in the DA File.

When I arrive, Aunt Anne is helping him spit mucus into a bowl. "I'm so sorry, Jordan," she tells me. I assure her that it is fine, that I can handle it.

She's brought him a sea salt caramel cheesecake from the store, as well as shampoo and body wash. "Happy Birthday, Dad," she says.

He's glad to see me. We cover a lot of the same ground as on my previous visits. But this time, his position on PawPaw Aubrey shifts, "He was a very, very strange man. I think he liked Mamou because he was a rich man in a little town. Mamou gave him everything he wanted."

"Would you say he was an ambitious man?" I ask him. He laughs.

"I don't think he was very, very, very ambitious. I think he knew what he was doing, where he wanted to go. And I wouldn't call that ambitious."

This time around, Uncle Sonny tells me he *was* at John Brady's trial, sitting in the back the entire time. It seems like something he would have written about in his journals—which he started in July of 1985, documenting every significant event, anniversary, or development in his life. But his father-in-law's murder trial didn't make the cut.

I ask him if he knew John Brady Balfa, before all this.

"No . . . I mean I knew who he was. I knew his crew. I knew his . . . I don't remember his name . . ."

"John Brady Balfa?"

"Yeah."

I ask Uncle Sonny if he'd ever heard anyone say John Brady wasn't the one who killed PawPaw Aubrey. That he had been wrongly accused.

"Well, that's who they were looking for . . . I think more people were thinking of him doing it than anybody else . . . What happened was, there was Balfa, and there was another guy who was . . . in Texas. And they killed him. And he was in the same . . . they were together. In Mamou."

"He was killed in Texas?" I ask.

"There was only one because no one ever saw him, because he was in a Texas jail."

Aunt Anne tries to get her dad to clarify: "But there were two that did it in Mamou, right?"

"Yes, but one of them was in Texas."

"When they caught him, he was already in jail?" I ask, bewildered, wondering how much of this is real, how much is muddled pieces of John Brady's own story—caught in a jail in Texas.

"Yeah."

"And you think he helped kidnap PawPaw Aubrey?"

"Oh yeah. Only one got caught."

"You don't remember the name of the guy in the Texas jail?"

"No, but I know where he was living—between Mamou and Eunice." Duralde, where the Balfas lived, meets this description.

Uncle Sonny then starts to mumble something about feet, about boots, about shoes.

"They had PawPaw's boots?" Aunt Anne asks.

"No . . . the way they got him . . . he had the boots, the shoes . . ."

"They had a print of his shoes?" I'm leaning forward in my seat.

"I don't know . . ."

I don't know it yet, but sitting in the DA file in the Evangeline Parish Courthouse are those two photographs of shoe prints in the mud. Could this be what Uncle Sonny is talking about? Is it possible there was another suspect that was never prosecuted? How can there have been not one single other record of it?

Uncle Sonny then, increasingly difficult to understand, his chin buried in the folds of his chest, starts to say something about receiving a call.

"Sit up, Daddy," Aunt Anne tells him. "We can't see your mouth."

". . . calling, kept calling . . ."

"Who kept calling?" Aunt Anne asks.

"One of the two."

"They'd call you?" I ask.

"My office.

"What were they asking for?"

"Money."

"Was that before they found Aubrey's body?"

"No, I think they had already found him. They . . . they hit him on the head and killed him."

I try to push forward, to draw out more, but the words are fighting a losing battle against the mucus building in Uncle Sonny's throat. I look through my questions and come back to the main points:

"Uncle Sonny, do you think John Brady Balfa did it, for sure?"

"Oh, it was him. The tires. The rims . . . it was him."

I ask him, then, if he had ever heard Jimmy Sylvester's name associated with any of this. Did he know Jimmy?

"I don't know . . . I know who Jimmy Sylvester was, but he . . . I don't remember him engaged to that. I wouldn't . . ." A smile breaks across his face, and he chuckles. "I'm getting pretty close to saying yes."

"Really? You believe he was involved?" I ask.

"Oh yes."

I've listened to these interviews countless times over the years. The interpretations are endless. Was this an old man's rambling, weaving sentences together from fragments of memory in a withering mind? Was this some combination of actual memories and myth?

Or was it all a performance?

One night some weeks after discovering the Watts letter—the first true, solid thing connecting Uncle Sonny to PawPaw Aubrey's murder—I meet my aunt Anne for dinner in Baton Rouge, where she now lives. I'm planning to broach the subject of her father, to see if she has any awareness of the things people back home say about him.

"Somebody once said to me, about Daddy," she tells me when I ask about him and Aunt Tot, "'Cinderella shouldn't have married the frog.' Because Mom was a princess."

We're peering out over the Mississippi River, at a sushi restaurant with the best view in town, sitting with her seventeen-year-old daughter Brenna and one of her DeVillier nieces. "And Dad wasn't from a good family. He was a DeVillier. The DeVilliers were brothel owners."

Veil DeVillier Sr. owned the Oleander Motel and Lounge in Eunice, which was indeed known by most as a brothel and general haven for the Louisiana underworld. In his journals, Sonny recalls working there as a child and meeting Carlos Marcello and Governor Earl K. Long. Both Louisiana legends had come to stay at the Oleander while hiding out—

Marcello from the US Marshals, who were pursuing him on a subpoena for the 1950–1951 Kefauver Hearings; Long from the press after an involuntary stay in a psychiatric institution in Galveston in the summer of 1959.

Still, Sonny's father, Veil, was one of the original shareholders at Guaranty Bank in Mamou. And somewhere along the way, his mother, Hazel, crossed paths with MawMaw Emily.

"The mothers set it up," explains Aunt Anne. "They considered it a good match, because Dad was going to *do* things."

By the time Tot and Sonny married in April 1961, Sonny had reclaimed the DeVillier name and inserted it into the highest levels of St. Landry Parish philanthropy, business, and politics. He opened his general law practice in Eunice in 1960 and led the local crusade for Kennedy's election as president of the United States that year, organizing the Eunice chapter of the Kennedy for President Club and hosting fundraisers selling barbecued garfish dinners. For these efforts, Sonny would later be one of the 1,600 people in the country invited to Kennedy's funeral.

During the 1963 Louisiana governor's election, he attached himself to John McKeithen—who would become a lifelong friend and ally. In journal entries, Sonny claims that in exchange for his work on the campaign, McKeithen promised he would help him establish a bank in Eunice, as well as a branch of LSU. Both dreams would come to fruition before the end of McKeithen's term, with Sonny at the forefront—a founder of Acadiana Bank, a key figure in opening LSU-E.

Over the next decade, Sonny would position himself, much like his father-in-law in Mamou, to be involved in virtually every significant dealing to be had in Eunice. The Jaycees, the Chamber of Commerce, the Kiwanis Club. In 1965, at age twenty-nine, he was working as the assistant attorney for the City of Eunice and the chief counsel for the Oil and Gas Conservation Department for the State. He became known in Louisiana as a talented "kingmaker," never holding office himself but forever circling the realm of power. More than once he was selected as a delegate at the Democratic National Convention, and in addition to his relationship with McKeithen, he was also intimately involved in the election of Edwin Edwards.

"He was Edwin Edwards's *padnah,*" my dad tells me. "His right-hand man."

\\\\\

"I WAS FORBIDDEN TO GO TO BAYOU COURTABLEAU, GROWING UP," Aunt Anne tells me. People would have parties at the camps there when she was a teenager, and her daddy never let her go.

It all goes back to a chilly January morning in 1967, when Sonny's father, Veil, was discovered in his fishing camp on the bayou, lying peacefully in his bed, a hole shining through his crown from beneath his chin. A .20-gauge automatic shotgun held in both hands.

Aunt Anne's grandfather had been a drunk, she tells me. A cheater and an abuser. Sonny writes in his journals that, in 1960, the reason he decided to start his law practice in Eunice instead of Baton Rouge was to help his mother deal with his father, "who tormented her life so very often." According to Aunt Anne, Veil held a special hatred for his eldest son, his namesake, because Sonny was more "feminine" than he believed a man was meant to be. That hatred burned especially bright, especially hot, after Sonny convinced his mother to get a divorce. He'd had the paperwork drawn up himself.

The only evidence of criminal charges I ever find against Sonny over the course of his entire life emerge just four months before his father's death, when a grand jury considered charges against Veil Sr. for battery toward Sonny, and against Sonny for attempted murder of Veil Sr. Neither resulted in indictments.

"The story is," says Aunt Anne, hesitating, "it wasn't actually a suicide."

By the early 1980s, Sonny was president of the Acadiana Bank and at the height of his wealth and power in St. Landry Parish. Selling himself as a more progressive businessman than the old farts like his father-in-law, who ran the other banks across the region, he brought computerized banking to Acadiana for the first time, and he often commented in the newspapers about the evolving industry.

It was during these days that my uncles and aunts best remember the staggering sparkle of the DeVillier lifestyle in Eunice, the expensive clothes Anne and her sister, Kaye, wore, the fabulous trips they took, the mansion they lived in—right beside the mansions of all of Uncle Sonny's friends. "Sonny DeVillier and his crowd" was how one journalist described them; another: "That very progressive group of Eunice citizens headed by Veil 'Sonny' DeVillier." The group included three or four wealthy businessmen who joined Sonny in various investments around the region, among them a handful of restaurants and lounges, a million-dollar office complex, a Trust & Savings bank in Opelousas, various oil interests, and two jewelry stores.

Sonny's downfall came hard, and it came fast. According to FDIC records, he made $1,767,661 in 1988 alone (equivalent to over $4 million in 2024). By October 1, 1989, his entire net worth was $834,426, and he was selling everything he owned to settle his debts. His law practice was losing money. The bank was failing, like so many other banks across the country, a trend sparked by increased regulations and set aflame by recessions. When Acadiana Bank closed its doors in December 1989, it was the twenty-first bank in Louisiana to do so that year. Sonny had stepped aside in July, partly because of debilitating grief after Kaye's death and partly at the insistence of the FDIC, whose audit revealed his involvement in multiple violations of lending and banking laws. On two occasions, Sonny had made loans through the bank to his family members (his mother and brother), before depositing significant sums of that money into his own account. The audit revealed he had signed hundreds of checks made to overdrawn accounts. At the end of it all, he was forced to pay off hundreds of thousands of dollars in improper loans, including one he had made directly to himself, and was fined over $500,000 (which would ultimately be lowered to $15,000 because he was deemed too poor to ever reasonably pay it; in the legal brief, the judge writes, "He is a wounded man."). He sold his house, all his stock, his restaurants, his properties, his cars. He sold his wife's finest jewelry, even her engagement ring. He tried to sell Aunt Tot's share of the LaHaye Brothers' estate, but an ensuing lawsuit confirmed he could not sell his stock without first offering it to members of the family.

"I think that's when he really quit coming around," says Aunt Suzette. "He spent all Aunt Tot's inheritance. And after that, he couldn't look at my daddy."

It's true that Sonny DeVillier sits entangled in so many of the threads winding around his father-in-law's murder. The thought of "who he knows" raises suspicions of all sorts, not to mention his wealth and the way he lost it. He was well known for his affinity to "adopt" young successful men attending LSU or LSU-E as "protégés," likely funding their way with scholarship money to some extent. John Brady Balfa, the student body president at LSU-E with aspirations to become an attorney like

Edwin Edwards, would have been exactly Sonny's "type." Then there was Sonny's own close association with Edwards himself. To this day, Aunt Anne still drives a vehicle with a Number 1 Louisiana license plate—a gift from Edwards to Sonny.

There is also the fact that Eddie Soileau, John Brady's employer and rumored benefactor, was Sonny's next-door neighbor and occasional business partner. When I ask Soileau if he's ever heard rumors of Sonny being involved in PawPaw Aubrey's death, he is one of the few people to tell me he has not. "I think he was way too smart to get involved in something like that," he says.

Even beyond Sonny's documented interaction with Carlos Marcello as a child, his friendship with McKeithen ties him to that particular ring of the underground at its height. It was during McKeithen's second term, after all, that Marcello was convicted of conspiring with McKeithen's aide to bribe state officials into giving him multimillion-dollar insurance contracts. That same aide was also involved in Marcello's deals with the Louisiana Teamsters Union, of which Jerry Sylvester—Jimmy Sylvester's brother—was a member.

In April 2020, four days after my week with the DA file, after finding Charles Watts's letter, I receive a text from my mom: Uncle Sonny died this morning, of COVID. Say some prayers for Aunt Anne, and for him.

He's gone; any hopes of extracting more details, any deathbed confessions, shattered.

But, strangely, I feel relieved. Freed to more seriously explore if he could have done this; freed from the specter of that old, trembling shadow to rediscover the hot-blooded, ambitious man he once was. That cunning, politically motivated millionaire. With Edwin Edwards and John McKeithen in his pocket, on JFK's mailing list, riding through Eunice in his Porsche—soon to lose hold of everything. How far would he go to try to keep it?

When the iconic May 24, 2020, edition of the *New York Times* comes out, its front page awash with a thousand names, all victims of the coronavirus pandemic, Sonny DeVillier's name is among them, one of twenty Louisianans included, of the 2,500 who have died of the virus so far. The micro-obituary: "driving force in establishing LSU-Eunice." I think to myself, *Oh, he would have loved that.*

\\\\\

WHEN JANE ASKS JOHN BRADY ABOUT THE CHARLES WATTS LETTER, he tells her he's never heard of Watts or Singleton. He admits to knowing the name Sonny DeVillier, but says he has never met him.

The letter is the first item of any substance that connects Uncle Sonny to PawPaw Aubrey's death—attaching him to the crime from as far as Harrison County, Mississippi. With the letter is a series of correspondence between Detective Rudy Guillory and the DA of Livingston Parish, Duncan Kemp. Kemp assured Guillory that "in return for Mr. Watts cooperating fully and truthfully with you in the charges presently pending against him in Livingston Parish, Louisiana, which I understand to be two burglaries," he would dismiss those charges. On August 27, 1984, Kemp wrote to Billy Pucheu to confirm that the charges against Watts had been dismissed. But there are no other documents regarding what occurred during this conversation, or what was learned—if anything.

Jane finds Watts serving a life sentence in the South Mississippi Correctional Institution in Leakesville. On the day that Sonny DeVillier dies, she sends me a copy of the letter she's forwarded to Watts, in which she's attached his letter from the DA file. She asks if he remembers writing it, explains John Brady's situation, and encourages Watts to contact her via letter or phone call. "I look forward to hearing from you, and I hope you stay safe in this pandemic," she closes. And we wait.

Postconviction Relief

ON JUNE 9, 2020, JANE SENDS AN UPDATE. THE DAY BEFORE, she had visited the Evangeline Parish courthouse and finally gained access to the DA's file. While she was there, the current district attorney, Trent Brignac, came to introduce himself. Brignac has held the office in Evangeline Parish since 2009, just narrowly beating out his predecessor. He ran on a tough-on-crime, "protect our families" platform that also emphasized an open-door policy—a commitment to accessibility he has come to be known for. For most of my life, I knew him best as one of the dozen dads at the ballpark or in the basketball gym; his two children are the same ages as my younger brothers.

He made a point to tell Jane, "If we got the wrong guy thirty-five years ago, I want to know, and I want justice to be served." This impressed her. "It's not often a DA comes to meet me and lets me know that he is willing to work toward exonerating someone or taking a second look at an old conviction." But when Jane laid out her theories to Brignac, he seemed to want more "definitive proof" of John Brady's innocence.

Jane filed John Brady's application for postconviction relief later that month. The fifty-page document—with five six-inch-thick folders of exhibits—lays out her case, issuing three claims:

1. That John Brady Balfa is entitled to postconviction DNA testing.
2. That John Brady Balfa is innocent, and his incarceration violates the Sixth, Eighth, and Fourteenth amendments to the Constitution.
3. That John Brady Balfa's conviction was obtained in violation of his Fourteenth Amendment right to due process when the state withheld exculpatory evidence.

To bolster John Brady's innocence claim, Jane includes the National Autopsy Assay Group's review of the conclusions drawn by Dr. George McCormick and Dr. William Rodriguez—calling into question their testimonies. This evidence, she argues, undermines the entire case against John Brady, discounting the "proof" that Aubrey LaHaye was killed in the early morning on January 6, 1983.

"Mrs. LaHaye's identification of Mr. Balfa was the only direct evidence tying him to this crime," Jane writes. "There were no other witnesses and the testimony about the physical evidence did not lead to concrete conclusions, only speculations that rope and tires may have originated from the same source. Eyewitness identifications are inherently unreliable and Mrs. LaHaye's identification of Mr. Balfa, one year and nine months after the crime, is no exception."

All this is now compounded, Jane writes, by the fact that information including the actual forensic physical evidence of the fingerprint and hair, along with Emily LaHaye's identification of Taylor Strother and Charles Watts's letter, were "deliberately withheld" from the defense and would have likely impacted the verdict.

In the requisition for DNA testing, Jane notes that FBI records stated the agency had preserved photographs of the fingerprint and a slide containing the blond strand of hair. Testing these pieces of evidence could result in a firm resolution regarding John Brady's guilt. In addition, DNA testing of other evidence such as Aubrey's clothing, the yellow towel, and ropes could result in the discovery of skin or sweat cell deposits that could lead to a suspect other than John Brady—using technology unavailable in 1985.

Even if testing is not possible, Jane argues that John Brady is still entitled to relief because "he is innocent of this crime and his continued incarceration violates the Eighth Amendment's ban on cruel and unusual punishment and the Fourteenth Amendment's promise of due process." For most postconviction applications, the statute of limitations expires two years from an applicant's conviction and sentence. This application, submitted thirty-five years after John Brady's conviction, calls on the exception available if the "application alleges and the petitioner proves, or the State admits, that the facts upon which the claim is predicated were not known to the petitioner or his prior attorneys." Jane argues that, in addition to the many problems with the existing evidence against John Brady—which she lays out meticulously—the mere existence of the new evidence bolsters his innocence claim, which he has maintained for almost forty years.

Finally, Jane accuses the State of knowingly withholding the above evidence from John Brady and Julie Cullen, which might have swayed a jury in his favor. "The cumulative effect of all the suppressed evidence undermines the reliability of his conviction and entitles him to postconviction relief."

October 7, 2020

There are nine people in the courtroom for John Brady Balfa's initial postconviction application hearing in Evangeline Parish. Up front are the court reporter; the minute clerk; the bailiff; the presiding judge, Gary Ortego; Jane Hogan; and Assistant District Attorney Nicole Gil. And in the gallery: me, Naomi, and John Brady's niece Bridget.

Naomi smiles at me from behind her mask, asks about my family. Bridget's eyes crinkle up too, though I get a sense of hesitation from her. She's wondering why I'm here. I sit a few pews behind them.

And John Brady's here too—kind of. His face looks out at us from a television arranged at the front of the courtroom, live via Zoom. He's wearing the blue fatigues of Angola, which from here look like any old button-down shirt. *Older than I've imagined him*, I write in my notebook. *Bald, white goatee, clean.* You can see the way the Bell's palsy has crumpled his face, the right side of his mouth sliding, the left side fighting it. He holds his hands behind his back, but when he goes to speak, there is no sound, initiating a shuffle up front, "Maybe he's muted," the court reporter says. "Can ya hear us?" Judge Ortego asks John Brady, in a thick-as-roux Cajun accent. After some time fiddling with the computer, they establish that while we can't hear John Brady, he can hear what is taking place in the courtroom. A paper and pen are provided to him so he can write out any messages, and Jane waives his "verbal appearance."

"Well, then let's get started."

The whole thing takes about fifteen minutes and is altogether casual, amicable. Jane has told me everyone in Evangeline Parish, including DA Trent Brignac and Assistant DA Nicole Gil, have been nothing but accommodating so far. She has high hopes.

Once the session starts, Jane presents that the logical place to begin is to see what evidence still exists that might be available for testing. The judge agrees, though he expresses doubt that anything *does* exist. To his knowledge, the only thing that remains from the Aubrey LaHaye case is that box of tire rims. But he orders the clerk of court to conduct a search, "a hunt," for any and all information regarding John Brady Balfa's investigation and trial. They ask John Brady if he understands what is taking place, and he nods.

"Okay, that's that. Court is adjourned."

I walk out with Jane, discussing our plans to come back and look at the box of rims in the coming weeks. In the parking lot, she approaches Naomi and Bridget, and I join them. Naomi thanks me for being there, and then there is an awkward silence.

I realize with a jolt that they are waiting for me to leave. I'm not part of this circle. I excuse myself, get in my car, and drive slowly past them—observing the excitement, mixed with frustration, on Naomi's face as she listens to Jane speak.

Danny Singleton

BACK IN JUNE OF 2020, JANE SENDS ME ANOTHER MESSAGE with a link: the Facebook profile of Danny Singleton, the man Charles Watts named in his letter, who said he was part of Aubrey's abduction. There aren't many posts, but there is enough to establish he is no longer in prison; some digging reveals he'd been released from a thirty-five-year sentence in April 2019.

The page is mostly devoted to promoting Singleton's self-published memoir *Sins of a Cajun Boy: The Legendary True Story of Louisiana's Famous Cat Man.*

Jane orders a copy. We both know better than to expect any confessions regarding Aubrey LaHaye within those pages. The man had just been released from prison; chances are he didn't want to go back. But there could be something. Associations. Patterns. Where was Singleton, after all, in January 1983?

"He was not in prison," Jane tells me over the phone a few days later. "He was free at the time of Aubrey's murder." She's already put the book in the mail for me. Within a week and a half, the tome arrives in my mailbox, a panther growling menacingly from the front cover, eyes glowing a neon green.

January 1, 2021

"This is the longest I've ever been crime free," Danny Singleton tells Barry Thompson, the host of the *Kajn Talk* program on Family Vision TV—a Christian television station broadcast throughout Acadiana.

In the clip, Singleton is wearing glasses that give him a professional persona, helped by the confidence with which he speaks. His Eunice accent has been corrupted, the rhythms rearranged to better imitate a Mississippi southern drawl. He holds his hands beneath the table, his thumbs pressed together like a steeple, just visible over the edge, tapping together while he speaks.

"And it's gone on two years, so I know God is inside of me. If he wasn't I would struggle . . . it's a struggle out here. God sees me through it every day. I'm tempted. I'm tempted a lot. But God's given me the strength to overcome that temptation."

"Amen to that," says Thompson.

Danny Singleton's career as a criminal began in 1960 in Eunice at age thirteen, when he saw a blue Pontiac Catalina sitting in a church parking lot and decided to take it. That night, he and a friend raced the cops down Highway 190 at a hundred miles an hour, the first time he'd ever driven a car. They ended up in a ditch, and Singleton ran. Hours later, he raised his thumb on the side of the road to hitch a ride to the nearest town, Jennings. The stranger who picked him up dropped him off at the police station, where—fate be damned—the wrecked Pontiac was parked. And Singleton still had the keys.

The cops caught him in Port Allen as morning broke. When they called it in, the Jennings police hadn't even noticed the car had been stolen again.

Singleton would spend most of his life chasing the high he had ascended that pivotal night—dabbling in high-stakes burglaries. By age twenty, he was in Angola, where, he writes, "blood mixed with the dirt to form Satan's dough." He wasn't there long, but it was long enough to make friends with many of Louisiana's most audacious criminals, to better educate himself on the tricks of the trade.

When he got out, Singleton committed himself to a career of thievery, traveling across the South and beyond, doing two "jobs" a day. His specialty was wealthy neighborhoods, his calling card his speed, his secret his good taste. His hauls were often worth over $300,000. Singleton quickly became a rich man, and he wasn't shy about it. He got himself a fancy car, used the best barbers in town, wore flashy suits and tons of jewels, and surrounded himself with beautiful women.

He developed his network, descending into the South's bustling underground, where "everyone knows, or knows of, everyone else. Each knows what the rest might provide if needed. Each knows who is weak and can be used. Each knows who is dangerous and best left to their own devices, except in an emergency." Singleton had the numbers for bail bondsmen memorized, secured himself meetings with some of the underworld's best lawyers, and got to know every shipowner in the South who was willing to sell stolen goods. And inevitably, he became involved with the Dixie Mafia. "I was up to my ears in that infamous organization."

From San Antonio to Biloxi, law enforcement started to make connections, labeling the slew of robberies the work of the elusive "Cat Man." There were a few prison stints, but Singleton always wormed his way out within a couple of years or so.

Amid the war stories and the jail stints and the name-dropping, at one point Singleton writes that he moved to Houma, southwest of New Orleans, with a couple of guys he'd grown up with in Acadiana, "both cold-blooded killers." One was Ralph Ortego,[1] the other Feryl Granger.

Singleton's time with Ortego and Granger was centered around the Gables Lounge, where they oversaw gambling operations, pimped out their girlfriends, and dealt drugs—all on the side of Singleton's usual activities. Singleton helped deal, but he didn't partake, by his own account. Working with the two addicts was getting riskier by the day. He abandoned ship just before each of the others got sent to Angola; Granger for his involvement in the Steve and Marjorie Anderson murders in Sugarland, and Ortego for armed robbery. We already know how Granger's story ends, but Ortego would—in a manner similar to John Brady—immerse himself in the ministerial vocations within Angola and ultimately devote his life to Christianity.

According to his memoir, Danny Singleton's own spirituality started to nudge at him around age thirty-five. He notes certain moments along his raucous journey where something greater seemed to be speaking to him, moments he had rushed right past. While serving time in the Dixon Correctional Institute in Jackson, Louisiana, he became overwhelmed by the fear that he would never be able to stop. He would always be a criminal. And so, he stopped eating.

Twice, Singleton attempted "hunger strikes"—which were really suicidal stunts, by his own admission. And each time, news spread across the state. He was at one point transferred to Angola to see a psychiatrist. Officials went to great efforts to bring all his loved ones in to convince him to end this crusade, which he vowed would not cease until they took him from the prison in a pine coffin. Each time, Singleton says it was the gentle urgings of his family and friends that convinced him to finally go to breakfast.

---

1 Ralph Ortego is of no significant relation to Judge Gary Ortego.

Singleton's memoir is structured as a story of redemption. A man changed; a man saved. His final stint in prison, from 1984 to 2019—a thirty-five-year sentence calculated as Singleton's life expectancy minus one year—forced him to face himself, and to face his relationship with God. "By the grace of our Father in heaven, the Cat Man was dead to the world. All that remains is Danny, the believer."

But in between the hunger strikes and the conversion are three years, 1981–1984, where Singleton was free in the world—struggling with the first true twinges of guilt about his life of crime. For the first time, the adrenaline rush was beginning to feel stale. But the Cat Man wasn't dead yet. The September 1983 robbery that would land him his last conviction was the first time he had ever carried a gun to a job, the first time he ever pointed it at someone. When he couldn't pull the trigger, the home-owner did—putting two bullets into Singleton's abdomen, and one in each leg. "I could never have done it," he writes. "There was nothing inside of me which would have allowed me that option, even in an adrenaline-filled 'tight spot.' I guess in truth I had known that all my life. I had merely never been tested."

I type Singleton's name into the newspapers.com search bar, with filters for "St. Landry Parish, Louisiana" or "Evangeline Parish, Louisiana" in December 1982–February 1983. He was free. He was battling something. Where was he?

A single entry comes up, published January 27, 1983. A speeding ticket for Danny Singleton. A fine of $40.50. Issued in Church Point, Louisiana. Thirty miles from LaHaye Road.

February 5, 2021

I'm shivering, trying to get as close to the door as I can to find some shelter from the loose, heavy raindrops descending from the gray day. I worry that I may not have knocked quite loud enough. I strum my fingers against my thigh.

Danny Singleton's mother's home is in the middle of Eunice, right off the main drag. Jane Hogan was able to track down the address. A sweet little cottage squeezed in with the other sweet little cottages, a front garden protected by a chain-link fence. Ethel is her name, as I've gathered from Mamou nightlife royalty Eugene Manuel, who knows every regular at all the major bars in the triangle that is Mamou, Eunice, and Opelousas from the last fifty years. And he knows their mamas too.

Ethel Singleton—"She used to be an Israel, though." I double-check my notes. John Brady Balfa's mother, Mildred, was an Israel, a name not particularly common around Acadiana. What are the chances they're family?

When the door opens, an old lady is standing there in slippers and a day dress. She looks out at me, suspicious. I stretch a smile across my face. "Hi! I'm looking for Danny? Danny Singleton? Does he live here?"

She blinks at me, shakes her head "Oh, no. No, he doesn't live here." Taking in my shivering, wet frame, she says, "Come on in, honey. I'm his mom."

He's moved, she tells me, once I'm inside the dark cocoon of her home. "He lives down the road in Church Point."

"Oh, do you see him often?"

She smiles. "Oh, I don't know. Because he's been involved with that book, he's all over the place. He don't have time for nothing."

She asks me if I'm a friend of his, and I tell her I'm not. That I've read his book and had some questions for him.

"You've got his phone number?"

I raise my eyebrows and tell her I don't. She rattles it off for me, then asks if I know where the Piggly Wiggly is in Church Point. Within minutes, I know exactly where to find Singleton. "If he's not working on his book, he's usually home," she says.

I thank her, and she wishes me luck. "Stay dry," she says. "It's nasty out there."

I find the house easily, even without an actual address. It stands alone, incongruous, in between a salvage yard and a graveyard—anchoring twisted metal and lost souls in humble multicolored brown brick. The yard is unlandscaped except for a single sago palm beside the sidewalk. I park on the street, lift the latch for the little gate on the chain-link fence.

Since the beginning, when I first started asking questions about Paw-Paw Aubrey, people have—usually with an uncomfortable chuckle—warned me to be careful. There could still be someone out there, someone dangerous, holding all these secrets. And my investigation could be a threat.

I'd never been scared. Not once. I'm not sure if it's foolishness, naivety, or if it's the line I've managed to draw between this story and my "real" life.

"This is your story," my dad tells me. "It's our story. It's your family's story."

And of course, it is. But this has always felt wrong, felt somehow untrue—even beyond the fact that PawPaw Aubrey died before I was born. It goes deeper. It goes back to my mother, a Texan among the Cajuns, sitting in the corner alone, watching as the family squeezed themselves together so tight. To the miles of rice fields and pasture separating our house on Heritage Road from LaHaye. To taking all those university French classes, only to retain so little. To being asked, when I tell people where I am from, why I do not have a Cajun accent; and telling them I don't know, but "you should hear my brother speak." To never having experienced true, devastating loss in my entire life.

It's this otherness, this sense of looking at it all from three steps away—this is what enables me to tell this story. This is what protects me, keeps the veil in place. There's this world, and then there's my world.

But today, I'm knocking on the door of a notorious criminal. Someone who once ran across the South with murderers and thieves. Someone who likely participated in my great-grandfather's murder.

"Last night," Jane told me when we spoke that morning, "after I told him where you were going, my partner had a dream. He dreamt I was hanging from a tree."

When Singleton answers the door, I'm struck first by how grandfatherly he is. He's tall, with great posture, a flannel shirt tucked into khakis. A tiny shaggy dog barks viciously at his ankles. "Are you Danny?" I ask.

"Yes?"

I'm married now. I'm no longer just a LaHaye, though I haven't relinquished the name entirely. But today I decide to shed my heritage. I won't lie, but I won't let Singleton know exactly who I am. "My name is Jordan, Jordan Fontenot."

I tell him I'm a local journalist, that I'm looking into historic crimes in the area, that I've read his book and have a few questions if he had the time. He invites me in. "Sure! Have a seat."

His living room is neat, practically bare. Carpeted, with a comfortable couch across from the front window. Singleton takes a seat in the rocking chair facing it. Fox News titters on low volume on the television.

"So how can I help?"

I tell him I've been researching a particular crime, speaking with various people from around the community who might know anything about it. "It took place in the eighties," I say. "And when I read you were connected with Feryl Granger, I figured you might know something, or know some part of the story I haven't heard, or know who we could talk to."

"Okay, now what murder was that?"

"The Aubrey LaHaye murder."

At this, Singleton starts laughing. "Oh, I know all about the Aubrey LaHaye murder . . . and I'm almost 100 percent sure John Balfa didn't kill him."

At this point, my nerves have shifted into adrenaline. I'm sitting on my fingers, and it's all I can do to keep my face neutral.

"Really?"

"Yeah, because somebody called me and asked me to get somebody to come see him, because he had to take care of something. And I'm gonna tell you, it was Aubrey LaHaye's son-in-law."

"Sonny?"

He nods. "Sonny was a good friend of mine. I used to sell him jewelry. He'd funnel it through the bank and the jewelry store."

"Oh my God," spills out of my mouth. But Singleton's in full-on story-telling mode now.

"You know they're trying to get John Balfa out now?"

"I did hear that," I say, curious about where Singleton's heard it. It's not like John Brady's postconviction appeal had been in the news.

"I'm almost certain he didn't do it, because I did send somebody to Sonny out of Georgia. A hit man for the Dixie Mafia."

"Okay . . . so Sonny had called you asking if you knew somebody . . ."

"He asked me to get somebody who could 'take care of something for him.' And I didn't know exactly what it was, but if it was like a safe job or to rob a jewelry store or insurance fraud, he'd have asked me to do that." Singleton wouldn't take violent assignments.

He said that after he heard Aubrey had been murdered, he put the pieces together. "Because I did send somebody to see him. Now what they did and what kind of arrangements they made, if that's really what happened . . . I don't know. But I believe that's what happened. He wanted somebody to hit him."

"Do you have any idea why?"

"Well, it was his father-in-law, Aubrey LaHaye. I'm sure he [Sonny] wanted his wife to inherit that money."

It's the same explanation Naomi gives, that the Balfas give, for their belief that Aubrey was killed by someone in the family. But again, this feels too simple. Too obvious.

"Wow, that's just . . . wild," I say, trying to reorder my thoughts. I hadn't expected so much to come out so fast. Singleton laughs and laughs.

"So I guess you couldn't give me the name of the guy you sent over there?"

He starts to shake his head . . . then seems to change his mind. "Well, it wouldn't do any good because the guy's dead . . . he was accused—have you ever heard of the Vincent Sherry murders? A judge in Gulf Coast, Mississippi? He and his wife were killed by contract killers with the Dixie Mafia. John Ransom was hired to kill them. John Ransom."

"That was the guy from Georgia?"

Singleton nods.

"And he was with the Dixie Mafia?"

"Yes, and I was too. He was a hit man for the Dixie Mafia. That's the guy I sent to Sonny. . . . I guess it doesn't matter anymore, Sonny's dead too."

I ask Singleton if Feryl Granger was involved at all, to his knowledge. "No, Feryl had nothing to do with it," he says. Then I ask about Jimmy Sylvester. Singleton says he knew him, but "As far as I know, he wasn't into anything. Let me tell you what Jimmy's deal was. He liked to gamble a little bit and run after the women. Other than that . . ."

I ask him if he knew John Brady Balfa.

"That's actually my cousin," he says.

Yep.

Singleton says he didn't know he was related to John Brady, or anything about him, until he was serving time in prison. His uncle had come to visit him and let him know that his grandson, John Brady, was in prison, too.

I ask him, one more time, "So you're sure he wasn't part of it at all?"

"No," he says. "I think somebody planted evidence, to make it look like he did it. Because them Dixie Mafia guys are pretty smart."

Singleton tells me the FBI and police did actually investigate him for the Aubrey LaHaye murder, had shown up at his wife's home in Eunice in January of 1983. He had been in Mobile when she called him. According to Singleton, he drove straight back from Alabama to the Sheriff's Office and delivered his alibi. And they let him go. There are, of course, no records to verify this, but it makes sense that Singleton would have been on the investigators' lists as a local criminal worth checking in on.

The fact that he was in Mobile clicks in my head though. In the letter, Charles Watts had written, "Danny had gotten a couple of fellows from Mobile, Alabama, and they had met with some other fellow concerning the deal. After the business was completed, Danny had took them back to Mobile, Alabama . . ."

"You mentioned that you heard John Brady's trying to get out . . ." I'm trying to figure out where Singleton has learned this.

He raises a pointer finger. "Well . . . let me show you something. I'll be right back." He stands up and steps into a back room. When he comes back, he hands me a sheet of printer paper.

"This letter was sent to a friend of mine, and it has to do with John."

It takes me a few seconds to realize what I'm looking at. *Shit.* It's a copy of the email Jane sent to Charles Watts, forwarded to Singleton with a short: "FYI . . ."

"You might want to talk to that attorney, Jane Hogan."

I nod. "I will."

Turning back to the letter, I start to ask Singleton about Charles Watts, "So you told him about this at the time?"

"Yeah, I had discussed it with him."

"Did you know he wrote this letter?"

"No . . . I didn't know he did that."

Nobody from the Evangeline Parish DA's office ever reached out to Singleton regarding Watts's accusation, he tells me. He never heard a word about it until now.

"If it ever came down to it . . . would you ever go talk to the DA and tell them what you know?"

"I sure would."

Before I go, I ask Singleton to sign my copy of his book. I tell him what an amazing story it is. "You liked it?" He smiles at me. "Tell your friends. They can order it on Amazon."

Within days, Jane and I each order a copy of Edward Humes's *Mississippi Mud.* The book follows the journey of Lynne Sposito, who spent years unraveling secrets behind the vicious 1987 murders of her parents, Vincent and Margaret Sherry in Biloxi, Mississippi. The book also serves as a deep dive into the inner workings of the Dixie Mafia during the 1970s and '80s—when several characters whose names float around the Aubrey LaHaye murder were a part of the organization, including

Feryl Granger, Clifton Thibodeaux, Henry Salisbury, John Ransom, and Danny Singleton.

Singleton, by his account, was only peripherally involved with the Dixie Mafia, maintaining strategic connections and conducting some "business" for them but avoiding the commitment of true membership. John Ransom, though, was high in the ranks.

As early as the 1960s, Ransom became known as a kind of grim reaper. Wherever there was a violent, mysterious murder, you could often find him somewhere nearby. He wasn't exactly conspicuous; Humes describes him as an "Ichabod Crane figure with long, spindly fingers, enormous knuckles, and a prominent Adam's apple that bobbed like a fisherman's lure." He walked on a peg leg, having lost the real one in a bar fight. In the trial for the Sherry murders, one witness described Ransom's face as haunting, "the personification of evil."

Despite this spectacularly recognizable persona, Ransom mostly managed to evade murder charges, slipping in and out of court with only a couple of years served at one time. This ended in 1989, when he pleaded guilty to a murder in Georgia and became a prime suspect in the Vince and Margaret Sherry case. At first, it was suspected that Ransom was the one who carried out the deed himself, though it was later proven he had merely provided the gun to the actual hit man. When questioned about the Sherry murders, Ransom told the investigators, "I would never kill a woman."

Was it possible that Ransom, called "the devil's first lieutenant," came to Mamou in January of 1983, on a job? It might explain why he left Emily alive.

But there are immediate problems with this theory. The first is that John Ransom doesn't match Emily's description. At all. In 1983, Ransom would have been almost sixty years old; and living the rugged life he did, it's unlikely he passed for someone in their mid- to late twenties or thirties. He had bright blue eyes and wouldn't have had a Cajun accent. MawMaw Emily certainly hadn't observed a peg leg, though by all accounts his limp was subtle and might have gone unnoticed.

But Ransom, I discover, does have a connection to this case beyond Singleton's accusation: he was an associate of "Little Henry" Salisbury, the "most dangerous man in the world"—whose Wanted poster had been loose in the DA file for the Aubrey LaHaye case.

It's possible that Ransom organized the hit and was not the person who knocked on the door that day. That there were others. This theory is supported by Charles Watts's 1984 letter, which of course also suggested that Singleton was more involved than he admits.

A few days after my visit to Danny Singleton's home, I hear from Jane. "I have an idea about this whole thing," she says. "I wonder if Danny had more of a role. Like if he was the local who helped abduct, or if there was another local who did this. I also wonder if Danny actually orchestrated the whole thing and read [*Mississippi Mud*] while in prison and is using John Ransom as a scapegoat."

For Danny Singleton to admit to being involved any more than he's shared would be confessing to acting as an accessory to murder. Two years out after a thirty-five-year sentence—fat chance we'll get that confession. And because Watts warned him by forwarding Jane's email, he has had time to come up with another story.

The entire operation of Aubrey's murder, though, is so contrary to Singleton's MO. In *Sins of a Cajun Boy*, he swears his criminal proclivities had a hard stop at murder. Even when his own life was at stake, during that last robbery in 1983, when he had the gun in his hand, he says, "I could never have done it."

This is reflected in the record. Of Singleton's dozens of arrests, rarely do they involve violence and never does anyone die.

What would have motivated him to take part in something so out of character? So risky? What transforms a professional jewel thief at the end of his career into a fumbling kidnapper? A murderer? More likely, I think, if Singleton was involved, his role was limited to the getaway, as suggested by Watts's letter. Someone who wasn't Ransom or Singleton knocked on MawMaw Emily's door that day. And it's possible Singleton knows exactly who it was. The fact that he won't say? That suggests the man is still alive.

The issues with Danny Singleton's story don't matter much to Jane. Even if he was involved, she has little interest in trading in one old man for another. What he's given us, she thinks, might be enough on its own.

Singleton's version of the story—which was preserved in an affidavit and filed with John Brady's postconviction application—conveniently allows him to assist in freeing John Brady while also legitimizing a narrative that keeps him blameless. He can "do the right thing" without going back to prison. And both people implicated in his report? They're dead.

Which, at first, is plenty good enough for Jane. She tells me, "John Brady is ecstatic about this development. I'm wondering if this could be the tipping point. Like if this is enough for everyone to recognize that John was wrongfully convicted and should be released. Who knows?"

In December of 2021, I receive a collect call from "Charlie," an inmate at the Mississippi DOC South Mississippi Correctional Institution. A few months before, I'd sent Charles Watts my own letter, leaving him my cell number.

Charles's voice possesses the Bible Belt twang of "redneck" Central Louisiana and Mississippi, with the tinniness of old age but a definite confidence. "Just what is it you want from me?" he asks.

"Yeah, absolutely. I wanted to ask you what you remembered about the letter you sent, all those years ago, what Danny Singleton told you about that incident in Mamou?"

"Ah." He pauses for a beat. "So, what was going on in that letter there . . . I was given instructions, by Danny, to write that letter."

I'm trying to gather my thoughts. "It said the son-in-law had hired some people to come kill that man. He told you that?"

"Yep, he told me to put that down there. That was all Danny. He would do things like that."

The automated voice comes on: *"You have one minute remaining."*

"Did he say he was involved?"

"What now?"

"Did he say he was involved? Danny?"

"I'm inclined to think he was. That's my contention. In order to have that information, he'd have to know something more about it. The only way to get that information, he was there. He participated in them kinda things."

"Right—"

"Like I say, Danny's pretty slick. I've been knowing him going on sixty years. Been a long time. And he's all about making money. He's always scheming on one thing or another. Like I said, he's pretty smart, but I don't think he's smart enough to—"

The operator: *"Thank you for using Global Cell Link."* And the dial tone.

Jane calls about a month later to let me know she visited Watts in Leakesville. When she showed him the letter, he told her it was definitely his

handwriting, and that he remembered being in a cell with Danny Singleton at the time. But he didn't remember the actual conversation that led
to the letter. I wonder about this, considering he took the time to forward
it to Singleton.

"What is an interesting takeaway from Charlie, though," she says, "is
he sent this letter, and the charges were dismissed, as we saw. But he
didn't know that. And in 1992, he wrote to Livingston Parish asking
about the charges, and the clerk wrote back to tell him the charges had
been dismissed in 1984." Jane has these records to confirm it.

"Oh, wow . . . So nobody ever even told him."

"Yeah, they never told him the charges got dismissed, and nobody ever
came and talked to him, which I find weird. The fact that the charges got
dismissed made me at least think somebody would have gotten to talk
to him."

"Right."

"It sucks," she says. "It's like because they zeroed in on John, they just
stopped investigating everybody else."

The timing supports this. The correspondence between the DAs' of-
fices regarding Watts spans June 1984 through August 1984. John Brady
was picked up in September.

But I'm not confident we can trust Watts, or his memories, here. He
gave Jane and me two different stories after all—either he didn't remember writing the letter, or he remembered Singleton telling him to write
the letter. Or something else. It isn't hard to imagine that Watts was visited by Rudy Guillory or someone else from the Evangeline Parish DA's
Office, and he simply doesn't remember it. But I can't find any records
of the event, and everyone else involved in the correspondence about the
matter—Guillory, Billy Pucheu, and Duncan Kemp—they're all dead.

Whether or not a conversation ever took place between Watts and the
Evangeline Parish investigators, within a month they'd have John Brady
as their suspect. And they were evidently far more interested in him than
Charles Watts, Danny Singleton, or Sonny DeVillier.

The Money Wouldn't Have Been Enough

ASKING AROUND UNCLE SONNY'S CIRCLES, I'M COMING UP empty: everything they tell me is either pure speculation, or I already know it. If anyone knows anything about his potential involvement in his father-in-law's demise, they aren't talking.

The motive issue continues to barb me: What ends did it serve for Sonny to have his wife's elderly father killed? To get Tot's inheritance quicker? By all indications, Sonny's real money problems didn't descend until the end of the 1980s, years after Aubrey died. There is little reason to believe he was desperate for cash in 1982 or 1983—he was trying to open a new bank for God's sakes, had just equipped the existing one with computers. The early '80s were Sonny's prime.

I do find, in the DA file, correspondence between Sonny and Dr. George McCormick from May of 1983. Sonny was requesting a copy of the autopsy report to submit to the insurance company; McCormick wrote that it was not yet complete, but that in Louisiana the death certificate should be sufficient to secure the insurance company's requirements. When I last visited Uncle Sonny in the nursing home, Aunt Anne had asked, "Did you know that the death certificate lists [PawPaw's] cause of death as a heart attack? Not his head injuries?" She knows this because she has it, the death certificate. It was in her dad's files. Later, she shows it to me, a form, filled in using a typewriter—the official record of what happened to Aubrey LaHaye. IMMEDIATE CAUSE: ACUTE CONGESTIVE HEART FAILURE, DUE TO: SEVERE CEREBRAL CONCUSSION, DUE TO: MULTIPLE BLOWS TO BACK OF HEAD. HOMICIDE.

It's tempting to attach suspicions to Sonny's being the point of contact regarding the life insurance. Why did *he*—of everyone—keep PawPaw Aubrey's death certificate in his records? But Uncle Sonny *was* the family's de facto attorney, and he was Aunt Tot's husband. On the face of it, there is nothing alarming about him being the one to oversee the dreaded task of securing the insurance payments. And Papa Wayne, Uncle Glenn, and Aunt Tot were cc'd on the messages.

People have questioned whether it's possible that Sonny took out his own separate life insurance policy on Aubrey. While an intriguing speculation, and an easy solution—the fact is that it's simply impossible to prove, short of paperwork from forty years ago turning up. And even if this were the case, Sonny would have had to get Aubrey's consent to buy the policy; the dollar amount couldn't have been outrageous enough to raise suspicion. But then would it be outrageous enough to justify killing him?

And if this is what happened, the money certainly wasn't enough to save Sonny.

Reading through his journals, I can't help but marvel at their vulnerability. I come from a family held together by men like my papa Wayne—unwavering steadiness, unaffected strength. Impenetrable. Uncle Sonny wasn't like this. He poured his sorrows, his self-consciousness, his failures, his loneliness out on pages he knew would someday be read—though I doubt he imagined I would be the person reading them. Part of me feels like a man so encumbered by his own story, his own legacy, might struggle to contain his secrets.

But then the other part of me sees the glaring absences in the journals. Aubrey's name is never mentioned. Neither is Sonny's father's.

"Have you ever . . . have you ever heard any rumors of your dad being involved in all of this?"

I'm sitting across from Aunt Anne at her dining table in Baton Rouge. I've dragged my feet for years now, have met with her half a dozen times before I successfully gather the courage to ask her outright. Part of me feels that it is impossible she has never heard this before. But she does live here, in Baton Rouge—across the Mississippi from the Acadiana rumor mill. She knows her dad and his faults more intimately than anyone else alive. But he is her dad, and I'm about to ask if she thinks it's possible he could be a murderer.

"Involved? In PawPaw's death?"

I nod. There's a beat of silence. Her face is contemplative, curious even—without a trace of defensiveness. "No . . . I thought you were going to ask me if I thought he was gay." She gives a kind of half laugh. "And I think probably."

But this, she doesn't think this can be true. "I mean, why would Daddy do that?"

I explain that I haven't been able to find a clear motive, that I've only come across whispers. "People say it had to have been about money." Aunt Anne nods.

"I mean, maybe . . . you know he and PawPaw were so connected in business. Do you know if he had any life insurance on him?"

I have no way to prove that he did, I explain, other than the life insurance he would have received through her mother, Tot. "Right. Like maybe people think he did it for the money, but it was Mama's money, and it was our money. He wouldn't have gotten anything himself . . ." She thinks for a minute, then shakes her head. "I mean he would have never done that to Mama, to us."

I tell her about Charles Watts's letter, sitting in the DA file for decades. About meeting with Danny Singleton, and his accusations. She gets caught up on the idea that her dad was selling stolen jewels: "Where did he come up with this shit?" she asks of Singleton's story. "I was in [the jewelry stores] a whole hell of a lot, and I don't recall ever seeing anything weird . . . I went in the back of the store a lot, they never said, 'don't go back there.'"

For a second, and it's really just a second, Aunt Anne reframes her childhood—imagining it with clearer, adult eyes. But her conviction holds fast. "No."

If this has been in the DA file all this time, she posed, doesn't that show it has been investigated? That the FBI looked into it?

I tell her it appears the DA's Office did investigate, but there's no telling where it led, only that they did not pursue it far.

"Some people think John Brady, and his conviction, might be a cover-up for your dad," I say.

"Well," she responds, "then they could have thrown that letter away; why leave it in the DA file if it would get them in trouble?"

It's a point I hadn't considered, a good one. If those letters were in fact indicative of malfeasance by members of the DA's Office—why did they still exist? Especially when so many other elements of the investigation did not?

"I just don't see it," Aunt Anne says. "And not just because he's my dad . . . I mean, do I think he was a saint? No. But I don't see what reason he'd have to do something like this."

Smokeless Guns

T ALL MOVES SO SLOWLY, THE COURT PROCEEDINGS. JANE HO-gan doesn't hear back from the Evangeline Parish clerk of court about any still-existing evidence until January 2021, and it's what we feared: all they've got is the box of rims—which, having been handled by dozens of investigators and in the courtroom, aren't great candidates for further forensic testing. Everything else is simply gone.

"I find it so weird," Jane says, "like, I mean, of all the things they keep—a three-hundred-pound box full of tire rims? Like that gets pre-served over thirty-seven years, but the envelopes full of hairs, pajamas . . . all that's gone. Like the heaviest thing you could have held on to."

In September 2021, the Evangeline Parish DA's Office finally submits their "Answer" to the June 2020 application for postconviction relief. They intend to fight it.

The entire document is only two sheets of paper. They assert that there is no forensic evidence to be tested and none of the new evidence "proves by clear and convincing evidence that no rational juror would have found petitioner guilty beyond a reasonable doubt." The State sub-mits that the National Autopsy Assay Group's report is not admissible in court because the issue of presenting expert testimony to counter McCormick's opinions had already been addressed in John Brady's first 1987 appeal and denied.

And to Jane's accusations that the State withheld material and ex-culpatory evidence from the defendant, the DA's Office issued a firm denial.

After considering both arguments, Judge Ortego disagreed with the DA's assertion that the matter should be dismissed. There was going to be a new postconviction hearing, to determine whether John Brady de-served a new trial. "I was hoping it wouldn't come to this," Jane tells me. "That we could figure something out. Going to a hearing, this could take years."

When I hear from Jane in January 2022, the hearing still hasn't been scheduled. "But I did go see Trent today," she says, referring to District Attorney Trent Brignac.

The meeting had lasted two hours, she says with appreciation. "That's way more time than any other DA has given me for a postconviction meeting," she says. "Usually, they're like, 'This case is too old, leave me alone.'" But Brignac was interested, asking lots of questions, walking through the case with her.

He was reluctant to entertain any possibilities of scheming by Billy Pucheu or Rudy Guillory. "He said, 'Those men were saints,'" Jane tells me. "I told him I don't think anybody would be like 'Let's go get some innocent person and make them hang for this.' That's not what happened. John was not a good person in the '80s. He wasn't sympathetic. He was a gambler. He had issues." *He was a rapist*, I add, to myself. "I think there's ways," she goes on, "you can look at the case and make it work. And the State made it work. I think they all *probably* believed they had the right person. But they didn't."

They went round and round, Trent coming back each time to needing more proof of John Brady's innocence. "He said, 'For me to go to the LaHaye family and say, 'I think I've got the wrong person, or I'm going to undo what's already been done, I need to be convinced. I need a smoking gun.'"

But anything that could be a smoking gun has been lost, argued Jane. And just because the proof isn't there doesn't mean his conviction is right.

"Well, what do you want from me?" Trent asked her.

"I want my client to go home," she said. "I don't want him to die in prison. He's done thirty-seven years for something he didn't do. And you know, you can keep your conviction. I don't want to fight about this in court for the next five years. Maybe I lose, maybe you lose. I don't think it's worth it. He's old. He's got health conditions. If there's a way we can come to a middle ground . . . he gets out. That's what I want." She's asking for a deal, despite her earlier insistence that John Brady would never take one.

"Well," Trent said, "what do you think the LaHayes would think about that?"

It's an idea Jane has probed at since the beginning, getting the LaHaye family's support.

At one point, she starts asking, almost every time we speak, whether

I think she could meet with my family members, to explain her findings, to show why she believes John Brady is innocent. I tell her she can try but stop short of volunteering to help her rally the troops. She's nudging at a boundary I can't immediately articulate. This isn't as simple as she thinks it is. Brignac is right, she doesn't have enough.

When she first starts talking about a plea deal, Jane asks if anyone in the family would fight it. I tell her many of them are openhearted, open-minded, inclined toward mercy. But not all of them. Not when it comes to this.

Then I find out, not from Jane but from my dad, that she's called him. He tells me this weeks after it happens. "She said that the Balfa family wanted the chance to sit down and talk about John Brady, about the case." He told her he would have to think about it, and then consulted his law-yer, a former Evangeline Parish DA—who told him "Don't go there. It can only cause you problems, and it cannot help their case. Nothing you say can help their case. All you gonna do is tear off scabs on bad wounds and hurt your own people."

It's disquieting for me, this interaction. I'd never told Jane *not* to speak with my family, or my dad—but I guess I had expected to hear from her before she did. That it takes my dad so long to tell me about the conver-sation, too, makes the entire thing feel more illicit. I feel simultaneously invaded upon and kept in the dark, as though I haven't done enough and as though I've done far too much.

I worry about the attorney's advice to my father; about the fact that it came from a former Evangeline Parish DA. The dark corners of my mind turn toward the pattern of secrecy, stemming from the DA's Office, that has historically plagued this case. Why are they so concerned with our family's wounds, even after all these years? *Don't go there*, he told my dad.

But now, here it is, laid out on the table: "I think Trent would maybe agree to reduce John's sentence," Jane tells me over the phone, "but I don't think it will happen without the approval of your family."

Somehow, according to Jane anyway, John Brady's future has fallen into my family's hands. We can save him, if we want to.

When it comes to John Brady Balfa, most of the time I feel pulled toward some merciful sense of justice, motivated by my ever-increasing convic-tion that he *is* telling the truth. That he is innocent. In these moments, I align myself with Jane Hogan. I want him out, reunited with his family.

I want him to have a garden in Naomi's backyard, to soak up what little life might have left to offer him. I want to rage against the corrupt system that allowed this tragedy to happen, and I want to tell him I'm sorry. I'm so, so sorry.

But even with everything I know, there remains the sliver of a chance John Brady *did* do it. This sliver is everything. When Jane asks me if I believe in his innocence, I cannot give her what she is hoping for. I cannot say I am all in. I want the smoking gun too. I want to know for sure.

When we'd first met, Naomi had told me, "The more you dig, the more questions you are going to find." I'd thought if I could just dig deep enough, I'd find *it*: that one kernel of truth that could tell us John Brady did it, or he didn't. But Naomi was right; there are only more questions, more ambiguities, scratched across time by layers and layers of unreliability. Beneath every bold statement is the possibility of a lie. One scientist says one thing, another says the opposite. Under every memory is the chance it is addled, faded, or simply wrong. Every story wears the gauze of rumor, and every written report lacks conclusion. Behind so many names are their obituaries, and dozens of unanswered calls. Every definitive bearer of certainty—recordings, cells, prints—has been lost to the abyss.

I'm driving out of St. Francisville, just miles from John Brady's cell, when the fact of the matter hits me, arising crystal clear: *If John Brady did kill PawPaw Aubrey, I don't think I want him to get out. I don't.*

Is it fear of an undoing? A sense that interrupting the trajectory I was born into—my family victoriously recovering from this unimaginable tragedy, the man who did it justly behind bars, forever—will break open everything? Will send us backward? Will wreak havoc on our paradise?

In the abstract, I know John Brady Balfa is not the man he was forty years ago. He can't be, in a world so small, so controlled. I believe that every day he awakes and prays and prays and prays, and that he spends those days teaching others to pray. I know that he has confessed to sins and asked for mercy. I know, in my heart, that he poses no true threat. And I see, so clearly, the absurd cruelty of imprisoning harmless old men, of holding tight the key to sorry criminals' lives for decades and decades, of the need for a hospice in Angola. I want to advocate for mercy. I want to stand for it, to fight for it. I want to be like Jane, devoted to a life of unclenching fists and finding humanity where people have given up on it. To seeing through the safety glass of the system and challenging the concept of justice. I pray, in a way I haven't prayed in years, for the ability to forgive. For my family to find it within themselves, too.

In March of 2022, I call Jane to see if there are updates. There aren't. She has followed up with Assistant DA Nicole Gil via email a few times, to no response. "Nobody does anything unless there's a fire underneath them. I'm going to start lighting fires and see where it goes."

Judge Gary Ortego has been appointed to the Third Circuit Court of Appeals, meaning John Brady's case will have to be assigned to another judge. "And I'll be on maternity leave at the end of May," she tells me.

"Oh wow! Congratulations, Jane, that's great!"

"Oh, thank you, yes, another baby. Another girl."

Since we met in 2019, brought together by our mutual interest in this case, each of our lives has changed so much. Both of us have moved in with our partners. I've gotten married. She's become a mother.

These luxuries of life moving forward with time, they feel obscene against our shared project. Naomi's words still haunt me, and every hour I'm not working toward unveiling some truth about this mystery, or at least toward sharing what I know, feels as though I've stolen it.

In 2021, my maternal grandfather succumbs to a long battle with Alzheimer's, and I lose my first grandparent. My mother is traumatized by the experience of having to decide to remove his feeding tube, is grieving his loss and worrying for my grandmother. And it's all coated in a thick sense of fear that this is our future. She tells me if it ever comes to it, with her, to stop them from putting the tube in at all.

On LaHaye Road, my mommee Susan keeps falling, and falling and falling. Her loose joints, which I and my father have each inherited, can no longer hold her up. The surgeries come one after another, until my dad admits to me that her body won't be able to take much more. That he's scared for the day she won't wake up from the anesthesia. The minute Papa Wayne stops working at the hospital at age eighty-two, the boredom curls his shoulders inward—channeling into a crippling fear of losing his wife. The conversations go on for years between my parents and my aunts and my uncles about how we will convince them to move downstairs to MawMaw Emily's old apartment. They are stubborn and their memories are fading side by side, their delusions shared. My aunt Suzette, who bears the brunt of it, says that as a pair the whole situation is so much harder. My dad reminds her that this is all anyone prays for, to grow old beside the person you love.

When I visit them, I am grateful they still know me, that my papa still kisses me on the face and my mommee can ask me to fix her a glass of wine. They rarely remember where I live or what I do, but when I pull out the old photo albums, everything lights up. When I come across a photograph of PawPaw Aubrey swinging a baseball bat, cigar in his mouth, Papa Wayne laughs and laughs: "Now that's a rare sight right there, he'd never play with us."

My brother, the one with the strongest Cajun accent, has married my best friend, and they have moved to Galveston, where he'll complete his medical degree at the place our parents met. Since then they've had two children—Cajun babies conceived, as I was, on a Texas island. Their second is named for my father, Frances Marcella LaHaye. She is a LaHaye with my best friend's face, and they ask if I will be her godmother. The world tugs at me to return to it, to step back into the present.

But at home, I'm rooted before this computer, my body growing soft and my Dupré joints cracking when I walk. My perfect eyesight blurs and I take ibuprofen like candy to quell the headaches. And we aren't trying because I said we wouldn't until this was done, but when I'm a little late and the test comes back negative, the tears, surprising me, run hot.

I'm waiting on the courts and I'm trying to make sense of this nest of information I've accumulated, pushed onward by some vague hope that the work might elicit some obscure meaning, might make some difference. I cannot save the man counting the dull days in Angola. I cannot even say with assurance that I want to. But I can keep asking questions, weaving tapestries, creating something that might pause the ever-forward moving world to turn back to 1983, to the question of John Brady, the question of Aubrey.

"You know you could do this forever," my dad tells me. "You might never find a place to stop asking questions . . . a way out. You might have to make one."

"I can't just make something up, Dad."

"No, but you can find an ending. A place where you can let yourself step away."

Forgiveness, It's Freedom

N THE SUMMER OF 2022, I SEE A FACEBOOK POST FROM JOHN Brady's niece Bridget on his sixty-fourth birthday—praying it be his last in prison. "We have PROVED HIS INNOCENCE," she writes, "and we didn't trade favors, pay someone under the table, or hide and destroy evidence to do it." I decide to message her, asking if she would share her perspective on the case. The next morning, I am struck dumb by the bitterness, the contempt, in her reply. I don't think u have a clue how much my family has suffered! And apparently don't care, because you know as well as I do what has been done and you and your family sit back and continue to do nothing about it.

I taste acid in my throat, and for the next several weeks I am riddled with anxiety. *Is there something I don't know?* More likely, I come to realize, this is the Balfa family's response to my family's refusal to engage with John Brady's case, my dad's rejection of Jane's invitation.

Months after the initial sting of her accusations has faded, I'm still kept awake at night, fretting about whether I should have done more. Could I have been wrong in assuming my family wouldn't collectively have mercy on John Brady? Should I have had more courage, more faith, or at least worked harder to give them the chance? Maybe I should have tried to change Dad's mind or orchestrated a meeting between Jane and all my aunts and my uncles, my papa Wayne. Maybe this is what they were made for—a pivotal moment in the shaping of their souls, missed. A chance to transcend their suffering and make meaning of it. To be like saints, or like gods—doling out forgiveness and freedom in one breath.

But other nights, I'm kept awake by anger and frustration over it all. With Jane Hogan, with Trent Brignac, with Billy Pucheu and Rudy Guillory, and with the entire damn system for putting this upon my family. How is it that a murder victim's family comes to hold the fate of the accused murderer in their hands? It's absurd, and upside down, and fucked-up.

At some point, it occurs to me that I know as much about this case, if not about the criminal himself, as Jane does. If Dad doesn't want to talk to Jane, or to the Balfas—well, I know he'll talk to me.

January 16, 2023

"The weather looks like it did the last time we visited the Nezpique," my dad says as I slide into his passenger seat. It's a Monday night, and I've rushed straight from Lafayette—trying to make it to Vidrine before the sun sets. The clouds are the color of the ocean at its deepest point, stretched swollen from one horizon to the next.

It's the fortieth anniversary of the day the Vezinats started shooting bullets into that mysterious mass in the Nezpique—ending the ten-day vigil with one final violence. It's been five years since my first trip there, to the place where they drew PawPaw Aubrey's body from the water.

I've asked my dad if we can go back. This time, though, instead of paying tribute to the spot where the search ended—the place of rims and ropes and rot—I want to visit our corner of the bayou.

It is more ours than it once was; my dad's bought up the seventy acres across the street, stretching all the way to the bayou's border. "There's a spot right here that would make a great homestead," he tells me, suggestively, as we pull onto the property. For now, the land is occupied only by our neighbor's cattle herd, by invasive wild hogs, and by the coyotes that have been tormenting the family dogs every night for the past month. Dad's loading a gun in case we see one. "This section of the property," he says, gesturing with his head toward the acreage right in front of us, "has the trees." But the one right next to it is his favorite. There is a hill for a house, and the yard goes right up to the Nezpique.

It occurs to me that if I were writing fiction, I'd end this story by bringing my character home. I'd revel in the poetic irony of submitting to Evangeline Parish's magnetic force, to making a home right on this storied bayou, our children spending summers setting hoop nets and imagining fairies on her banks. In this world, I'd learn enough French to tell them Pépère Marcellus's folktales, to sing his songs. We'd walk across our own little LaHaye Road to have lunch at my parents' house every Sunday, ride four-wheelers and horses back and forth between our homes, cousins everywhere. We'd claim this paradise.

I'd tell them of the darkness too. Of the truth that Acadie's story cannot be separated from her suffering. Evangeline was pure and beautiful and resilient, but she was also sad until her dying day. The world is not only darkness, nor only light—but dappled and sometimes gray. The Nezpique can be heaven, but it can also be hell.

But if this were fiction, there would be resolution elsewhere too. Someone would come forward, a witness who'd seen everything. Reconciliation would be within reach. John Brady's innocence would be certain. Someone far less ambiguously evil would clash into the halls of justice. If this were fiction, those answers would lead us to a happy ending—to a world where righteousness always wins out, and John Brady Balfa can return to Evangeline Parish to live out the rest of his days. And I could sit upon the Nezpique's banks and tell my children of how I helped to solve their great-great-grandfather's murder, how I stitched up a half century of open wounds, how I returned a lost man to his family. And then, I returned home.

In life, though, you cannot write your own endings. We might never know what happened on that day forty years ago, this story remaining forever ragged at its ends.

And this very morning, Julien and I planted dogwoods in the front yard of our house in Lafayette, an investment in the future. When I tell Dad this, there is a sadness in his eyes, but he smiles. "Dogwoods are beautiful trees. We used to have them all over, and then a blight killed every single one in Evangeline Parish. You just don't see them anymore."

We climb up onto the ridge, the levee rising out of the bayou. It's been years since I've been here, but the trail opens up, it invites—even as thunder gurgles from behind us. The ground is soaked soft, a layer of dead leaves slicked across it, barely crackling underfoot.

"There's your Nezpique, honey."

There she is, full to the brim, reflecting everything between her and the sky, just at a slant, just for us. We walk for a while, me following behind him. The wildlife's on his mind, the holes dug in the levee, a turtle poking its head out from the water's surface, pig tracks, armadillo tracks, deer tracks. Across the water, someone's left their folding chair on the bank, a fishing line hanging from a tree branch right in front of it. I step over a ball cap, smashed into the mud.

When we make it to where the bayou bends and the levee ends, Dad tells me he cooked dinner for Papa Wayne and Mommee Susan the night before. He wasn't going to mention it at first, but something had made him say, "You know, tomorrow is the fortieth anniversary of when we found your daddy's body." And Papa was just quiet. "Oh?"

I ask Dad to tell me again about that day, what he remembers of it.

"I just remember hugging my daddy. And my daddy wasn't the kind of man we hugged a lot. I think that is the only time in my life I saw him cry, I remember holding him, and he was shaking."

It's started raining now, the drops fat and wet, plopping on our heads from between the branches, slowly soaking us through. But we don't budge.

I ask him, "When you think about the last forty years, and everything that's happened, and who we are now . . ." The question trails off. I'm not sure exactly what I'm asking. But he has an answer: "Well, we survived. I kinda can't believe it but *we survived*. I mean, look at us! Look at you."

When we get back to the house, my mother orders pizza from the gas station and we all fix whiskey drinks. Mom takes hers to the back office, leaving Dad and me in the living room: him on the couch, me on the floor, my laptop balancing on my knees. I tell him I want to present the case to him, and he leans forward. The case of John Brady Balfa's innocence.

I walk him through Jane Hogan's list of grievances, the details hidden from John Brady and Julie Cullen all those years ago—the shadow box of broken paths to another potential murderer. He's intrigued by the fingerprint, by the hair—"But couldn't it have been old? Do those things actually mean anything?" The knives found by PawPaw Aubrey's house earn a raised eyebrow. That law enforcement had other leads and other suspects, Taylor Strother among them, doesn't particularly impress him. "They were checking everybody out," he says. "We knew that."

"But the problem is," I try to explain, "it looks like Pucheu and Guillory were maybe intentionally trying to keep a lot of these details from John Brady and from the jury." I tell him about MawMaw Emily's first identification of Taylor Strother. I walk him through the drama of the autopsy report. I explain that the National Autopsy Assay Group has effectively debunked the time of death. He's nodding, he's getting it. "So [Guillory and Pucheu] found a way to make the time of death fall exactly in that slot when John's alibi didn't work. And that . . . Yeah, that was convincing, to me."

"Well, what do you think? About whether they manipulated things?"

"Well . . . honestly, I'll just tell you what's going through my brain right now," he says, bringing his hands to a temple in front of his mouth. "For what it's worth . . . if they were as convinced by the evidence they had as I was, with no question that he did it—they had the power to say, 'Let's not let all this other shit muddy it. Let's forget all this other stuff, get it out of the way. We got our man.' And that wasn't right, but that was how they could be sure to get their conviction."

The trial had failed to convince my dad that John Brady killed Paw-Paw Aubrey over a bank loan—and the *why* has plagued him for forty years now. But he's never seriously questioned that John Brady did it. "From what I saw, with the rope and the tires and the alibi—there was no question in my mind. I'm telling you . . . That's what got the jury to say 'guilty.' I was there. I saw what the jury saw. It was impressive."

"Let me show you something." I pull up the photos I took of the rims, lined up in that plywood storage box. Multicolored and of different sizes, they so obviously don't resemble one another.

"These are them?" he asks. "Wow . . . they don't look the same at all."

Then I pull up the transcript. I read him what the experts said that day about the ropes and the rims: It wasn't even the rims themselves, I tell him. The top layer of paint on the rims "could have come from the same source." The paint on the two pieces of rope "could have come from the same source" as the paint in Harry Balfa's workshop. The two pieces of rope "could have come from the same source."

". . . it's such a small town. Everybody gets their rope from the same places," Dad observes.

Finally, I show him Charles Watts's letter. I've told him about this before, about the implication that Uncle Sonny may have been involved. But this is the first time he's seen it for himself.

Reading aloud, when I get to the sentence, "It was a fake ransom demand, and the banker had been killed for someone—" Dad interjects.

"—I would believe that one hundred percent," he says.

I go on, reciting: "His son-in-law has a deal made—"

"—I honestly don't have trouble believing that either."

When I'm done, I already know where Dad stands. But I ask anyway. "Is there anything here that might convince you John Brady could be innocent?"

Dad takes a minute, stirs his drink with his finger. And then he says it, "No." He's grappling with the narrative as he's known it, trying to see if it can be undone. "We were so biased at that time, perhaps . . . but still today it's hard for me to think of this man as anyone but the asshole who killed my grandpa. I mean, what we walked out of that courtroom believing— there's really nothing new, nothing big enough . . . I mean, that's still where we are. Even after tonight, all our discussion, in my mind, that's still where we are. It's not enough."

There's some doubt raised, sure, he allows. But it's so easy to fall back on the system, to relegate justice to a place outside of oneself. "The system, it supports where we want to be," he acknowledges. The system said the man who killed PawPaw Aubrey has been punished. The system made sure he would never hurt anyone again. The system allowed the LaHayes to close the door on that dark chapter of their lives, to move forward. Or to at least try. "If the system's against you, you're more likely to criticize it. In this scenario, it was on our side . . . we never questioned it."

If John Brady were to get another trial, Dad says, and the court were to deem him innocent—he could accept that. If this evidence was brought before a new jury, who came to a different conclusion, he could accept John Brady's innocence as fact. But like me, like Trent Brignac, he doesn't want to make the call.

The Watts letter, Dad says, is the only thing I've shown him that's resonated. And it's because it serves to answer missing plot holes, it offers something resembling a *why*.

"This is why we're still talking about this, right?"—this vortex of possibilities. He goes on, "There are these questions . . . Is there more to the story? Does it involve Sonny DeVillier? Does it involve big Mafia business? *Why did this happen?*"

It's the question that has come to define so much of my life. But what I offer next is the bleak alternative: "Sometimes, though, I step back . . . there's the possibility too that it *was* just some random act of violence . . . just this guy who needed money, who was angry at Aubrey for denying him a loan . . ."

"You're right," Dad says, leaning back in his chair. "And in all practicality . . . it probably was. It probably was that simple. It probably didn't involve Sonny or anyone else. It probably was that fucking simple. This guy was a lunatic and got denied that loan, and that's what happened. We want it to be this bigger story. We want it to make more sense than just such a wasted life on such frivolous bullshit. But in reality . . . I mean, I change my mind about this every day . . . yesterday I would have said something different. But today, if you ask me, I think, yeah. Maybe it's that simple. Dumbass was pissed and angry and already troubled, and that rich asshole wouldn't give him the money he needed, and so he's gonna kill him. And he did. We all walked away feeling like 'That don't make sense, you can't have killed my grandfather for that.' But maybe he did. *Probably* he did. And that's what the court said. And you know, even if you say we're corrupt and small-town, they couldn't have made all this shit up. These were intelligent men. The data was there . . . So, what do you got? You've got what the court found. And yeah, we've got hundreds of theories and conspiracies and complications of a complex man with all these connections. But no one's been able to disprove the court's story. No one's been able to truly, definitively, say otherwise."

"But what if we're wrong?" I ask him. "What if John Brady *really is* innocent, and there is absolutely no way to prove it? What then?"

Dad nods, sits silent for a minute. "It's terrible to think about. It really is. I almost think it would be better for him if he had done it, and he just said he was sorry."

Back when I first started writing about Aubrey LaHaye's murder, Dad spoke of how badly he wanted to know the *why*. He wanted me to find it, if I could. He said that if John Brady Balfa would only tell them this, if he would explain what happened, answer all these unyielding questions— well, then Dad would open the prison gates himself.

He still feels this way, he tells me now. Regardless of John Brady's innocence, my dad sees little use in imprisoning an old man whose family misses him. He wouldn't fight Jane's efforts. "Personally, I don't mind if he goes free," he says. "I think he's harmless. He can die with his family. I think everybody deserves forgiveness . . ."

But Dad can't speak for the rest of the family. He can't speak for his father, who has spent the last forty years wearing what the court told him as armor, who Billy Pucheu once promised, "Balfa's never getting out, we'll make sure of it."

"I'm trying to see it through Papa's eyes," my dad contemplates. "My dad is a forgiving person. But he doesn't allow himself to think about all of this. He shuts it down."

My dad thinks it would do everyone good to forgive John Brady, to dismantle any residual hate, to unburden this last living remnant of suffering. "Forgiveness, you know, it's freedom," he says. "But it's difficult to forgive someone who doesn't admit what he's done," someone who—in my dad's mind—is still withholding the piece of the story that prevents everything from settling. My dad believes John Brady knows what really happened on January 6, 1983—whether it was an elaborate conspiracy or a random act of violence. But the fact that he won't tell, this is what is so hard for my dad to let go of, to forgive.

May 22, 2023

Standing in the lobby of the police jury meeting room at the Evangeline Parish courthouse, Uncle Richard comes up to me. "You lit a fire, huh?"

I'm instantly defensive. "Oh, this wasn't me, Uncle Richard. I didn't do this."

I'd been afraid of this since the minute I'd learned about the meeting. A couple weeks before, all of Aubrey LaHaye's grandchildren had received a letter from the Evangeline Parish District Attorney's Office, informing them that the hearing to consider whether John Brady Balfa's case should be retried was scheduled for June. Trent Brignac requested members of the family come to the courthouse before the hearing, during which he'd be available to answer any questions.

I'd mentioned to various family members that the case had been reopened, but over the course of the three years since Jane filed the postconviction application, there had been so little progress. I don't think anyone took me seriously. Until now. The timing, coinciding with my ongoing conversations with them around PawPaw Aubrey's death, easily makes it look like I'm responsible, that I've asked one too many questions.

Of course, this would have all happened anyway, I try to explain.

Representing Papa Wayne's family are Dad, Parrain Danny, and Uncle Jay. Representing Uncle Glenn's are Uncle Jody, Uncle Richard, and Aunt Dusty. Aunt Anne didn't want to make the drive from Baton Rouge, and most everyone else was fine learning about the results later. I try to make myself small as we seat ourselves in the police jury meeting room—hyperaware of the cavern between my connection to this case and theirs. Sitting here with them, I align myself with the LaHaye family, and I try to radiate my support for them outward. But the journalist is here, too. And I'm afraid that they know it.

What's more, a few weeks before the meeting I'd had a conversation with Jane. As soon as I'd picked up the phone, I could tell she was nervous. "This is . . . I mean. I don't want to put you in any kind of weird position," she started. I felt my neck tighten, anxious. "But part of what I have to show at the hearing is that John was diligent in trying to get records that would help his claims . . . and that there was this continued suppression of evidence." She never said it outright, but I understood. She wanted me to testify, to tell the judge about how Richard Vidrine had been so protective over the file the first time I visited the DA's Office in 2017. "I can't subpoena you because you're technically a victim, but if you agreed . . ." She trailed off. It was the one thing I'd asked her from the beginning, to avoid putting me in this position—testifying before my family, on the side of John Brady Balfa. But I didn't hesitate. There was a legacy of secrecy around the case, and my refusal to share my experience of it—out of loyalty to the LaHaye family, no less—would only contribute to a cycle I'd been striving to break open. "I could do it," I told her. "I could get up there and say that." I'm sitting with the LaHayes, but I'll be testifying for the defense.

Once we are seated in the front few pews, Trent Brignac emerges from the back with Assistant District Attorneys Nicole Gil, Jacob Fusilier, and Stan Vidrine. Standing up to the mic, Brignac opens with an explanation of why we were invited here. "We're concerned enough about the family to keep y'all abreast and informed, especially when things have gotten to the point that they've gotten now, when you're going to start hearing some rumors." He explains that postconviction applications come in all the time, but that this one was different. Never had the court received an appeal from *this* long ago, where almost all the main figures were now deceased. When Uncle Richard asks if they've tried to track down FBI agent Ellis Blount, who he remembered fondly from the investigation, I can't help myself from interjecting, "He's dead." Aunt Dusty follows up, "What about Dr. McCormick?" My dad answers, "Him too."

The room goes quiet, and Trent continues, "I was a freshman in high school when this happened." From the pew in front of me, Dusty corrects him. "You were in eighth grade, Trent. Because I was in seventh."

He smiles at her, "That's right. Eighth grade."

He goes on: "Now, God forbid there is an innocent man or woman in jail for the rest of their life. I hope we have never put someone in that position. But we know it does happen. We do not believe it happened in this case." An exhale from the pews around me.

Brignac tells them about Jane Hogan, who he describes as "someone not with the Innocence Project, but akin to it." "I'm gonna say it like it is," he goes on. "I don't dislike Jane Hogan. I'm surprised I don't dislike Jane Hogan, because I had a couple of interactions with her where I expected her to be confrontational and argumentative. And she was not." His answer to Jane and her case, he explains, has been that because all the people who came before him—the investigators, the attorneys, the judges, the appellate courts—deemed John Brady Balfa guilty, he has to assume they got it right. "Unless you show me the proverbial smoking gun, then it's not our office to make this decision." So the question had to go before a judge, who would decide whether he thinks the new issues warrant a new trial.

"To be clear," inserts Jacob Fusilier, who had been assigned lead on the case, "we're opposing this at a trial level, at the appellate level, as far as they can go. It is our position that he's had his time in court multiple times, it's time now to just let this go. We need some finality for everyone."

One of the office's biggest concerns, Brignac explains, was Jane's allegations that the DA's Office had failed in 1985 to adequately provide Julie Cullen with evidence that might be exculpatory to John Brady. *My concerns from the beginning.*

Today, the Evangeline Parish DA's Office practices a policy of open file discovery. "If we can't beat you fair and square with the information we have, we just can't beat you," says Brignac. The reason he employs this policy is precisely to avoid accusations like this one—that evidence was hidden from a defendant.

"But that's not how the office practiced forty years ago," he admits. "They didn't do anything wrong. They did what was the practice of the times. Not all the information Rudy Guillory had was turned over to the defense counsel."

The question the DA's team would ask is whether what was left out would have actually resulted in a different verdict. "And that's where, in our opinion, their argument gets a little bit weak," says Trent. "Because... I knew Rudy Guillory. I know most of you knew Rudy well. As far as I'm concerned, that was an honest, fair man that would not have tried to put anyone away he thought was innocent. Same to Billy Pucheu."

The DA's Office was requesting that the family have a presence at the hearing. "We want the judge to know—unless y'all tell us something different—that this is still something the family is paying attention to, that the family cares about the outcome of the decision he makes." The Balfas would have a big turnout, says Brignac. "I've already had people from his extended family come talk to me."

From the pew in front of me, Uncle Richard booms, "Well, we're gonna haul a crew in, if that's what it takes. But just so I'm not misunderstood—I'll speak for myself. *He better not get free.*"

"I really think it's a very, very low probability," Brignac assures him. "Very, very low."

Before he dismisses us, he notes that he has an obligation to pose to the family the possibility of a renegotiation of John Brady's sentence, outside of court. Jane had never formally requested such a negotiation, he says—which I find interesting, considering my conversations with her. "The only thing she said, and she said it multiple times, is that the Balfa family does not want to see him die in jail." Had Jane not been clear with Brignac when she said she was interested in a deal?

"If there was a fairly compelling case, or he was in his eighties or something, or had a terminal condition, I might ask y'all if you really wanted to go through a new trial and put your family through that," says Brignac. "There are people in the family that don't want to relive this. If he's willing to acknowledge his guilt, we could just let it die . . . But that's not the case, is it?"

Before anyone else can even process what he's said, Uncle Richard replies, "No. It's not."

The rest quietly shake their heads, in agreement. *No.*

Later, my dad will tell me how this frustrated him—the way the La-Hayes operate as a single body behind the loudest person in the room, without room for conversation, for nuance.

After the hearing, Assistant DA Nicole Gil—who has done all the groundwork on this case until now—approaches my dad and me. Dad says to her, "It sounds like y'all are pretty confident you've got this in the bag." She shifts her eye contact to me, shakes her head. "I wouldn't say that."

The June 2023 hearing gets rescheduled for February 2024, then to May—making it almost four years after Jane's original June 2020 filing of the postconviction application. "I really don't believe it's ever actually going to happen," my dad tells me.

Over the course of all this time, the DA's Office fails to fulfill their promise to reach out to the FBI to learn whether or not the fingerprint and hair samples were still available for testing. So Jane takes it upon herself.

When the FBI responds, they confirm they do indeed have the fingerprint, but they can't test it without a court order. That process takes months. Jane and I wait anxiously. Could this be the key to everything? The answer? There is no mention of the hair.

Finally, in November 2023, Jane emails me the fingerprint report.

It confirms what we mostly already knew: the print is not a match for John Brady. It is also not a match for anyone in the CODIS system.

Like so much else, it leads us nowhere.

"Balfa Speaks"

SINCE OUR FIRST MEETING IN 2019, JANE HOGAN AND I HAVE repeatedly discussed the possibility of my meeting with John Brady, or at least exchanging correspondence of some sort. He has always expressed reluctance to speak with me. The reasons are plenty, of course: I'm a LaHaye, and according to Naomi he's always believed our family was involved in his wrongful conviction; I'm a journalist, and he might see my motives as questionable; and he is, of course, in the middle of legal proceedings concerning the very case I'm interested in.

I have to try, though, one last time. "If there's any chance at all he might be open to it . . . this story is his, too."

After consulting John Brady, Jane gives me a final no. "It's not personal," she says, though I suspect it might be. "Where we are with this criminal case, I just don't . . . he said if he gets out of jail, he'll be glad to speak with you. But until that happens, he's just really cautious."

I'm disappointed, but not at all surprised. I tell her I won't push it any further.

"I'll let you know if he changes his mind," she promises.

In January 2024, I receive a text message from my dad: Balfa speaks. There is a link to an article published in the *Ville Platte Gazette* that morning. Before even opening it, I respond: Has Papa seen it?

My dad and his siblings have mostly tried to keep Papa Wayne, in his diminishing health, out of the courtroom drama. "This will only cause him grief," my dad insists. "And he probably won't remember what we tell him anyway." But my papa reads the Sunday paper religiously.

My phone pings. Your parrain is going over to talk to him.

The article is the entirety of a letter written by John Brady to the newspaper. "My name is John Brady Balfa, and since 1984, I've been seeking to correct the injustice done to me in the wrongful conviction of the murder, abduction, and armed robbery of Aubrey LaHaye." He goes on to accuse District Attorney Billy Pucheu; his successor, Brent Coreil; and the current DA, Trent Brignac, of withholding evidence regarding his case. "For almost 40 years, the FBI, Evangeline Parish district attorneys, and Dr. Wayne LaHaye (the victim's son) knew of this withheld evidence and said nothing."

Oh God. They named Papa.

He goes on: "This crucial withheld evidence consists of a fingerprint, blond hair, and perjury committed by Emily LaHaye (the victim's wife)." *Perjury.*

I'm sick to my stomach. *Is this the route they're taking?* I don't know what reason John Brady or his family, or Jane for that matter, would have for accusing Papa Wayne of knowing about this evidence. But I feel instantly protective of my grandfather. And of MawMaw Emily. *Are we really going to call whatever happened that day perjury? The traumatized victim's testimony?* However possibly grave the error might have been, MawMaw Emily had no reason to lie.

While awaiting updates on John Brady's court proceedings, I find myself wading through the archive of the Louisiana State Penitentiary newspaper, *The Angolite.* John Brady is featured in several articles, all of them concerning his involvement in ministry. I'm reading one from 2012, in which the Angola inmates celebrated their first ever "Day of the Dead" Mass—held in the historic Angola cemetery. In Catholic tradition, this holy day is meant to honor the souls of the dead, especially those suffering purification in Purgatory, awaiting Heaven. For the occasion, the inmate ministers placed baskets in all of Angola's camps, where anyone could write the name of someone who has passed. The basket was then presented at Mass as an offering, these intentions elevated toward the Lord in hopes that he might grant them mercy. John Brady Balfa, on this day, told a reporter that the name of "his victim" was among them.

My breath catches, and my brain turns over, reaching into my deep internal archive for all the possible explanations. Maybe he didn't mean PawPaw Aubrey. Maybe he was talking about his rape victim—was it possible that she had passed? Maybe John Brady was just trying to fit in among the other inmates, to take on the persona of a converted killer. Why, after maintaining his innocence for so long, would he tell a reporter about his victim?

I keep flipping through, now just scanning the articles, distracted. I come across one story about a Catholic high school retreat held on the prison grounds in 2007—part of Burl Cain's faith-centered publicity campaigns. Twenty-five teenagers were touring the grounds and attending seminars put on by Catholic inmate ministers, including John Brady. One by one, these ministers stood up to witness, to tell their story of spiritual awakening. "I understand that I have been forgiven," one inmate told them. Another testified to discovering Christ's mercy through suffering, and another to how his life had changed after putting his trust in God.

When I get to John Brady's testimony, I find myself blinking. Reading it again. And again. I stand up with my computer, zoom in. And I screenshot what I see, afraid it'll disappear in an instant. John Brady told these teenagers to guard their decisions, to recognize that evil acts come with consequences—that they affect your family and your victim's family. Then, there it is, so plainly said, in his own words: "In 1983, I killed a man."

For months, I agonize over what to do with this revelation, this singular, simple confession. I go back and forth over whether it means anything at all.

When I lean toward rejecting it, toward painting John Brady as a man playing a role, willing to use the ugliest piece of his history, truth be damned, to cast that momentary glow of redemption, I wonder if I'm self-sabotaging. Has the truth been so elusive that I can no longer recognize it? Have I convicted myself to a fate of perpetual doubt, doomed to question every single thing about John Brady, about PawPaw Aubrey, about the reliability of justice in America and the virtue of my traumatized family and the similarities of paint and the way a body decomposes?

At night, my mind turns to old insomniac habits—repeating "Hail Marys" over and over and over again. When it doesn't work, I open my eyes and stare up at the ceiling. I try, as I've tried from the beginning, to conjure my great-grandfather's spirit. *What do I do with all of this?* I ask him.

I think of the certainty with which PawPaw Aubrey operated, the way his judgments shaped his world. Sitting behind his desk, chewing on his cigar, all so serious. *Who are your people?* he'd ask his loan applicants, assessing the way they dressed, the way they spoke. *Where are your roots?*

And more often than not, whatever the answers were, he'd grasp their hands. He'd trust them at their word.

Even he hadn't trusted John Brady, though.

The words are there, publicly available to anyone, if they know where to look. I just happen to be the only person who knew to look. Whatever they may mean, John Brady said them. And I can't keep it to myself, can't continue the tradition of suppression that has brought me, and my grandfather, and my dad, and John Brady, and Naomi, and all of them here. This is just one more piece of the incomprehensible puzzle that has become the question: What happened to Aubrey LaHaye?

If the State uses this correctly, if they find the journalist who wrote the article and bring him into court to verify what he heard, they can use what I've found as an admission of guilt. And likely, the judge will use it to dismiss John's claims of innocence. This keeps me up at night too— the thought that, after everything, it may have come down to this, to me. Again, I waver, straining against the unknowability of it all. The fear remains that he is, despite everything, just a lost soul at the wrong place at the wrong time. If this is the case, what great irony that a lie told on a pulpit would be the thing that dooms him. There is irony in the opposite reality too, of course. That his conversion finally spurred the truth, even if he didn't mean for it to.

I call my dad, and I tell him I've decided to turn the *Angolite* articles in to the District Attorney's Office. He tells me I'm doing the right thing.

"No more secrets," he says.

Epilogue

LIFE, AS WE KNOW, IS MESSIER THAN STORY. IN MY PURSUIT for answers, I've found myself with more questions than before—awaiting resolution that feels ever-imperfect, and like it may never come.

As of this printing, John Brady Balfa's postconviction relief application is still pending in the district court, plagued by a stream of ineligible judges, futile efforts to get evidence tested, and attorney turnover.

Judge Marcus Fontenot[1] was assigned to the case in 2022, following Judge Gary Ortego's departure. He recused himself soon after, citing his prior relationship to the case, brought to attention by a series of motions by Jane Hogan. In 2013, in the position of assistant district attorney, Fontenot had responded to a records request from John Brady and his family and had been responsible for overseeing the files' delivery. What the Balfas received did not include the FBI reports, information about the fingerprint or hair, the Charles Watts letter, and other information that could possibly be considered exculpatory to John Brady. This made Fontenot a witness to the State's pattern of withholding information from John Brady regarding his case, and, as Jane argued, ineligible to act as judge. In addition, as she pointed out, Fontenot's wife is an employee of my uncle, Dr. Nick LaHaye.

At this point, Judge Chuck West, the other 13th Judicial District Judge, took over the case, and a hearing was scheduled for June 2023. By the time May rolled around, Jane had issued a continuance to allow her time to get the fingerprint tested; the (inconclusive) results of which didn't arrive until November. The hearing was then rescheduled for Valentine's Day 2024.

Toward the end of January, my dad got a call from a clerk in the District Attorney's Office letting him know that the Assistant District

---

1 Marcus Fontenot is of no relevant relation to my husband, Julien Fontenot.

Attorney Nicole Gil, who had up until that point been leading the research and on-the-ground efforts of the case, had retired. The hearing would have to be rescheduled yet again.

"The timing is certainly interesting," my dad said of Nicole's retirement. "In fairness, I felt a whole lot better with her on this case."

I agreed. Nicole was the fourth woman attorney ever employed by the Evangeline Parish District Attorney's Office. I'd attended high school with her twin daughters. She was smart and no-nonsense, but also reasonable and avoided dramatics in her pursuit of justice. She respected Jane as an attorney, describing her as "like me, if I truly believed someone was wrongly convicted. I respect that." Nicole had read through the transcript with the same meticulousness I had and come to similar conclusions. "Julie Cullen, she was 'good ole boyed' the whole way through," she said. "She fought this case hard, and asked for the right things but was denied, denied, denied. She was told 'no' at every turn and 'Cher little darling, you little woman,' almost directly."

With Nicole retired, the case was firmly in the hands of the office's other ADA Jacob Fusilier, who is close friends with my uncle Richard LaHaye. Jacob, aggressive and showy in court, would fight this case in a way reminiscent of Billy Pucheu. He would fight the case, I surmised, as the former DA had, *for the LaHaye family*. And that made me nervous. A repeat of history would get us nowhere nearer to justice.

"I wish it would just go away," my dad told me, over the phone.

"I know."

A few days later, I received a text from my brother's wife's sister asking to meet. Sydia Robin was finishing her law degree at Southern University in Baton Rouge and had been working for the Evangeline Parish DA's Office part-time under Jacob Fusilier. She wasn't getting her degree until May but had been promised a position as ADA pending her passing the bar exam. And she'd been officially made second chair on the John Brady Balfa case.

Sydia has social ties to the LaHaye family from multiple angles: she attended high school with my older cousins, dance classes with me. She'd grown up with us, and now her children are my niece and nephew's first cousins. I'm once again disturbed by how elusive objectivity is in a place like Evangeline Parish. At the same time, Sydia was someone I trusted, someone who could grant me even greater access to the inner workings of this case, now from the side of the State. She was a new attorney, too, hungry to make a difference in her hometown, still interested in justice as a goal rather than a tool.

The hearing was scheduled for May 30; Sydia and Jacob had four months to get up to speed, to wade through the piles of records in the forty-year-old file. When I met with them a few weeks after she texted to go over my research, it quickly became clear that they'd only just dipped their toes in. Without Nicole, they hardly knew anything.

But Sydia was a quick study. She had been carefully following my progress on this project for years and knew I was a valuable resource. She asked all the right questions, texting me often with inquiries I could answer in minutes with a quick dive into my massive digital archive of FBI records, the transcript, newspapers, and the DA file itself. I told myself I wasn't playing double agent so much as ensuring both sides had access to the most accurate information possible. I'd given Jane everything I had, too. A just resolution would never be reached if the facts weren't there. And a hearing would never happen if the State kept finding ways to delay to better familiarize themselves with the case. But when the DA's office offered to pay me for my consultation services, I refused. I was queasy about articulating such clear partisanship.

Sydia let me know that the *Angolite* articles I'd provided to the DA's Office were going to be the jugular blow of their case. She and Jacob had managed to track down the prison journalist who'd reported on John's address to those high school students in 2007, who had written the words as he'd supposedly heard them: "In 1983, I killed a man." "It's an admission of guilt," Jacob told me. "I don't think the judge is going to undo a forty-year-old conviction when the guy's publicly admitted to the crime." I nodded, my stomach clenched, my fingers fluttering. "I'm going to hang that around his neck," he said. I swallowed.

Weeks before the hearing, I heard from Jane: "Did you find some article from the *Angolite* about John?" My heart sank into my gut. I knew she'd find out when the articles entered the case file. But I'd hoped she might not learn they came from me. I sent them to her in an email, writing, "I understand this doesn't amount to a real confession, nor does it dismiss the very real concerns you are bringing to this case. As with everything else, it just complicates all of it. It is *something* though . . ." I haven't heard from her since.

I learned later that Jacob had gotten into a yelling match with Jane after the Valentine's Day hearing had been postponed.

"We can't keep pushing this off. How can you sleep at night, keeping an innocent man in prison like this?" she'd demanded.

He'd laughed. "What do you mean? He *said* he did it! We've got it in print!" She'd looked at him blankly. And, with glee, he'd proceeded to tell her about the articles, and where they'd come from.

"You can't send a coonass to talk to some city lawyer," he'd told my family, recounting the interaction. A few of my uncles chuckled. I locked eyes with Sydia, sitting next to Jacob. She subtly shook her head, looked down.

We'd gathered for another family meeting at the courthouse, about a week before the May 30 hearing. Jacob went on to explain the significance of the articles, as well as his strategy to argue against a new trial. He admitted the State's weak spots: the claims of a pattern of suppression of evidence. "I'm not going to blow any smoke," he said. "We can't say the reasons why Mr. Pucheu didn't turn it all over. We just don't know. And he's dead. I can't ask. I assume if I could talk to those people, and if they were to remember, they'd have a reasonable explanation." Richard Vidrine, it should be noted, was at this point suffering from dementia, and could not be effectively consulted either. Then there was the issue of the missing evidence—the ropes, Aubrey's clothes, everything but the rims. "Where is it?" my aunt Sandy asked.

"It's crazy," said Jacob. "It just evaporated. Disappeared. I'm trying not to laugh, because it's just so wild. We have no explanation we can give them why they don't have access to that material."

Once again, Jacob encouraged the family to attend the hearing en masse. "Nothing would make me happier than if Judge Chuck West was out there smoking cigarettes and he just sees LaHayes strolling in here by the dozens," he said.

The weekend before the hearing, there was a LaHaye wedding. In my bridesmaid's dress, champagne in hand, every corner I turned I found a cousin or an aunt or an uncle, asking, "Will you be there Thursday?"

On Wednesday, at 3 p.m., a text from Parrain Danny made the rounds. The hearing, which was to begin in less than twenty-four hours, had been canceled again. Judge Chuck West, it turned out, had briefly represented John Brady as a public defender during his 1998 postconviction application. When I received the news, I quickly turned to my archive—*how did I miss this?* Sure enough, there is West's name, mentioned exactly one time in a handwritten letter from 1999 addressed to him, in which John Brady asked for a postponement of a hearing so that his new hired attorney would have time to prepare.

Under those grounds, Judge Chuck West recused himself from the case.

"It feels to me that the DA's Office is dragging this out," my dad told me shortly after we'd learned the news. They were less interested in Judge West's bias than in trying to buy more time. "It indicates to me that they aren't as confident as they'd like to be. They don't want to have this fight."

According to Sydia, though, the move was necessary. They all needed the hearing to be watertight, to avoid weak spots susceptible to future appeals.

As of October 2024, Judge John Conery has been appointed as an ad hoc judge on the case, though a new hearing has yet to be scheduled. The truth is that whether the court deems John Brady deserving of a new trial, or not, this case will drag on for years. The losing side will appeal, likely all the way up through the Louisiana Supreme Court.

"Is there a chance he's going to be on the streets one day?" Aunt Dusty asked Jacob.

"There is," he said. "But at absolute soonest, we're talking five, probably seven years from now." And John Brady Balfa is now in his sixties, an old man by prison standards.

My dad no longer asks me, because he knows the answer. But others from across Louisiana still pose the plaguing question, at family gatherings, in the coffee shop in Ville Platte, in private messages on Facebook. After the last family meeting, Aunt Suzette asks it to me in the elevator on the way out of the courthouse: "Jordan, do *you* think he did it?"

And I still can only shake my head. I simply don't know.

Acknowledgments

In 2016, when I was hearing this story as something more than a myth for the very first time, I was an undergraduate English student without any discernible direction, desiring nothing more than to run off to some vague *big* city and never look back. So, I must begin my thanks with my thesis adviser, Joshua Wheeler, who in teaching me to write about place, helped me to look at Louisiana with new eyes. Thank you, Josh, for helping me fall in love with my home again, even as I rooted around in its darkest moments. You are the first person to tell me that the story I had could be a book. Without your mentorship and encouragement, *Home of the Happy* would never have gotten its start.

Thank you as well to my fellow students in those creative nonfiction workshops at LSU, whose enthusiasm and feedback in my earliest drafts were invaluable. Thank you to Jennifer Davis, Margaret DeFleur, and Robert Mann, who sat on my thesis committee and not only passed me but assured me that this book had a future.

To James and Ashley Fox-Smith, and the team (past and present) at *Country Roads* magazine, thank you for giving me such a rich and supportive space to grow as a writer and a Louisiana storyteller. It has had a tremendous influence on this book's evolution. Thank you especially to James, who provided such valuable feedback to an early draft of this project, and whose approach to the personal essay continues to inspire me. Other early readers I'd like to thank include Lauren Markham and Chris Feliciano Arnold, whose Story Board creative nonfiction course provided a much-needed structure and challenge to my writing process postgrad.

To my dearest girlfriends—Anne Christian Ardoin, Victoria Billeaud, Addyson Burke, Olivia Creel, Jenifer Endsley, Andee Fontenot, Ainsley LaHaye, Tori McDowell, Ardhyn Parks, Emily Picard, Kenzi Pumford, Grace Simpson, Emily Soileau, and Amy Sylvester—many of whom were early readers of my work, and all of whom were my loudest cheerleaders: thank you for never tiring, these past eight years, of hearing me talk about my ancestors, the Dixie Mafia, and the reverberations of family trauma.

This book has had many champions, none the least of which is my brilliant agent, Mina Hamedi at Janklow and Nesbit. What a privilege it has been to work with someone whose vision for this book so immediately aligned with mine. Thank you for embracing a story by a Cajun girl from the middle of nowhere and helping me bring it to the rest of the world. We wouldn't be here without my former editor, Molly Gendell, who originally acquired *Home of the Happy* for Mariner and made all my dreams come true. Thank you to her successor, Ivy Givens, for taking over this project with such enthusiasm. Each and every brainstorming session with you was a thrill, and I'm forever grateful for your keen eye in deciphering the story from the mountain of words you inherited. A huge thanks, as well, to the entire team at Mariner Books for getting this book to the finish line, and especially to Ploy Siripant for designing such a gloriously ominous cover.

To Olivia Perillo, I knew from the moment I discovered your photography and film work that your creative aesthetic was exactly how I wanted readers to imagine our Acadiana. Thank you for lending your talents to this project, for providing the photograph for the cover, and for coming out to the prairie to capture the world of Evangeline Parish. My author portrait is all I could have dreamed of; thank you for spending those sunset hours on Lake Martin, catching my flyaways, and reminding me to soft smile.

I have to thank Peg Ramier and George Marks, and the other folks at NUNU Arts & Culture Collective, who twice allowed me to escape into the "Shiny Tiny" for a week at a time to work on this book. Thank you to Megan Broussard and Louis Michot for providing some of the Cajun French translations included in the text; to Tony Marks at the *Ville Platte Gazette* for allowing us to reprint articles from the newspaper's archives free of charge; and to the staff at the Evangeline Parish Clerk of Court's office for your assistance over the years. Thank you to Professor Jay Shelledy, without whom I might never have found the complete transcript of John Brady Balfa's trial for the murder of Aubrey LaHaye.

None of this would have held any meaning if it were not for the immense generosity of my many sources for this book, who give voice and scene to a world, devastating as it was, that I was not present for. Thank you to Kurt and Beulah Vezinat, for welcoming me into your home and sharing with me the details of one of the most traumatic days of your lives. Thank you to Bob and Katy Marcantel, Greg Monier, Ted Smith, Stephen Deville, Gayle Fontenot, and Faye Parrot for helping me to piece together the world of Aubrey LaHaye's Guaranty Bank; to Eva Guillory for offering insight into the mind of the late Rudy Guillory; to Mawdry Williams for sharing your memories of LaHaye Road during those dreadful ten days; and to Eddie Soileau, Tanny DeVillier, and former FBI Agents Ed Grimsley and Ed Pistey for sharing your recollections of the investigation. Thank you to Doug Pucheu, Eddie Soileau, Lori Parks, Brian LaHaye, Mark LaHaye, Greg Bergeron, and Colleen Jackson for granting me an elusive glimpse into John Brady Balfa's past. And to the many others I spoke to over the years whose names do not appear here or in the text, you also were vital in helping me to understand this story as a collective trauma, an enduring mystery. Thank you for your time and for your trust.

I am especially grateful to Naomi Nero, for reaching across the barrier between our families and sharing your perspective on this case with me—and even more than that, your love for your brother. I heard your voice in my heart, every step of the way.

To Jane Hogan, thank you for bringing me behind the curtain in the fight for John Brady Balfa's freedom, for granting my theories and fears some validity after years of carrying them mostly alone. Thank you for being such a fierce advocate for him when I could not; and for being an advocate for so many lives ruined by the failures of our justice system. Thank you for showing me what it means to believe in people, even when the rest of the world has turned away.

To Trent Brignac, thank you for allowing me to take up a brief residence in the back room of the DA's Office in 2020 and for granting me open access to a file that had beforehand been treated with such secrecy. Thank you, Nicole Gil, Jacob Fusilier, and Sydia Robin, for always speaking openly and honestly with me about John Brady Balfa's case and how the State plans to fight it.

Most of all, thank you to Aubrey LaHaye's descendants, my family: Papa and Mommee, Parrain and Aunt Michele, Aunt Suzette, Uncle Jay, Uncle Nick, Uncle Jody, Uncle Richard and Aunt Cindy, Aunt Sandy and Uncle Paul, Uncle Billy and Aunt Kristy, Aunt Dusty, Aunt Anne, and Maggie. Thank you for opening your hearts to me, for revisiting those darkest days, and sharing what memories emerged. I know that it was not easy. Without your generous vulnerability and your trust, I could have never told this story. Thank you, even more, for building such a beautiful world for my generation—for finding ways to interrupt the cycles of trauma in our family, even when it was perhaps detrimental to yourselves, all to grant us futures PawPaw Aubrey and MawMaw Emily could have only dreamed of. Thank you for holding on to LaHaye Road, and all that it stands for, so that we might share it with the next generation, too. I wish to offer a special thanks to my papa Wayne, for whom I know this book's publication will be especially difficult. Thank you for never telling me no, even when you might have wanted to. Thank you for always being there, sitting in the recliner as your father once did. A pillar in all of our lives, a kiss on the face, a burst of pride. Thank you for all you've given us.

This book's beginning and its end can be attributed to no one more than my father. Dad, you gave me this story and walked with me all the way through it. Over the past eight years, you've played the part of source, confidant, liaison, and devotee. Thank you for sharing your fears and hopes alike with me. Thank you for all the leads you gathered from that hot spot of Evangeline Parish gossip that is your office, and for pushing me to the end—even when I felt I might never find it. Amid distractions and self-doubt, you never ceased reminding me that this book needed to be written. Thank you, also, to Mom—for your endless support, friendship, logic, and love. Thank you both for planting us beside the Nezpique, for teaching me what it is to have a happy home, and teaching me to be grateful for it.

Finally, thank you to Julien Fontenot—who met me when this book was only an idea, a dream. Thank you for bearing with the laptop glow on all those late nights, so that I might be near you even when my mind could not be. Thank you for loving me all the while, for being my joy, my escape from the turmoil. My home.

Selected Bibliography

Books

Ancelet, Barry Jean. *Cajun and Creole Folktales: The French Oral Tradition of South Louisiana*. Jackson: University Press of Mississippi, 1994.

———. *Cajun and Creole Music Makers / Musiciens cadiens et creoles*. Jackson: University Press of Mississippi, 1999.

Bernard, Shane K. *The Cajuns: Americanization of a People*. Jackson: University Press of Mississippi, 2003.

Brasseaux, Carl A. *Acadian to Cajun: Transformation of a People, 1804–1877*. Jackson: University Press of Mississippi, 1992.

Elliott, Todd C. *A Rose by Many Other Names: Rose Cherami and the JFK Assassination*. Walterville: TrineDay, 2013.

Gahn Sr., Robert A. *The Opelousas Country: With a History of Evangeline Parish*. Baton Rouge: Claitor's Publishing, 1972.

Garrett, Brandon L. *Convicting the Innocent: Where Criminal Prosecutions Go Wrong*. Cambridge: Harvard University Press, 2012.

Hume, Edward. *Mississippi Mud: Southern Justice and the Dixie Mafia*. New York: Gallery Books, 2010.

Longfellow, Henry Wadsworth. *Evangeline: A Tale of Acadie*. Boston: William D. Ticknore & Co., 1847.

Rideau, Wilbert. *In the Place of Justice: A Story of Punishment and Redemption*. New York: Knopf Doubleday Publishing Group, 2011.

Ryan, Joann and Stephanie L. Perrault. *Angola: Plantation to Penitentiary*. New Orleans: US Army Corps of Engineers, 2007.

Savoy, Ann Allen. *Cajun Music: A Reflection of a People, Vol. 1*. Eunice: Bluebird Press, 1984.

Savoy, Marc. *Made in Louisiana: The Story of the Acadian Accordion*. Lafayette: University of Louisiana at Lafayette Press, 2021.

Singleton, Danny and Virgil Breeden. *Sins of a Cajun Boy: The Legendary True Story of Louisiana's Famous Cat Man*. Sulphur: Wise Publications, 2016.

Newspapers

The Angolite. (Angola, Louisiana), 1995–2016.

The Atlanta Constitution. (Atlanta, Georgia), 1959–1982.

The Atlanta Journal. (Atlanta, Georgia), 1959–1982.

The Daily Advertiser. (Lafayette, Louisiana), 1935–1996.

The Daily World. (Opelousas, Louisiana), 1940–1997.

The Eunice News. (Eunice, Louisiana), 1948–1997.

The Longview News-Journal. (Longview, Texas), 1982–1985.

The Mamou Acadian Press. (Mamou, Louisiana), 1967–1985.

The Sun Herald. (Biloxi, Mississippi), 1972–1990.

The Town Talk. (Alexandria, Louisiana), 1931–2020.

Ville Platte Gazette. (Ville Platte, Louisiana), 1930–2024.

Articles/Papers

American Civil Liberties Union. "Captive Labor: Exploitation of In-carcerated Workers." Chicago: University of Chicago Law School Global Human Rights Clinic. (June 15, 2022).

"Balfa is elected SGA President." *Bayou Bengal.* Eunice: Louisiana State University (October 18, 1978).

Cardon, Nathan. "'Less Than Mayhem': Louisiana's Convict Lease, 1865–1901." *The Journal of Louisiana Historical Association,* Vol. 58, No. 4. Baton Rouge: Louisiana Historical Association (Fall 2017).

Chammah, Maurice. "What Angola's Resigning Warden is Leaving Be-hind." *The Marshall Project.* (December 14, 2015).

Committee on Scientific Approaches to Understanding and Maximizing the Validity and Reliability of Eyewitness Identification in Law En-forcement and the Courts; Committee on Science, Technology, and Law; Policy and Global Affairs; Committee on Law and Justice; Di-vision of Behavioral and Social Sciences and Education; National Research Council. "Identifying the Culprit: Assessing Eyewitness Iden-tification." Washington, DC: The National Academies Press. (2014).

Donze, Beth. "Louisiana Inmates lead Catholic ministries for incarcer-ated, visitors." *CatholicPhilly.com.* (May 10, 2016).

Eckholm, Erik. "Bible College Helps Some at Louisiana Prison Find Peace." *The New York Times.* New York City: The New York Times Publishing Company (October 5, 2013).

Quigley, William P. "Louisiana Angola Penitentiary: Past Time to Close." *Loyola Journal of Public Interest Law,* Vol 19. Loyola University New